MEDIA IN MODERN INDIA

MEDIA IN MODERN INDIA

DR. MANOJ RAJAN
Department of Gandhian Studies,
Panjab University,
Chandigarh

Foreword by

DR. JAI NARAIN SHARMA
Professor and Hon. Director,
Gandhi Bhawan
Department of Gandhian Studies
Panjab University, Chandigarh, and
President, Indian Society of Gandhian Studies

DEEP & DEEP PUBLICATIONS PVT. LTD.
F-159, Rajouri Garden, New Delhi-110027

MEDIA IN MODERN INDIA

ISBN 978-81-8450-352-4

Typeset by S.S. COMPOSERS
3190, Mohindra Park, Shakur Basti, Delhi-110034.

Printed in India at MAYUR ENTERPRISES
WZ Plot No. 3, Gujjar Market, Tihar Village, New Delhi-110018.

Published by DEEP & DEEP PUBLICATIONS PVT. LTD.
F-159, Rajouri Garden, New Delhi-110027.
Phones: 25435369, 25440916
E-mail: ddpbooks@yahoo.co.in • ddpubs@gmail.com
Showroom:
2/13, Ansari Road, Daryaganj, New Delhi-110002 • Telefax: 23245122

Dedicated

To my father who

showed me a dream

&

To my mother who

helped me to fulfil that dream

Contents

DR. JAI NARAIN SHARMA
Professor and Hon. Director,
Gandhi Bhawan
Department of Gandhian Studies
Panjab University, Chandigarh, and
President, Indian Society of
Gandhian Studies

Foreword

The media surround us. Our everyday lives are saturated by radio, television, newspapers, books, the Internet, movies, recorded music, magazines, and more. In the twenty-first century, we navigate through a vast mass media environment unprecedented in human history. Yet our intimate familiarity with the media often allows us to take them for granted. They are like the air we breathe, ever present yet rarely considered.

Let's take the simple act of watching television. Nothing could be easier. Sit yourself down and "click," it's on. Click, change the channel. Click, click, click.... Most of us do it almost every day without thinking much about it. But what if we stepped back to look at television in a broader context? What would we find?

Or take the Internet. The buzz and hype have been almost deafening. "Revolutionary", "explosion", "a new era in communication"—this is the sort of language that has surrounded the Internet's growth. But again, what happens if we pause and take a look with a more critical eye? What do we see?

One thing we see is change. The "old" television networks are losing their share of the audience. New broadcast networks are springing up, along with dozens of cable channels and satellite options. Television has gone digital, and soon viewers have hundreds of channels to choose from. The Internet is changing even faster. The technology bringing audio, video, and text is getting more sophisticated as the Internet is becoming accessible to more and more people. The Internet has gone commercial too, with e-commerce now well established—despite its ups and downs—and advertising proliferating. More Web sites, more channels, more choices, more media.

But if we focus only on change and growth, we risk missing the forest for the trees. That's because surprisingly, when we step outside of our routine media habits and move away from all the media hype, we also find that some enduring questions and issues face all types of mass media. From the printed page you are reading, to the television set you watch, to the virtual world of cyberspace, we can examine all of these.

This book by Dr. Manoj Rajan invites us to step back and seriously consider the mass media and the issues they raise. It asks us to put your everyday media activities into a broader social, political, and economic context to better understand them.

It is true that the media has no sanction of law behind it. It has, however, a greater sanction—the sanction of the public opinion. In fact the sanction behind the law is also of the public opinion. If there is no sanction of public opinion behind a particular law, it becomes a dead letter. It is for this reason that the media has become the most powerful organ. Hence, it is imperative to consider the ways and means of harnessing this power for constructing a value-based society.

It is notorious fact that in spite of development in many fields, such as industrialization, the agricultural development, scientific and technological advancement, the spread of education, the spread of health care facilities, one confronts several problems and ailments. The problems of ignorance, of poverty, population explosion and environmental destruction are the principal problems facing this country. At the same time, there is an increase in white collared crimes of corruption, various scams, misappropriation and embezzlement of public funds and property and also in the street-crimes and violence, casteism and communalism. In fact, problems and ailments have increased in depth and width and also in depravity since independence.

The question is what can the media do in such circumstances. When we ask this question, we are at the very inception confronted with a question as to whether the media is qualified to do so. The media has no doubt the capacity. But has it the will to do it, and can it do it as it is practised today? It is a notorious fact that for a long time, the media has resisted even formulation of a code of ethics for itself, although it has always insisted on a code of ethics for others and has attacked viciously even the smallest deviation from the ethical standards on the part of others. That resistance, among others, led to the establishment of the Press Council which is entrusted with also the task of building up a code of ethics for the print media and to take cognizance of its deviations from code. That has also brought in a voluntary agency like Advertising Standards Council. That has also seen the emergence of the Censor Board which applies its scissors whenever necessary. The point that in spite of the code of ethics which has been built up so far for the print media by the Press Council and the Advertising Standards Council, and for the small screen as well as big screen by Censor Board, we find many, and more, degrading deviation from them. At present the Press Council is flooded with the complaints against the press. The point is when media itself is indulging this misconduct, can we assure ourselves that it help to create a society which is value-based? Unfortunately again, for the last few decades commercialism has entered the press in big way. With its commercial values and practices, no value is sacrosanct on the altar of the Money Goddess. More and more profit has become the only goal. That is why we see sensationalisation of news and events, encroachment on the privacy of individuals, blackmailing, character assassination, obscene and indecent pictures and language and so on and so forth. All the vices that can be catalogued. As if this was not enough, the corporate sector has entered the field.

The corporate sector is not interested in promoting the freedom of the press but in promoting interests of their other businesses and want to use the enormous clout that the media wields for its own purpose. This presents a dark picture for the future. Fortunately for us the dark picture or the dark side of the picture as yet comparatively faint and small. There are many in the media who are on the other side with the purpose of seriously considering how best one can help create a value-based society. There are many in the media who are doing an excellent work exposing scams, exposing hawala rackets, exposing individuals responsible for corrupting the society and its private and public are also those who are devoting space and time to developmental work, for focussing attentions on individuals and organisations who are doing constructive work in many fields. They are crusading for certain social causes, and throwing light on the neglected areas and people. There lies hope with this section of the media, however small the section may be, however their cry may sound a cry in wilderness today. What they do will pierce the darkness and spread light all around.

There are certain guidelines or ethical principles which they must follow if they are to succeed. The first is that you have to crusade for a new social order without which it will not be possible to build a value-based society. You cannot keep gutters open and ask people to maintain hygiene. Therefore, let us first crusade for the creation of the new social order. Secondly, we must develop a spirit of inquiry and try to go to the root causes of the events and phenomena. Don't just report a case of corruption or of murder. That is news. That is no information. That doesn't educate the society. You will have to find out the root cause of each of these events and phenomena and educate people if you want them to understand what exactly went wrong, who was responsible for the act and for what reason.

Ultimately, it is the people who are going to create the value-based society and it is they who are going to nurture it. Unless, therefore, there is sufficient information with regard to real causes and consequences of the events, they will not be enlightened. The third thing is you have to be truly independent. It is not enough that you are free. Freedom and independence are two different things. You may be free in the sense that you are free from the external restraints. When we say that you are independent, it means not only freedom from the external restraints but also from the internal constraints. We have our own predilections, preconceived ideas and biases, and prejudices nurtured from childhood. I remember, once Pandit Jawaharlal Nehru said, "We are all rationalists, socialists, humanists and what not, but that is only from the platform. We wear masks when we speak from the pulpit and the platform. It is what we say casually that reveals what is within us and that comes to the surface very often on crucial occasions. You have to be truly independent, objective, fair and impartial while discharging you duties as media persons. You must be like a judge. When he puts on his robes, he has to disrobe his other clothes, his own inclinations towards particular philosophy and ideologies and his own preconceived ideas and go strictly according to law. That is what is expected also of those in the media who are the educators of the masses. The judgment given by the judge may affect the individual parties in the case. But what you say and don't say or suppress, affects the entire society." He further said:

"And last but not the least important thing is to be above corruption and hypocrisy. Today if the fair name of the media, which is the legacy of the past, coming from the stalwarts in the journalistic world who were also stalwarts in social, religious and political fields, has been tarnished, that is because corruption has entered the media in no small measure right from the bottom to the top. I can quote instances of misinformation, disinformation and suppression of news and planting of news. Unless you are above these malpractices, nobody will believe you, much less respect your words. Therefore, doctor heal thyself, if your word is to carry conviction. You must therefore remain above these practices. Not only that, you must also expose others who are indulging in such practices. That is also your sacred duty." Panditji said these words almost 50 years ago. The situation today amply proves that how prophetic he was.

In the age when the print media was the only source of widespread communication Mahatma Gandhi made maximum use of it for the dissemination of his ideas, for organizing the movements he lead, for educating the people while at the same time building the nation. His wide repertoire of communication skills were supplemented and complimented by the use of media. He made a fine distinction between liberty and licence in so far as media was concerned. His responsible handling of the press set standards of journalism. The media bosses who thrive on media can learn a lesson or two as to how to use media for educating the people for the right cause and making the cause a success. All these have been discussed in this work.

The study is based upon his Ph.D. thesis completed under my supervision and guidance in the Department of Gandhian Studies, Panjab University, Chandigarh. Dr. Manoj Rajan is very serious and hardworking scholar. I hope he will continue his pursuits further in his chosen field of interest. I wish him all the best in his future endeavours.

Chandigarh JAI NARAIN SHARMA

Preface

The modern times have seen a major breakthrough as far as the media's role and reach is concerned. There was a time not so long ago when media was limited to newspapers and people would wait 24 hours to get an idea of what was happening around them. The last decade-and-half has seen the rise of multi-media, with TV and Internet emerging as big players. News now is like instant coffee, 24 hours, seven days a week and 365 days a year. You don't like the coffee, change the flavour—you want news of a different kind, switch your TV channel or the webpage. In this scenario, and faced with huge threat from TV and Internet, newspapers have also changed face: they are pacier, more frivolous and more in-your-face than ever before. The media now is the most powerful tool in the society as it helps form opinion and helps the weakest in the society to air their voice. Its reach and imprint has also grown multifold and people are also dependant on the media for each and every small need of theirs. Just that the media needs to be responsible and sensitive.

Being accredited as the fourth pillar of Democracy has laid a greater onus upon it to work in the best possible way, thereby helping the nation in adhering to the norms of being a welfare state. As press progressed from its preliminary stage to the one it has achieved now, it witnessed phases of all the eras. From being an alien product, it went on in becoming the means adopted by the freedom fighters to realize the dream of a free India. It was press that went on hand in hand with Tagore and Bose to voice their call for Independence. It was press that conveyed the motives of young revolutionaries to British. The might of Press can be understood from the face that the Father of the Nation, called the press the guiding light, which he believed was an excellent means to unite country thereby strengthening the foundations of the movements against the British.

Mahatma Gandhi reached out to millions of people across the world through his communication skills and journalistic approach, put an ever lasting impact on Indian National Movement's and waging a battle, single handly against mighty British. He took journalism as a medium to educate the common masses and to install patriotic feeling in their hearts for the cause of others. In his journalistic career, which roughly spanned four decades, he wrote articles on various topics, simple and clear with passion and burning indignation. Gandhi was not a journalist in the popular sense of the term. His life and writing had a symbiotic relationship with each other. Gandhi wrote with a purpose. Writing for him, was not a writer's pursuit for creativity for a role, it was a duty bound to perform. He vouched for the freedom of the press, but at the same time he was critical of the tendency of the journalists to pick up the bits from here and there and dish them up for the purpose of creating sensation was, according to him, back door journalism.

Press thus was not a profession, rather a practice, preached by those who believed in its potential to rise above the multitudes and restore order and justice in a democratic set-up. As media progressed, it widened its arena. The motives and objectives were no more limited to a nation or a group, but the whole world. Thus the media, since then, has been playing a pivot role in bringing the whole world under one roof. This was the onset of globalization, wherein there were extensions of all the genres, namely, print, broadcast and radio, and the latest being the Internet.

Global journalism is the product of the digital technology provided by the big international companies, the multinationals. Some of these huge companies are news corporations; but an increasing number aren't. They are more to have electrical pods or washing powder, or Hollywood, as their foundation but incidentally also own an international media corporation. The standard of information and its dissemination also seems to have suffered. Media Barons have western origins and empires and as a result the informational gratification of the third world countries is being forsaken for lucrative deals. Since media graduated to a global level, it was expected to play a much more responsible role, but, it some how seems to have lost in the fray of commercialization and misplayed responsibilities and priorities of the media persons. The sufferers in this ethical battle are of course the viewers, who have over the years become puppets at its hands for it the media that influences their lives so intrusively. Agreed that the journalist, atleast some of them have had the courage of forfeiting temptations and practicing in depth as well as investigative journalism, but on the whole, the media today is clearly aware of this mighty position that it has gathered and has started to act superfluously. The media has yet to come to terms in resisting the temptation of building brand images, which blur the other aspects of reality on vital issues like combating communalism and problems of the common people. Media organizations must realize the need to draw out a system to prevent the necessary process of investigation degenerating into a "trial by the media."

Never hang a person till proven guilty. That has been the dictum for long as far media was concerned but recent years have seen a sharp U-turn where a minute-by-minute blow has coined a new term for the media: 'Present-tense Journalism'. There have been several cases where, in an effort to be ahead of their competition, the media has resorted to reporting false claims and counter claims without fully verifying the facts. This will obviously raise many a question over the credibility and utility of the media as besides news, they also form the opinion of the society. Investigative journalism should be mindful of the reach of the media and its role in the society. Many instances come to mind in recent years, like the Tehelka Tapes and Operation Duryodhan which proved an eye opener for all of us. But the moment certain media twists the evidence for their own convenience and to make their story authentic, the problem begins. We do get to see the glass half empty in specific stories but only when the glass is also shown half full will the media have done their job.

India is no longer a land of snake charmers. It is one of the booming economies in the world today, that too as one of the powerful voices internationally. All this would not have happened but for the change in the social set-up across the country. The mass reach of the multi-media has created an impression on the minds of the Indians, across all ages and genres, and created Brand India. Today, countries like the US, UK and others want to do business with India. They want to open shop in India. They want to accept and embrace the Indian-ness because they have realized the power of Brand India. Satellite TV in the early 90s led with the way. India wanted to progress. India wanted to shed its old skin. India wanted to compete with the best. India wanted to be a step ahead of the others. The emergence of multi-media gave impetus to that dream and showed us how it could be done. The tolerance level among different genres in the country went up, people became more aware of their needs and roles and the media gave them the platform they craved for.

The media also acted as the watchdog of the society, highlighting corruption and the Government and bureaucratic level. The Government was on its toes, aware it can't pull the wool over anybody's eyes now and the impact on the society was such that democracy became the biggest tool in our hands. The most encouraging signs of the media were its penetration into rural and semi-urban areas. The youth there got the focus it needed and most success stories being scripted today have come from such backgrounds. Even though the evils of caste, creed and religion haven't died down completely, the percentage of eradication has gone up. People are more worried about their bread and butter, civic amenities and education for their children than the social taboos the country reeled under for ages altogether.

Here lies the responsibility for the media. It has to play a constructive role and realise that present-tense journalism will just be a short-cut to doom. The basics for the media will remain the same—truth and nothing else. Many feel that the multi-media are in its infancy right now and will learn from its mistakes as time goes by. May be a mature media will push the social and political reforms in our country with double force. It's good to conclude that the glass is half full than being half empty. There is hope that the dream for the Indians will turn sweeter.

Thus media, the fourth estate has an onerous role of transforming the society and leading masses. In fact, a country's socio-economic set-up can be gauged well by the status that it accords to its press. Media especially in a democratic set-up needs to exercise itself as an independent body, sans any control. This independence and freedom must not misused by its beholders. Thus is a grave need for the media fraternity to play a constructive role in the society. A role not tarnished by the prejudices of commercialization and growing market domination. At the same time, the same onus can be allocated to the consumers of this media, who are alert and intelligent enough to choose the kind of informational package that they are served by their media. Thus with the coordination of the source (media) and the receivers (viewers/readers/listeners), a nation can go a way ahead in deciding its fate.

Thus media needs to become participatory in its approach and live up to the ethics that have been associated with it. It has to restore the sanctity attached to it and shed away the prejudices that unshackle it. It needs to realise its potential and channelize it and not to misuse its authority and influence, atleast not in Gandhi's India.

Chandigarh MANOJ RAJAN

Acknowledgements

On the successful completion of my Ph.D. thesis, I express sincere gratitude to my distinguished supervisor, Dr. Jai Narain Sharma, Professor, Department of Gandhian Studies, Panjab University, Chandigarh. I would at first, like to thank him for his judicious and scholarly guidance, continued and active interest, sustained encouragement, constructive criticism and sagacious counseling at every stage of my work and without his support this thesis would not have materialized.

I owe immense gratitude to Dr. (Ms) Ashu Pasricha, whose keen perception, pieces of advice, words of inspiration and immense knowledge enabled me to accomplish this thesis. I am also thankful to Professor M.L. Sharma and Dr. Manish Sharma for their kind cooperation during my research work.

I am highly thankful to my parents, brother and bhabhiji and my two smart and lovely nephews, Manan and Karteek for their kind cooperation, sincerity and affection during my research work.

I will be failing in my duty if I do not acknowledge my profound thanks to my better half Ms Tawinder Kaur Chandel for her kind support, patience, valuable suggestion and ever smiling face, which motivated me in all circumstances to finish my thesis.

Last but not the least, thanks are due to my little daughter Aastha, who behaved like an angel and her charming face let me pursue my thesis without disturbance.

My thanks are due to my friends and relatives for helping me in the arduous task of moving around for collecting the necessary material and complete my research.

I am also grateful to the Librarian, A.C. Joshi Library, Panjab University, Chandigarh for helping me in procuring the relevant material for my study. Facilities provided by The British Library, Chandigarh, State Library, Chandigarh, National Gandhi Museum, New Delhi and The American Library, New Delhi are acknowledged with thanks. At this juncture, I also would like to thank the Almighty who has given me strength to complete this research work.

Chandigarh MANOJ RAJAN

Introduction

Men communicate information and ideas through the spoken word to individuals, small groups, large audiences in schools; they share their opinion and experience, in meetings and crowded auditoria. The effectiveness of men's words with any audience depends as much on the manner speakers say, what they have to say, level and background of audience as well as venue, electronic devices and the contents of subject/topic. At its best, his superior influence of speaking over writing lies in the ability of the speaker to impress his audience with his personal characteristics and his manner of delivery which includes non-verbal part, say body language. Communication is not only a human phenomenon but also among the infra human species such as chickens, bees and ants and there are signs and signals which give order to their living settings. However, human beings have the programming capability and that is how they get differentiated from the infra human species which are incapable of having a language.

Man alone of all the living organism kingdom has acquired the knack of translating sound into written symbols. At first man communicated to his follows through gestures, then pictures and signs/symbols and finally he learned to speak, to use words, he discovered how to turn his words into written symbols which others could see and understand. He scratched them first on the cave walls or carved them deep in stone columns and monuments and later he wrote them on which could be carried around or sent from place to place. Untold centuries went into the perfecting of this unique achievement, but its possession has done more for the human race than any of the men's other learned activities in this universe. To communicate means to share, to make common ideas, views, opinion and experiences. Human beings because of their social and economic living, have to share a wider range of perceptions, beliefs and ideas. In this process of interaction, they evolve a symbol system which relates them to a commonly understood code representing various objects and subjects having significance in their day to day living. In short, communication is an exchange of facts, ideas, opinions or emotions by two or more persons. Communication is also defined as an intercourse by words, letters, symbols or messages and in a way that organization members share meanings and understanding with one another. Communication is the sum of all the things one does when he wants to create understanding in the mind of others. It involves a systematic and continuous process of telling, listening and understanding.

Communication sets in a process of development. Communication also acts as a complement of technological change. In fact, communication mediates in the production, consumption and accumulation of goods and services besides promoting political, social, psychological and cultural processes of development. Modern communication system reflects the philosophy and achievements of society in all spheres by fast flow of information and thus paves way for homogeneity of culture not only within its geographical unit but also beyond it. Free flow of information is one of the objectives in the process of globalization which is aided by the Press. Press is one of the effective means of communication which produces the publication of news and views on various aspects of human activities in newspapers and periodicals. In a broader sense, the functions of press are to convey national policies, programmes and development/ progress of various projects to the public. Information is the key to human progress. Mankind has traveled a long way to reach this present stage of development. All along, it was a story of advancement that kept moving the wheels of civilization. From the Stone Age to the atomic age, it was always a journey forward and the driving force of this journey was information. The eternal urge of man to inform and to be informed widened the horizons of knowledge, and provided a strong impetus to the development of the society.[1]

Mass communication communicates messages to large, heterogeneous and anonymous audiences. It communicates the same message to mass audiences simultaneously; sometimes in public, other times in private. On July 10, 1962, Telstar I was launched, which marked a significant event in the history of worldwide communications. Telstar was an experimental "bird" that was the first to receive, amplify and simultaneously retransmit telephone and signals. It was in fact, a forerunner of the modern communication satellite. Today, communication satellites by the scores are traveling through space, orbiting the earth and making possible a new era in communication. Mass communication is the term used to describe the academic study of the various means by which individuals and entities relay information through mass media to large segments of the population at the same time. It is usually understood to relate to newspaper and magazine publishing, radio, television and film, as these are used both for disseminating news and for advertising.

To perform its duties with entire independence and consequently with the most public advantage, the press can enter into no close or binding alliance with the statesman of the day, nor can it surrender its permanent interest to the convenience of the ephemeral power of any government. The first duty of the press is to obtain the earliest and most correct intelligence of the events of the time and instantly disclose them, to make them the common property of the nation. The duty of the press is to speak; that of the statesman to be silent. The duty of the journalist is the same as that of the historian;, i.e. to seek out truth above all things, and to present to his readers not such things as state-craft would wish them to know, but the truth as near as he can attain it.[2]

Press helps to keep the Government at local, state and central levels, informed of public needs and public expectations. It is through press, again, that the reactions of the affected groups due to omissions, commissions, wrong-doings and indifference to the public's complaints and grievances, on the part of public servants, are known through articulated feedback. It also brings out public reaction to Government policies and decisions. In addition, it keeps the public and the government informed of events and happenings at home and abroad. As Jawaharlal Nehru rightly points out, "The press is one of the vital organs of modern life especially in a democracy. The press has tremendous powers and responsibilities. The press must be respected."[3]

Human life is a cooperative enterprise. One lives in society and for our very living, one have to cooperate with others. In order to be able to do this, one must understand and exchange information with others. Even where one competes with others, one have to understand them otherwise our efforts would prove futile, or even counter productive. Doing this involves some kind of exchange of experience with others. Now experience is basically private and personal, but along with this personal component, experience has also a public component. This public component is embodied in concepts which are either pure or empirical, embodied in experience and contains essayistic elements.

Democratic freedom is, therefore, the very condition of a vigorous intellectual life. Most of all, it is the very condition of virility of the press, which was proved in a historic manner in the water-gate scandal. It was, therefore, because of the basic duty of the press to fight for preservation of the freedom of information and comment, and what all was more important for an active exercise of it. In doing this, the press is only exercising its rule at the home level of democracy, its rule of creating a healthy, truth-seeking public opinion, which is the operant factor in the successful functioning of the democratic order. A public opinion formed by distortion of news may succeed in pressuring a corrupt government or pulling down a just one thereby installing in its place, a government, which may betray the voter.

Printing was an ancient art long before it was used to

reproduce lettering or books. The Japanese were the pioneers as they were engraving wood blocking and impressing them on paper in the eighth century AD. A Chinese, Wang Chien, printed a book in the memory of his parents and dated it with the equivalent of 11 May, 1868. The Chinese are believed to have invented the first movable type, by using small blocks where each carved character was independent and inter changeable. Pi Sheng is said to have done this between 1041 and 1049. But, to compile character of the Chinese alphabet, with its multiplicity of picture symbols, made this a slow and tedious process.[4] It was not until the fourteenth century that moving type was introduced in Europe. Johan Gutenberg set-up his press is Mainz, Germany in 1454-55 and began to print Papal indulgences, the document authorized by the Pope to grant forgiveness to sinners, for which there was an understandable demand. In 1456, Gutenberg and his assistant printed 300 copies of the Bible. It was in Black Gothic lettering and the initial letters were left blanks and later ornamented to give the impression that the work had been written by scribes. Within a few years, the skill spread to Italy, particularly to Venice. Before the end of 15th Century, printing had started in France and Switzerland, where, for a time, the great scholar Erasmus was the press corrector. Then printing was brought to England by William Caxton. Soon presses began to be set-up all across the world.

NEWS

News, as you may know, is the substance of a newspaper. News is a kind of timely information of interest to many people. It usually concerns events that have just taken place or sometimes about to take place. The event is largely physical such as the collapse of bridge; sometimes it is principally intellectual, such as the discovery of a cure for a dreaded disease. The fresher the information, the better is its use in newspapers. It can also be called as anything timely that interests a number of persons and the best news is that which has the 'greatest interest for the greatest number'. News is anything you did not know yesterday. Another aspect here is that news is perishable. It must be delivered to its consumers while it is still fresh; otherwise, it is no longer news.[5] Reporters compete with each other to get the news into the paper fast, so that it will be fresh, and their's will be the first publication to print it. Certain information can be timely and not news worthy because it does not interest enough people. Thus editor must decide what timely information interests a considerable number of his readers. The origins of the world 'new' lies in the Latin Term 'nova', which means 'new things'. The first three letters spell out the freshness and originality that underline all accounts of news-worthiness. The Oxford English dictionary defines 'News' as newly received or noteworthy information, especially about recent events, again emphasizing the topicality of the revelation. So, to put at its simplest, news is a record of the latest events, incidents and developments that in some way touch on the lives of a news papers' readers.[6]

Thus there has been no definition of news which is satisfactory to all. What passes for news in Indian newspapers and American newspapers are familiar. And what appears is British and American newspapers may not be understood as news by the Indian reader. The definition of news, therefore, varies from country to country or from one continent to other continent. The obsession with speeches and governmental activities has continued till today in this country with politicians and politics claiming a lion's share of the daily newspaper space to the exclusion of news of other aspects of life, except for the coverage of news like riots, natural calamities or major accidents. Apparently, Indian newspapers have not recovered from the hangover of colonial rule and the readers themselves have not been educated to expect or demand anything different from what they have been used to so far. Herbert J. Gans says, "News is about the economic, political, social and cultural hierarchies which we call nation and society. For the most part, news reports on those at or near the top of the hierarchies and on those particularly at the bottom who threaten them, to an audience most of whom are located in the vast middle range between top and bottom"[7].

When common man says something it's not necessarily

news, but the same statement by a person in authority is news. When unknown people do something, it may not be news, but the same act by a celebrity is news. News comes from the things people or groups of people have done, are doing, or plan to do. That covers everything except natural phenomena, and you can be sure that Mother Nature will make big news all year[8]. News must consist of facts and truths on which people can depend. Newspaper subscribers read the news to get the facts. They base their judgements on those facts, and later act on those judgements. News that is false or inaccurate may lead to all kinds of troubles. Every successful newspaper-man must develop the habit and the zeal for accuracy, a goal that may take a lifetime to realize fully. Every reporter in the world has made mistakes and may continue to make them occasionally. No human being can attain perfect accuracy, but the person who strives for it will come nearer and nearer to success. Experienced words are always preferable to colourless ones—when the facts justify them. The facts do not justify all the active expressions used in journalism. Some reporters, eager to capture attention, colour the news in a way that is more captivating than true e.g. Arushi murder case where media led the case where it could fetch more TRP's. It is true that in general people do not like to be distressed or disturbed and the news of the day is often distressing and disturbing. Therefore, one element of popular press might be called the 'familiarity factor' of Pulp entertainment, of simple reassurance that the world is still turning, that the popular press feels, it must include in its pages. The 'familiarity factor' is important. It must not be despised, for to get through to its readers, its listeners or viewers, journalism must lay down some guidelines to lead the public from what is familiar to what seems strange, dangerous and frightening. Journalism is an agent of change in a society, which must not stay too comfortably in the familiar present.

The broad/public nature of 'News' is indicated by the way the word NEWS is derived. The four letter word is the initials of the four directions of the earth, namely, North, East, West and South. This means that news is constituted of reports from all quarters, from all sides, from all directions.

The only criterion of selection of News is the 'public interest'—interest of the reading public at large. It means the vital interests of the people and it also means the things in which the people are some-how interested. If the water supply of the town is to be stopped for a day, this news concerns the vital interest of almost every one of its residents, but if cricket match is abandoned because of rain, it might concern the interest—which is not so vital—of only the cricket fans.[9] News is no more a luxury to be indulged in by a selected few. It has become a necessity for the people at large. It is information which a man must get in under to survive and get along in the complex society of today. One must remember that man's life depends on a regular supply of information. The variety of news of comment is an important means of securing the truth. This variety is possible only if there is freedom of gathering the news to commenting on it. If the sources of information are restricted and channeled through a prescribed way then there is a major chance for its losing the objectivity which is an integral part of any good news. It is the nature of perception, which is at the root of information to be conditioned by the past of the perceiver and, therefore, all perception is, in a way, biased. The only way of correcting this bias is to have a large variety of perceptions of the same event and sort them out with a view to secure objectivity.

Anything that enough people want to read is news, provided it does not violate the canons of good taste and the laws of libel. It comprises all current activities which are of general human interest, and the best news is that which interest most readers. News is an account of an event which a newspaper prints in the belief that by doing so it will profit[10]. The tendency to provide unpartisan news is likely to continue, since the gathering and the distribution of most important national and international news is conduct by press associations. The association by the very nature of their existence must be non political and non partisan. The freedom of printing has never accorded a publisher or writer the right to injure others. News happens wherever there are people. It comes from formal sources such as police, fire, ambulance and coastguard, from business and other organizations and from the less formal setting of clubs and societies. It comes, too, from individuals with a good story to tell. Having a nose for news as it is sometimes referred to is an essential requirement for any journalist being able to unearth fascinating and stimulating ideas for coverage; it is vital to ensure that news is never old, stale or, worst of all, plain boring.

News must reflect the diverse events, issues and interests that make up for the every day news requirements of its readers. News must be contemporaneous if they are to achieve prominence. There is no point reporting yesterday's news in print today, when your readers may have already been well briefed by broadcast and other media or in a worst case scenario, your rivals. Newness will very much depend on the individual news cycle of the output. News is about people rather than things. As a society, we place tremendous importance on the integrity of human existence, which means that stories involving the most vulnerable people attract must coverage. Johan Galling and Mari Harolmoboe Ruge[11] in 1965 identified twelve recurring factors in news stories, as list of their criteria and a summary of their meaning is reproduced:

- Frequency—how close a story happens to the movement of publication?
- Threshold—the level the event must reach in terms of scale for it to stand out.
- Unambiguity—the story should be clearly understood.
- Meaning fullness—the story should be relevant to the reader's frame of reference.
- Constance—the build up to an expected event.
- Unexpectedness—how predictable an event is.
- Continuity—a big story will remain in the news or days or weeks.
- Composition—a story may be selected because it helps balance the other stories.
- Reference to nations—some places are covered more than others.
- Reference to event—event affecting famous people.
- Reference to persons—news that has a human focus.

- Reference to something negative—bad news usually contains more of the above criteria than good news.

Newspaper

Thomas Jefferson, one of the founding fathers of the American Republic said, "Were it left to me to choose a government without newspapers or newspapers without a government, I would not for a moment hesitate to prefer the latter."[12] The modern newspaper is a complicated and many faceted organization whose interests and activities encompass the entire world. It is no exaggeration to claim that the world is its stage and its readers are its audience. By the very nature of its gigantic task—purveying news, opinion and pictures from all parts of globe—it cannot be anything but the big business. It is as much a commercial proposition as any other trade and it has to make profits as any other business if it is to survive even for a day in a world of rising costs and inflation.[13]

The newspaper today must have the good-will of the people. Its editions know they cannot occasionally deceive readers and still keep them as good customers. Consistent honesty must be their watch word. Even today, a scrupulous person is tempted to earn money or to gain notoriety through false news which even the most alert editions may fail to detect. Once such news is discovered, however, good newspaper will quickly acknowledge the error and make every effort to have the offender punished. It is even more difficult for newspapers to maintain a high standard by inclusion of unbiased news. For the sake of making news sensational, some reporters and editors add embellishments that are entirely imaginary although the basis of the story is factual. The public wants the facts so that they can judge the right or wrong of the matter. To present such an unbiased story, the modern reporter writes his news from what is known as the objective points of view, rather than the subjective, that is, reports the news as it exists apart from him, keeping prejudice and his own opinion and feelings out of him.

To appeal to readers and attract subscribers, newspaper

editions play up the stories with the greater news value, that is, give them prominent space and conspicuous headlines. News value depends on the degree of timeliness and mass interest, which means a given piece of news has impact on the numbers of readers' interests and on the extent to which it interests them. Thus the news story in a given issue of the paper and the one that merits the leading headline on the front page is the story that interests the greatest number of persons to the greater extent. The Press has been very slow to catch up with this change, and to revise its methods of operation, so that the newspaper still has a function to perform. Newspapers are achieves of record of event and objectives. They can be referred to, checked back on, in a way that the television or radio cannot. They can describe events at great length, add more relevant details, reproduce authoritative comments from the people to be in a position to observe trends and tow the likely lines in which a news story will develop.

A great editor of the Manchester Guardian, C.P. Scote, made keen observation and made statement of main principle of journalism. He said, "Comment is free; facts are scared. A Newspaper must have coverage and fairness, and a sense of duty to the reader and community. Its primary objective is the gathering of news, at the peril of its soul; it must see that the supply is not tainted."[14] A newspaper man should be an educationist and not a propagandist. His job is to furnish facts, to inform his reader about the things as they are and guide them in assessing their significance. In order to supply correct information to the readers, a newspaper must itself be able to get correct information. Its sources of news must themselves be impeccable. This implies that its correspondence should have the capacity and the integrity to collect unvarnished news. Newspaper correspondent, these days, are open to many kinds of corruption or coercion.

To fight for the preservation and furtherance of democratic freedom is its most natural and necessary duty, for the very simple reason that a newspaper is a newspaper only in a democracy. In a dictatorship, a newspaper is not a newspaper but a view paper, in fact a government hand out. A newspaper contrary to what many people think is not an instrument of propaganda but a means of education. Propaganda aims at converting the people to a particular point of view, education aims at enabling them to think for the universe. Propagandists insist that theirs is the truth, educationists recognize that truth is a vast thing, almost co-equal with the universe, and that it is the duty of us all to participate in the research for it. Education does not believe in standard manufacture of truth. It aims at discovering facts and the laws which bind them together. Newspapers in a free society tend to adopt conflicting points of view with one another. But a study of conflicting views has a better chance of gaining, at least a glimpse of truth, than the reading of newspapers in a dictatorship. Newspapers in a dictator ruled country are not the means to disseminate information, but to doctor it in a manner found necessary and convenient by the rulers for themselves. They are not newspapers but vehicles of propaganda. Just as people get the government they deserve, so do the readers who get the newspapers they deserve, as a result of which the Indian newspapers are neglecting their duty not only towards their readers, but towards themselves—a duty that obliges them to be the true pillars of democracy, to be the educational organs of public opinion; an obligation they seem to be increasingly unmindful of.

The newspaper as an institution has been no more better than other institutions of a democracy. The newspaper has become primarily a business, the desire of the holder is to earn a living to make money, to achieve power through the newspaper. In a democracy, freedom to write is not just for good but for the wise men, for good taste. It is for all, those of good principle and those of evil principles or of no principle."[15] "What is the power of the press." The reply is, "it is the power of words." Newspapers also use pictures which lend beauty to their look. But rarely can a picture make sense to a newspaper reader without the help of words. We think we read a newspaper to get information. We survey to get a good deal of knowledge about our surroundings. But in process, we also get affected and therefore influenced. The newspaper, therefore, by employing words which embody concepts, inculcates emotions in their readers. The newspaper readers do not receive cold information from their newspapers. The information is callused by emotions it arouses, of course in varying degrees. That is what makes newspaper reading interesting. The information that touches the sensitive spots in the reader's psyche, arouses strong emotions are more demanding than the other kind which would affect them only slightly. The power of press consists in the power of concepts embodied in words. Apparently, they supply information but in doing so, they touch upon many sensitive spots. Their expressed purpose may be to supply cold information affecting their readers. But all information is not really that cold. The interpretation of news, except where on some occasions, it is purely abstract or merely explanatory that arouses emotions, some times identity. Life is practically action-oriented and emotions points towards action, emotions help man keep himself action-oriented and this is what life would appear to demand.

Newspaper has to live according to its character. Therefore, in the 21st century, it must not merely look after the economic side of its existence, but fight for its freedom as well. The only thing the newspaper has to do is providing the true facts of a situation with logical background and rest would leave to its readers. Further, a newspaper not merely provides news, it interprets it also to make the news story understandable to the common man. However, interpretation of news is likely to encounter opposition from some powerful quarters, who may not agree with the views expressed in the newspaper. But in doing this, it cannot lose its sense of solidarity with the reader. Therefore a newspaper has to ultimately care for the well being of the community to which it belongs. For an example, while reporting a rape case, a newspaper is bound to honour the dignity of a woman and for that purpose, it must desist form publishing certain details like her name, her identity, etc. This particularly exists in our society in which we would look down upon the raped woman, even though we know or ought to know that the woman is in no way to blame. Another example is of a communal riot. A newspaper must report in a way that would not inflame further emotions to already inflamed passions. The newspaper delivers different forms of news, with differing effects on the consumer. As a print medium, the readership demands news published in an interesting manner, as reading is a more difficult process than watching TV. Thus polycot, a higher degree of discernment, if not actual intelligence, is needed to process news stories in print media as opposed to TV stories in which someone else is reading the story to deliver it in an animated manner.

Newspapers are said to be easiest and cheap medium to inform, educate and entertain. But the balance of emphasis varies widely among various newspapers. The importance of solid and accurate research and meticulous recording of information cannot be emphasized strongly enough. Once a newspaper gains a dis-repute for inaccuracy or floppy research, it can be very difficult to regain good reputation. M.H. Deyong Said, "A great NP should be concerned with the accomplishment of great ends for benefit of the public, rather than be designed simply to solely be a gainer of money for the benefit of the stockholders of the corporation."[16]

MAJOR PLAYERS OF INDIAN JOURNALISM

Amrita Bazar Patrika

In India, five English dailies have crossed the century mark, out of these three namely the Amrita Bazar Patrika, The Hindu and The Tribune, were owned and edited by Indians and the other two, the Times of India and the Statesman were owned and edited by the Britishers. All these newspapers have played a major role in the evolution and growth of Indian journalism.

The Amrit Bazar Patrika[17] is the oldest Indian-owned daily. It was born as a weekly in Bengali in February, 1868, in the village of Amrita Bazar in Jessore district (now in Bangladesh). It was started by four brothers to fight the cause of peasants who were being exploited by indigo planters. Sisir Kumar, the more famous among the brothers, was the editor and the story of Patrika was the story of Sisir Kumar's relentless fight against the alien rulers that were determined to suppress this mouthpiece of the poor and downtrodden Indians. The Patrika moved to Calcutta in 1871 and functioned as bi-lingual weekly, publishing news and views in English along with Bengali. Its anti-government views and its influence among the people provoked the Government of Lord Lytton to take action against the language press. But before the Vernacular Press Act of 1878, (said to be mainly directed towards the Patrika) was enforced to crush this language paper, the Patrika overnight became an English weekly and thus escaped the clutches of the law. With increased circulation and greater influence with the people, the Patrika continued to remain a thorn in the side of the administration. Every effort was made to buy the Patrika by English people but Sisir Kumar refused to be tempted. The Patrika became a daily in February, 1891, and plunged into the nationalist movement which had received a fillip with the formation of the Indian National Congress in 1885. The Patrika created history during the term of Lord Lansdowne as Viceroy when it published a confidential document of the Foreign Office concerning Kashmir. It created a sensation among official circles and a law was passed to prevent disclosure of official circles, documents and background material without prior permission. Sisir Kumar fought for the freedom of the Press and those in the profession. He launched vigorous campaigns against restrictions on civil liberties and economic exploitation. He pleaded for the establishment of representative institutions for Indians to have a say in the administration. He contributed much to arouse the political consciousness of the people and he founded the Indian League in 1875, which probably was the first political association in India. Sisir Kumar and his brother, Motilal Ghosh, were deeply attached to Bal Gangadhar Tilak. When Tilak was prosecuted for sedition in 1897, they raised funds in Calcutta for his defense. Such was the editors of first Indian daily and their writing and courage speak about them itself.

The Times of India

The Times of India[18] is the oldest English daily in India and it is also a great newspaper which has played an important role in the development of journalism in this country. Before the advent of political freedom and especially in the closing years of the 19th century and beginning of 20th century, it had been a controversial newspaper which had stood as a bulwark of colonial rule and had nothing but contempt for Indians and their aspirations to freedom. It was incepted in 1838 and since then, The Times of India is not only India's largest selling English general daily but also the leading English general daily broadsheet in the world. It attracts a daily circulation level of about 22 lakh copies. It is the largest selling English daily between Tokyo and Paris. Its own history constitutes an authoritative slice of the history of Journalism in India. It has witnessed and reported the making of the phenomenon called Modern India. It has been published by dozens of the English editors and put a mark in revolutionalizing journalism across the world. Officers, executives, decision-makers, businessmen, government executives, politicians, intellectuals and students form the highest percentage of The Times of India readership. The Times of India has highest percentage of sole readers indicating its leading position and has eight regional editions which include Mumbai, Delhi, Ahmedabad, Hyderabad, Pune, Bangalore, Lucknow and Patna.

The Hindustan Times

Hindustan Times Media Limited is a major player in the print media in India. It too has a leadership position in the English newspaper market in North India and the second position in the Hindi newspaper market as Hindustan in the North and East. The group now intends to consolidate itself as vibrant and modern media powerhouse through strategic partnerships, ever increasing scope of operations and a consumer focused approach. Hindustan Times, the flagship publication from the group, was inaugurated by Mahatma Gandhi in 1924 and has established presence as a source of newspaper editorial par excellence and full of integrity. Today, Hindustan Times has a circulation of over 1.2 million and is the fastest growing mainline English newspaper in terms of readership. Hindustan Times, Delhi, is India's largest single edition daily. In July 2005, Hindustan Times made successful entry into the commercial capital of India, i.e. Mumbai.

The Hindu

The Hindu,[19] started in 1878 as a weekly, became a daily in 1889 and from then on, has been steadily growing to the current circulation of over 1000,000 copies and a readership of over 3 million. The Hindu's independent editorial stand and its reliable and balanced presentation of the news has over the years, won for it the serious attention and regard of the people who matter in India and abroad. The Hindu uses modern facilities for news gathering, page composition and printing. It is printed in twelve centers including the Main Edition at Chennai (Madras) where the Corporate Office is based. The printing centers at Coimbatore, Bangalore, Madurai, Hyderabad, New Delhi, Vizag, Thiruvanathapuram, Kochi, Vijayawada, Mangalore and Tiruchirapalli are connected with high-speed data lines for news transmission across the country. Six young men, all in their twenties, founded The Hindu in Madras on September 20, 1878. Two of them, G. Subramanian Ayer and M. Veeraraghavacharier, stayed on later to become joint proprietors of the paper, which started as a weekly and became daily in 1889. They all belonged to a society called the Triplicane Literary Society, which was a forum for discussion of political and social topics and attracted to it the elite of Madras. The immediate reason for starting the paper was the criticism by British owned newspapers of the appointment of T. Muthuswami Ayer as judge of the Madras High Court. In the words of Subramanian Ayer: 'Unable to stand this unfairness, six of us joined together and started The Hindu. When we started the newspaper, we had no idea of the responsibility which its publication would involve, of how to conduct it, of the expenditure to be incurred, etc. Since we had no money with us, we borrowed one rupee and three quarters and printed and published 80 copies'[20]. In its first editorial, The Hindu wrote: 'We are inclined to be conservative as much as it is consistent with the national progress of the natives. The principles that we propose to be guided by are simply those of fairness and justice. It will always be our aim to promote harmony and union among our fellow countrymen and to interpret correctly the feelings of the natives and to create mutual confidence between the governed and the governors'[21]. At that time when The Hindu appeared, public opinion in Madras Presidency was stagnant and there were very few recognized forums to voice the feelings and grievances of the Indian population. It filled a vacuum and instantly become popular. This helped The Hindu to be accepted from its very birth as an all-India paper even though it could not claim any large all-India circulation.

The Hindu changed hands in 1905 when S. Kasturiranga lyengar, a lawyer, bought it and became its editor. A. Rangaswami lyengar became the editor in 1928 and he performed the duties of Secretary of the Indian National Congress for many years and was also a leading member of the party in the Central Legislative Assembly. After the death of Rangaswami lyengar, Kasturi Srinivasan, took over as Managing editor of the paper in 1934 and remained in that post till his death in 1959. In 1958, The Hindu's page one became news page when it abandoned its policy of over 80 years of carrying only advertisements on that page. His brother's sons, G. Narasimham and G. Kasturi took over after Srinivasan's death.

The Statesman

The Statesman[22] is one of India's oldest English newspapers founded in Kolkata in 1875 by Robert Knight, who was one of the early British journalists, who like Silk Buckingham, encouraged critical analysis of the government's actions and policies, which set him besides other British-owned papers, which while supporting the government, steadfastly also indulged in denunciation of Indians and particularly the nationalists. The Delhi edition of The Statesman began publication in 1931. It is said that Jawaharlal Nehru read the Statesman every morning during the days of the freedom struggle when he was out of prison and it was one of the newspapers supplied to him when he was in prison which happened frequently. In 1928, when the nationalists organized a boycott of the Simon Commission which came to go into constitutional reforms, the Statesman appealed to them to cooperate with the Commission and this led to a campaign to boycott the paper and copies of the paper were burnt. But it did not deter a prominent nationalists' leader from reading the paper's editorials. The Statesman, which was described as the Manchester Guardian of the East, has had a long line of able and dedicated editors who have left their mark deep on it. There were several occasions when it got into trouble with the government. On one such occasion, Gokhale had to use his influence to rescue its editor, Samuel Ratcliffe, from government displeasure. This happened during the viceroyalty of Lord Minto. The paper had published a secret minute of Lord Curzon on the partition of Bengal and the Home Department withdrew from it government advertisements and other privileges as a punishment. Gokhale spoke to Dunlop Smith, private secretary to the Viceroy, who supported to arrange an interview for Ratcliffe with the Home Member, Arundel. The Statesman published an apology and the government withdrew the ban.

The Statesman Weekly is a compendium of news and views from the Kolkata and Delhi editions. Primed on airmail paper, it is also popular with readers outside India. The Statesman is the leading English newspaper in West Bengal. The Statesman has distinguished itself through objective coverage of events, its value as an honest purveyor of news, emphasized at times of crisis such as the Bengal famine of 1943 and the infamous internal emergency of the mid 1970's. It is forthright in the expression of its views. Its pursuit of the truth has been relentless and often at considerable cost to itself; first, when the government of Indira Gandhi, in gross abuse of power, attempted to suppress its voice and secondly, when the government of Rajiv Gandhi interfered with the grant of statutory clearances to its modernization plans unless the paper changed its editorial stance.

The Tribune

The Tribune[23] is one of the powerful newspapers which had made its footprint not only in the freedom struggle of India but also enlightening the contemporary times with its editorials and news. Gandhi once said in 1932: 'The Tribune is the best newspaper. Its editorials, readings and analysis of events are unsurpassed'. He said of its great editor: 'Long lives Kalmath Ray'. Kalmath Ray was to the Tribune what G.

Subramanian and Kastunranga lyengar were to The Hindu and Motilai Ghosh to the Amrita Bazar Patrika. He was a Bengali who had worked on Surendranath Bannerjee's Bengalee in Calcutta before he came to Lahore in 1917, to take over editorship of the Tribune. He was tireless writer who bravely faced the risks involved in fighting the strongly entrenched alien government. His fierce attacks on the Punjab Government and particularly on General Dyer, villain of Jallianwala Bagh in 1919, led to his being arrested and sentenced to two years' imprisonment. On appeal, however, it was reduced to three months. Ray had his differences with Gandhi. He did not believe in non-violence and the methods adopted by Gandhi to achieve freedom but he was a good Congressman and took an active part in the freedom struggle. He told Mulk Raj Anand, the novelist: We Bengalis do not agree with Gandhi that India can win freedom with non-violence. We can embarrass the government with non-cooperation. Some of our young students have turned terrorists. You know one of the men who threw the bomb at Lord Harding in 1911 was a Bengali called Rash Behari. He escaped to Japan afterwards. And one of our writers, Sarat Chandra, has written a novel lauding the gospel of 'Tit for Tat'. Amolak Ram, a former editor, has said that Ray who edited the Tribune for 28 years was known for his uprightness, integrity, and independence. He neither did nor allowed his judgment to be influenced by personal or sectarian considerations. Nor did he brook any interference, internal or external, in the conduct of the paper. It was a treat to read his analytical editorials particularly at a time when the British bureaucracy was out to suppress all patriotic aspirations. Kali Babu, as his admirers affectionately called him, was generally disinclined to meet any VIP. He rarely attended any social function. He had a deep insight into the affairs of state and the working of various political organizations. He differed with Gandhi on certain aspects of the non-cooperation programme and expressed his opinion candidly and freely. But he had a high regard for those with whom he happened to differ. In spite of his differences, he gave unrelenting support to Gandhi in the long and arduous fight for freedom. Ray passed away in 1943 and the Tribune passed through many ups and downs until the final calamity in 1947 when, on the eve of independence, two of its staff members were stabbed and the publication of the paper in Lahore was suspended.

Sardar Dayal Singh Majithia, who was a great admirer of Raja Ram Mohan Roy and the Brahmo Samaj started the Tribune as a weekly in Lahore in 1881. He was helped by Surendranath Bannerjee in buying a printing press. The Tribune, which became a daily in 1906, had a number of Bengalis as its editors in its early career, including Kalinath Ray and Bipin Chandra Pal. A great philanthropist and prominent nationalist of northern India, Sardar Dayal Singh established a trust, for the Tribune, which continues to function till date. In its first issue on February 2, 1881, the Tribune said: "The aim of the Tribune will be, as its name imparts, fairly and temperately to advance the cause of the masses. We shall strive as much as lies in the compass of our humble abilities to create and educate such opinion."

On the eve of independence when Punjab was partitioned, riots rocked Lahore and the mob attacked the office of the Tribune. Two members of the staff were killed; the printing machinery, building and land were lost. The paper suspended publication. In a telegram to Patel, home minister, the manager of the paper said, "Tribune Lahore has lost property, cash, machinery, newsprint, etc. worth Rs. 25 lakhs. Newsprint worth Rs. 2 lakhs removed under orders of the West Punjab Government to Government Printing Press, Lahore. Our van and six typewriters have also been given to Pakistan Times. The government has sealed our press and office. I learn that our press and building are being given to Pakistan Times." Patel asked the Rehabilitation Minister, K.C. Neogi to give all facilities to the Tribune to resume publication from Indian soil. The Tribune had opposed partition but when it became a tacit accompli, its trustees decided to continue to publish it from Lahore and its editor wrote an editorial supporting Jinnah's views. Jinnah appreciated the Tribune's stand but the chaos and anarchy that followed partition left no option for the paper and it moved to Shimla and later to Ambala in May 1948. The Tribune moved to its present home in Chandigarh in 1969.

The paper, whose editor then was Madhavan Nair, got into trouble with the Government of India during the Emergency in 1975. It was one of the three papers blacklisted by the government and denied advertisements and other facilities. Two sister papers, one in Punjabi and the other in Hindi (Punjabi Tribune and Dainik Tribune) were started in 1978 and were an instant success. Till today, the Tribune is putting its mark in the development of the masses and society.

Journalism

Journalism is both an art and a profession which records events and opinions and seeks to interpret and mould them for the benefit of public. Herbert Hoover says, "Honest difference of views and honest debate are not disunity. They are the vital process of policy making among free men"[24]. Today, we read and hear much about the importance of being well informed. To be successful in any activity, you must be equipped properly with all the knowledge possible concerning that activity. Journalism is the business of timely knowledge. The business of obtaining necessary facts, of evaluating them carefully, of presenting them fully and of acting on them wisely is a part of journalism. Journalism entered the twenty first century caught in a paradox of its own making. We have more news and more influential journalism, across an unprecedented range of media, than at any time since the birth of the free press in the eighteenth century; yet journalism is also under widespread attack, from politicians, philosophers, and the general public and even from journalists themselves.[25]

Definition of journalism varies from the flip to the pompous and the ones that matter lie between those extremes. Journalism is about finding things out and then telling other people in as interesting and accessible way as possible. Taking it a step further, journalism is about discovering things various interested parties would prefer left undiscovered. Another popular definition says journalism is about comforting the afflicted and afflicting the comfortable. It is about finding out what is really going on. It is about holding those who wield power—political, commercial, financial, legal and social—to account, representing those over whom power is exercised. The powerful are kept in check, the powerless supported. Journalism, thus exercises a critical role in a free society and is always checked, constrained or out lawed in undemocratic societies.[26]

The press on one hand performs the utilitarian purpose of giving information through news and imparts education through comments, views, opinions, features, interpretative writing and articles on subjects and topics of various sorts, while on the other hand, it provides entertainment to its readers by publishing short stories, poems, sports events, film features, reviews (of books, films, policies and programmes), comic strips, caricatures, anecdotes, etc. Newspaper, particularly, is said to give taste to the reader's morning coffee or tea. It is so much socialized that it is important part of life of readers. The main function of journalism is to bring to light to the people what its members feel and think. Journalism has focused solely on its primary political function, which is to inform the public and has therefore neglected its secondary but complementary function, which is to engage with the broader life style and entertainment requirements of the readership. In its secondary function, journalism has contributed enormously to wider cultural politics. In short, journalism in both printed and electronic format is best seen as the continuous recombination of novelty, information, opinion and entertainment.[27]

The ascent in journalism's influence is easily explained. Its underlying cause is the growth in the cultural, political and economic value of information, facilitated by the emergence of new, cheap electronic technologies to distribute and display news. It is now widely understood that without abundant and accessible information, we can have neither the democracy in which we believe nor the economic growth and consumer choice we desire. Journalism is that part of social activity, which is concerned with gathering information about events, happenings, and occurrences, assessing their newsworthiness or news value, before writing story for dissemination of the news and views about and concerning the society. Modern journalism feeds many departments of mass communication through specialists of diverse subjects, topics, technology, art, skills and presentation. "Journalism is communication. It is the events of the day distilled into a few words, sounds or pictures, processed by the mechanics of communication to satisfy the human curiosity of a world that is always eager to know what's new", said David Wainwright.[28]

All activities concerned with the communication of mass media is not journalism but only that part of the activity which involves writing, preparation and production of the communication messages to convey information containing concern or interest to the readers, listeners, viewers, society, is journalism. Thus, journalists essentially are writers, authors, reporters, correspondents, editors, sub-editors, interviewers, story-writers, script writers, scenario editors and a host of specialists—in diverse subjects, disciplines, critiques of literature, in skills like designing pages, page layout, typography, calligraphy, art, printing technology, etc. In the present times, freelance journalism is catching on—like travel and tourism, photography, biographical sketches, brief profiles, and so on.

Journalism is primarily an educational experience, not a business enterprise. It is designed, not to make you become an expert in any or all phases of newspaper work, but to familiarize you with the functions and responsibilities of one of the most powerful means of communication in modern society. It will enable you to become aware of the importance of timely information in every day life and how that affects your beliefs and actions. It will help you to exchange more intelligently your views and opinions with others. A study of Journalism will make you a more effective citizen in a more effective community.[29]

> "I want to tell you how I look at journalism. It is becoming an increasingly exciting profession. Journalist is becoming not just a collector of interesting items that people want to hear about; it is becoming increasingly a teacher in a world that has grown extremely complex to explain. I think journalism has improved, but improvement has not proceeded as far as the problems it has to report and explain have grown more difficult. Journalism is about people. It is produced for people.

> The newspaper has to be aware of the changes in the lives of its readers. It is not enough for it to print the 'hard news' of the evening to its readers till morning, since its readers who look at the paper over breakfast will have heard most of that and seen many of the public figures and significant events on television the night before."[30]

The only qualities essential for real success in journalism are rat like cunning, a plausible manner, and a little literary ability. The ratline cunning is needed to ferret out and publish things that people don't want to be known. The plausible manner is useful for surviving, helpful with the entertaining presentation of it, and even more useful in later life when the successful journalists may have to become successful executives of their newspapers. The literary ability is of obvious use. Some journalist would deny that it is their purpose to form opinions or change society, but simply to give the facts. But as one has seen, the relevant facts are not identified as easily as all that, and whether we like it or not, journalism in the press or on radio or on TV is a contributory factor—mingled with other factors—in the transformation of society. Always be aware of change and the prospect of change. One reason why journalism used to appeal so much to young people as a career was that it did not seem to need long and boring periods of study.

Power recognizes power and the newspaper is a power of words which can reflect and evoke public passions. In fact, the power of press lies in its capacity not only to tap the public emotion but to create it. The power of the journalism is the power of the public passion and that is why government power is always apprehensive of the power of the press. The government of democratic countries tolerates the freedom of the press because the people of these countries are emotionally committed to freedom. This indeed is the secret of their cultural and instinctual progress. Journalism is a highly competitive profession in contemporary times. Newspapers are surviving on the good-will of their readers and they are rarely having enough time to cope with the flush of news. Moreover, a large number of readers do not read their newspapers with the serious intent of having objective knowledge. They read it more as a pastime and an entertainment purpose. This tends to affect their consideration of the news or views offered by their paper. Because of this, newspapers are tempted to make the news colourful and their views entertaining more than instructive, and since Indian readers, by and large, lack no hesitation, they tend to err on the cheap side.

Self-respecting journalism, in all its forms, strives constantly to meet this obligation to fulfill its duties to society. John Thadens Deleon, the great editor of "The times" of London from 1814 to 1877, who turned that paper into "The Thenderer" [31] eloquently set forth this principle. The better writers and the better papers seek to avoid deliberate and intentional partiality. The ideas of fairness are achieved by journalism which avoids errors, bias, prejudice and false colouring. Fair journalism is peculiarly the medium for the expression of the immunities because it is not under government control. Journalism includes the printed word in the daily and weekly press in pamphlets, magazines and books, and the spoken word through its various channels, notably radio, TV, etc. In the beginning, it was the word. Even before the dawn of history, men spoke to inform, to convince and to persuade their fellows. Men today are still hard at it and with the same ends in view. Through the centuries, the spoken word has lost none of its power and in our own century, science and invention have widened the range of its influence by increasing its audience manifold. History is not only written in words, it is made with words. Adolf Hitler once said, "The Power which set sliding the greatest historical avalanches of political and religious nature was from the beginning of time the magic force of the spoken word alone."[32]

Pioneers of Indian Journalism

Journalism in India was an alien concept in its present form though in its natural form, it was indeed present but it was one of the benefits of British rule. In the beginning, it was present and confined to the interests of ruling class and rarely had to do with its main subject say people. Even

British officials were suspicious of journalists and newspapers and intolerant of criticism. However, the press in Britain was gaining power and the Press in India drew its strength from the power of press in England.

James Augustus Hicky

He was the first pioneer of Indian Press and first one to launch the first newspaper in India. An expatriate Irishman and a fiercely independent journalist, James Augustus Hicky, published India's first newspaper, "The Bengal Gazette", "Hicky's Gazette" or "The Calcutta General Advertiser" in 1780.[33] Hicky quickly realized that truly distinguished newspapers should serve society, even at the risk of official displeasure. Hicky's newspaper made interesting reading with its ample dose of scurrilous reporting, unique advertisements reflecting the low morality in society, and scandalous accounts of the misdeeds of British administrators in India. Soon enough, the British rulers charged him of libel. Hicky was harassed, attacked and jailed. Undaunted, Hicky continued to edit his newspaper from prison. But his publication did not survive long and the British rulers caused him immense harm. The Britishers made all efforts to scuttle the freedom of the Bengal Gazette, though it was not a daily at that time. Its masthead proudly and courageously proclaimed itself unbiased as "A Weekly, Political and Commercial Paper, Open to All Parties but Influenced by None."[34] However, in actual practice, it was not so for it being highly partisan in nature. Compared to current newspapers, the Bengal Gazette was smaller in size, twelve inches in length and seven inches in breadth. It consisted of only two sheets with three columns on each page and was printed on both the sides of the pages. Hicky's Gazette had a limited circulation, not exceeding 200 copies. Its readership consisted of employees of East India Company and other Europeans, mostly traders. Regarding the contents, the Gazette's predominant feature was 'Addresses to the Public' from Mr. Hicky wherein the editor spoke, rather wrote, directly to the readers. There were a large number of letters, which sang the praises of Hicky. A section was devoted to amateur verse, named 'Poets Corner'. The Gazette printed many advertisements mainly about auctions and goods for sale and so also came to be called the Calcutta General Advertiser.

James Silk Buckingham

Jawaharlal Nehru has described James Silk Buckingham[35] as among the earliest pioneers of the press in India and freedom of the press who is still remembered for his advocacy of free press. He came to India in 1818 as the editor of Calcutta Chronicle, which was started by some local merchants to propagate their interests. The first issue indicated that it would be a chronicle of political, commercial and literary news and views. Mr. Buckingham faced this challenge of versatile editor and proved a breath of fresh air in polluted scandal mongering, flippancy and easygoing life of Europeans. He emphasized on conditions of local community rather than fashions and the life of popular Europeans in India. He published drawings and charts to drive home his point on any subject and introduced special feature section in the paper. He made the newspaper the mirror of the people. Buckingham was one of those who are born journalists rather than made.

Raja Ram Mohan Roy

He was one of the founders of the India owned Press, though most people remember Raja Ram Mohan Roy[36] as the man who fought to abolish Sati and also founded the Brahmo Samaj. But his contribution to Indian society was a great deal more than these social reforms. Roy was born in Radhanagar village in Bengal's Hooghly district on May 22, 1772, to a conservative Bengali Brahmin parents. Roy did his elementary education in the village school in Bengali, in his mother tongue. At the age of 12, he mastered Persian and Arabic. His knowledge of Arabic enabled him to read the Koran in the original, as well as the works of Sufi saints. He also devoured Arabic translations of the works of Aristotle and Plato. In 1803, he secured a job with the East India Company and in 1809 he was posted to Rangpur. Roy was drawn to certain aspects of Christianity that led some of his followers of the religion to suggest that he convert; but he politely declined.

Roy's understanding of the different religions of the world helped him to compare them with Vedantic philosophy and glean the best from each religion. To pursue his interests, Roy resigned from the East India Company a few years later and came to Calcutta in 1815. Dissatisfied with the system of education and the wrong method of teaching English, he formed an association of English and Hindu scholars. He also invested his own money in the starting of a school where he introduced subjects like Science, Mathematics, Political Science and English. Roy felt that an understanding of these 'modern' subjects would give Indians a better standing in the world of the day.

Though initially antagonistic towards British rule in India, Roy later began to feel that the country would benefit in terms of education and by exposure to the good points of Christianity. Along with a group of like-minded people, Roy founded the Atmiya Sabha in 1815. The group held weekly meetings at his house; texts from the Vedas were recited and hymns were sung. 'Atmiya Sabha' used to publish a weekly called 'Bengal Gazette'. Roy's efforts to abolish the practice of Sati were largely driven by his concern for the moral dimensions of religion. It was the sight of the burning of his brother's widow on her husband's funeral pyre and his inability to save her that spun Ram Mohan Roy into action. Ram Mohan Roy, who first published a newspaper in an Indian language, made thousands of people understand many things in their own language. Besides, Ram Mohan was himself bringing out newspapers called "Mirat-ul-Akhbar" (the Mirror of News) in Persian and another one called 'Sambad Kaumudi' (the Moon of Intelligence), a Bengali weekly. In those days, items of news and articles had to be approved by the government before being published. So, there was no freedom of the press and Roy protested against it. He argued that newspapers should be free and that the truth should not be suppressed simply because the government did not like it. Newspapers should have the right to uphold the truth. It needed much courage to speak out like this 150 years ago, when India was under the British rule. The press secured freedom by the constant efforts of Raja Ram Mohan Roy.

Rudyard Kipling

English short-story writer, novelist and poet, who celebrated the heroism of British colonial soldiers in India and Burma, Rudyard Kipling[37] was the first Englishman to receive the Nobel Prize for Literature in 1907. His most popular works included The Jungle Book (1894), with such unforgettable characters as Mogli, Baloo and Bagheera and Walt Disney's cartoon version, was produced in the 1960s. Rudyard Kipling was born in Mumbai. India was at that time ruled by the British. An ayah, who taught him Hindustani as his first language, brought up Ruddy. In 1878, he entered United Services College, a boarding school in North Devon and returned to India in 1882, started working as a journalist in Lahore for Civil and Military Gazette and an assistant editor and overseas correspondent in Allahabad for Pioneer. In 1892, he married Caroline Starr Balestier, the sister of an American publisher and writer, with whom he collaborated a novel, The Naulahka. The young couple moved to the United States. Kipling was dissatisfied with the life in Vermont, and after the death of his daughter, Josephine, Kipling took his family back to England and settled in Burwash, Sussex. During these restless years, Kipling produced a collection of animal stories for children. Soon after Kipling had received the Nobel Prize, his output of fiction and poems began to decline. Kipling died on January 18, 1936 in London, and was buried in Poet's Corner at Westminster Abbey. His autobiography 'Something of myself', appeared posthumously in 1937.

Bal Gangadhar Tilak

The beginning of 20th century was the age of alien rulers and persecution of the Indian press, especially the language press which had spread to all parts of the country. The centre of activity was shifted to Maharashtra where new revolutionary leader, the lion of Maharashtra, Bal Gangadhar Tilak, was born on July 23, 1856, in a village near Rainagiri, into a middle class Chitpavan Brahmin family. Tilak was an avid student with a special aptitude for mathematics. He was among India's first generation of youth to receive a modern, college education. After graduation, Tilak began teaching mathematics in a private school in Pune and later became a Journalist. He became a strong critic of the Western education system, feeling it demeaning to Indian students and disrespectful to India's heritage. He organized the Deccan Education Society to improve the quality of education for India's youth. Tilak founded the Marathi Daily, Kesari, which fast became a popular reading for the common people of India. Tilak strongly criticized the government for its brutalism in suppression of free expression, especially in the face of protests against the division of Bengal in 1905 and for denigrating India's culture, its people and heritage. He demanded the British immediately give the right of self-government to India's people. Tilak joined the Indian National Congress in the 1890s, but soon fell into opposition of its liberal-moderate attitude towards the right for self-government. Tilak opposed the moderate views of Gopal Krishna Gokhale, and was supported by· fellow Indian nationalists, Bipin Chandra Pal in Bengal and Lala Lajpat Rai in Punjab. In 1907, the Congress Party split into the Garam Dal led by Tilak, Pal and Lajpat Rai, and the Naram Dal led by Gokhale during its session at Surat in Gujarat. When arrested on charges of sedition in 1906, Tilak asked a young Mohammad Ali Jinnah to represent him. But the British judge convicted him and he was imprisoned from 1908 to 1914 in Mandalay, Burma (now Myanmar). Upon his release, Tilak re-united with his fellow nationalists and re-united the Indian National Congress in 1916. He also helped found the All India Home Rule League in 1916 with Annie Besant and Mohammad Ali Jinnah. Although he was basically a proponent of Advaita Vedanta, he differed from the classical Adrian view that jnana (knowledge) alone brings release. Tilak added a measure of karma yoga (the yoga of activity) to this, not as subordinate to jnana yoga, but as equal and complementary to it. Tilak proposed various social reforms, such as a minimum age for marriage and was especially keen to see a prohibition placed on the sale of alcohol. His thoughts on education and Indian political life have remained highly influential—he was the first Congress leader to suggest that Hindi, written in the Devanagari script, should be accepted as the sole national language of India, a policy that was later strongly endorsed by Mahatma Gandhi. However, English, which Tilak wished to remove completely from the Indian mind, remains even now an important means of communication in India. But the usage of Hindi and other Indian languages has been reinforced and widely encouraged since the days of the British Raj, and Tilak's legacy is often credited with this resurgence. Another of the major contributions relates to the propagation of Ganesh festival which contributed for people to get together and celebrate the festival and provided a good platform for leaders to inspire masses. His call for boycott of foreign goods also served to inspire patriotism among Indian masses. Tilak authored Arctic Home in the Vedas in 1903. In it, he argued primarily on the basis of astronomical statements, that the Vedas could only have been composed from an Arctic location. Tilak authored 'The Orion', and researched into the antiquities of the Vedas in which he used astronomy to establish that the Vedic people were present in India—at least as early as the 4th millennium B.C.

Bhartendu Harishchandra

Bharatendu Harishchandra was multi-faceted personality and father of the modern Hindi Literature, Hindi Journalism and Hindi Prose. He made major contributions in the field of journalism, drama and poetry. He edited the magazines, Kavi Vachan Sudha, Harishchandra Patrika, Harishchandra Magazine and Bal Bodhini. Bharatendu Hanshchandra Awards have been given by the Ministry of Information and Broadcasting, Government of India, since 1983 to promote original writings in Hindi on journalism and mass communications.

PIONEER EDITORS IN INDIAN JOURNALISM

B.G. Homiman

Homiman[38] came to India as an assistant editor of the Statesman. He was the son of a former Paymaster-in-Chief of the British Navy, brother of a Rear-admiral and a famous actor. He was a staunch advocate of Indian independence and was soon disgusted with the uncongenial atmosphere of

Calcutta (now Kolkata) where the Statesman was printed. He resigned his job in 1912. By recommending him to Sir Pherozeshah Mehta, who was in search of an editor for his newly started Bombay Chronicle, Surendranath Bannerjee wrote: 'I may assure you that Homiman is as good an Indian as myself. During the days of the partition of Bengal, he used to walk with us barefooted through the streets of Calcutta (now Kolkata) with a shawl on his broad white shoulders.' Before Homiman arrived in Bombay and took charge of the Bombay Chronicle in 1913, vigorous dynamic public life was unknown. An Englishman as editor of an Indian newspaper necessarily had to work under great strain but Homiman had the advantage of professionalism, which made him an expert. There had been British champions of the Indian cause before and after Homiman, but none is as eminent for personal identification with the causes as he took up and for the vigour with which he pursued them. To his qualities as a trained journalist, he added emotional involvement in the fight for Indian freedom. He was an indefatigable worker, active in public life and in movements for relief to the people. By his incessant attacks on the British owned press, he shook the Times of India (which virtually enjoyed a monopoly until the arrival of the Chronicle) out of its smugness and exposed its views and prejudice. It soon became a habit for the citizens of Mumbai to read the Chronicle first in the morning. A European bureaucrat said, "I hate Homiman though 1 can't help admiring his articles which are a tonic." The officials branded him a traitor to his motherland and Homiman defended himself through the columns of the Manchester Guardian. He wrote: 'Though the government was strongly criticized as it deserved and the strongest protest was made in my paper regarding the public flogging of people in streets, the dropping of bombs on unarmed crowds, machine gunning of demonstrators without adequate provocation, the whole of my personal influence and that of my paper were used in support of restoration of order and the inculcation of the doctrine and practice of Satyagraha—the very negation of violence—both before and during the disturbances that occurred' In a letter to the Chronicle in September 1919, he related the circumstances under which he was deported. He was ill and under doctor's orders after an operation not to leave the house, the police came and carried him from his house in an ambulance and placed him to board the ship.

Arthur Moore

Arthur Moore[39] belonged to a rare group of editors, who have a mind of their own and do not care what others think about it. Moore enjoyed in letting people in high positions in government or in politics know what he thought and wrote which was not always palatable to the parties for whom it was intended. He was an unconventional editor of the Statesman for 10 years. K.P.S. Menon, the veteran diplomat said that Arthur Moore was non respecter of persons. Some VIP's disliked him and he reciprocated their sentiments cordially. On the whole, he was regarded by the Establishment as a difficult person to deal with. Moore succeeded Alfred Watson as an editor of the Statesman in 1932. Watson was the target of terrorist attack twice and he was injured in the second attempt when a young terrorist shot him. The attacks were a sequel to some articles published in the Statesman and according to Muggeridge who had just then joined the paper, as an assistant editor, that they had been written by Moore. Watson resigned his job and returned home. Before he came to India, Moore had worked as a reporter with The Times of London and was considered an authority on Balkan and Persian affairs. He served as The Times correspondent in Persia for some years. He came to India in 1924 and joined the Statesman as an assistant editor. His most famous brush with authority was during the viceroyalty of Lord Linlithgow to whom he was like a red rag to a bull. Maulana Azad remembered him in his autobiography by saying that Moore was also a part of Satyagrah in 1947 when Gandhi was fighting against the communal riots in Calcutta.

S. Sadanand

In the history of Indian journalism, S. Sadanand,[40] has an important place as an able editor, an innovator and a fearless patriot. Born in Tamil Nadu, he made Bombay his headquarters for his multifarious ventures in journalism. That was where he held sway during the Salt Satyagraha of 1930-33 when his newspaper Free Press Journal, was a rage and eclipsed all other nationalist papers. He was a pioneer of popular journalism in English, who sold his papers at six paisa a copy, an unheard of thing in those days. He created a mass base for himself by espousing popular causes and airing public grievances in a big, spectacular way that caught the imagination of the educated masses. He, more than any other journalist, strove to instill pride and devotion among the people for their country and for the epic battle for freedom waged by the Congress under the leadership of Gandhi. He was a powerful supporter of the Congress movement and his newspaper Free Press Journal had to pay the penalty when the alien government persecuted it by demanding securities and forfeiting them and demanding fresh deposits. Sadanand did not flinch and survived the ordeal even after paying Rs. 70,000 in one year alone. He revolutionized editorial writing. Instead of the writing like a song and meandering editorials, very often going above the head of the ordinary reader, which were a feature of the nationalist newspapers then, Sadanand introduced the sharp, telling and pungent editorial paragraphs which, with their mythical allusions and anecdotes, went straight to the heart of the readers and enabled them to grasp with ease what was being conveyed to them. The reader became emotionally involved in whatever was suggested and their cooperation was assured. And that was how the Congress gained its supremacy in Bombay. His right hand man on the Free Press Journal was Stalin Srinivasan who was an able and experienced journalist. The sobriquet, 'Stalin', was given to him by his colleagues in the profession because of his moustache, which closely resembled that of the Russian dictator. Sadanand started his career as a journalist in Burma in the 1920s when it was part of India. He worked in a Rangoon newspaper and later came to India. He purchased the Indian Express from Dr. P. Varadarajulu Naidu in 1932 who had started it a year earlier. Sadanand ran it for some months and soon got tired of it as all of his concentration was on the Free Press Journal in Bombay. He went to C.

Rajagopalachari in April 1932, and urged him to take over the Indian Express. Rajaji told him that the man who could help him was K. Santhanam, who had just been released from prison where he had undergone an imprisonment. When he came out of prison, he had decided to renounce politics but fate had stored something else for him. Rajaji advised him to take over the Indian Express as its editor. For Santhanam, Rajaji's words were a command and he started a new life as a journalist. For him, editing and running the Indian Express was a national service and a mission. The Indian Express became a morning paper and spokesman for the Congress. It was sold at half an anna in line with Sadanand's innovative seal. Very soon, a sister Tamil daily was added, and the Dinamani in a short time outstripped its rivals. The Indian Express, however, fell into a financial crisis and it finally passed into the hands of Ramnath Goenka who later became a newspaper baron and the owner of the largest chain of newspapers.

Frank Moraes

Frank Moraes[41] was a journalist of great courage and always called a 'spade a spade'. Long training and apprenticeship in a British-owned and edited newspaper had given him a discipline and keen sense of what was right and what was wrong, and integrity and clear thinking, so that when he came to assume positions of responsibility in a newspaper, he commanded great respect and authority. He asked himself once: 'What did England give me?' and provided the answer: 'Primarily, I think, a sense of tolerance combined with a habit of evaluation which while enabling one to listen to the other man's point of view, did not necessarily imply that one necessarily accepted it. I suppose this attitude of mind really adds up to democracy. England also taught me to recognize the importance of standards in human relationship and individual conduct, which in a way spells civilization. I think the most valuable gift England gave me was a sense of proportion.' It is this sense of proportion, which marked his editorship of the Times of India and later of the Indian Express. He occupied the editorial chair of India's two leading newspapers at a time when the country was facing enormous problems of reconstruction and survival. He was a constructive critic whose writings were valued in the highest quarters of Government and paid the greatest attention. A close associate described him as 'one of the most straightforward journalists and a gentleman'. He was of a reserved nature and a man of few words. He had the advantage of moving with the leaders of government on an equal footing, which developed intimacy and trust, and he established high level contacts in all spheres of public life. His close friendship with Jawaharlal Nehru and Indira Gandhi was a great asset. His involvement with and appreciation of, Nehru was so much that he became his biographer.

Son of an Indian government servant, Moraes was born in Bombay in 1907. He graduated from St. Xavier's College, Bombay, and later took a degree from Oxford. He was also a barrister of Lincoln's Inn, and practiced law for some time before he entered journalism in 1934. He worked with The Times of India as a junior assistant editor. Of this period, Moraes writes: "The Times of India then on the eve of its centenary was a British newspaper whose senior editorial and production staff were exclusively British and I was at that time, the only Indian assistant editor." The editor, Sir Francis Low, was a competent Scotsman, who had worked his way up through various departments of the paper. Outwardly, he appeared to be reticent and diffident but he was not easily overawed or taken in. The Times of India then was a firm supporter of the government since it was British-owned. He was, for instance, not invited to use the senior staff canteen, which was exclusively for the British. He was also excluded from the daily morning conference with the other assistant editors, which was otherwise attended by all British Editors. In accordance with government office routine and the practice of European commercial establishments, the senior staff worked by the clock and only very rarely worked round it. Our daily office hours were from 10 a.m. to 5.30 p.m. with an hour and a half for lunch and in my 19 years on the Times of India I do not believe I came more than a dozen times to the office at night."[42]

TYPES OF JOURNALISM

Print Journalism

Print journalism can be split into several categories: Newspapers, news magazines, general interest magazines, trade magazines, hobby magazines, newsletters, private publications, online news pages and others. Each genre can have its own requirements for researching and writing reports. In it, editors usually ensure that reports are written with as few words as possible. Feature stories are usually written in a looser style that usually depends on the subject matter of the report, and in general granted more space[43].

Photo Journalism

Photo journalism[44] is a particular form of journalism (the collecting. editing, and presenting of news material for publication or broadcast) that creates images in order to tell a news story. It is now usually understood to refer only to still images, and in some cases to video used in broadcast journalism. Photo journalism is distinguished from other close branches of photography (such as documentary photography, street photography or celebrity photography) by the following qualities:

Timelines—the images have meaning in the context of a published chronological record of events.

Objectivity—the situation implied by the images is a fair and accurate representation of the events they depict.

Narrative—the images combine with other news elements, to inform and give insight to the viewer or reader.

Photo journalists must make decisions instantly and carry photographic equipment under the same circumstances as those involved in the subject (fire, war, rioting) often while being exposed to the same risks. Photo journalism, as a descriptive term, often implies the use of a certain bluntness of style or approach to image making. A wedding photographer would not typically be described as a 'photo journalist', even though he covers a timely event and his images may be published in the press.

Broadcast Journalism

By broadcasting events such as the Tehlka hearings, Gujrats riots, Parliament attack case, Watergate hearings, controversial Supreme Court's hearings, and sensational criminal trials, television has, in some ways, rewritten the role of journalist in contemporary times. Yet reports by journalists of the World Service of the British Broadcasting Corporation and Cable News Network, owned by Ted Turner based in Atlanta,[45] are transmitted around the world and provide news to world leaders in times of crisis. The proliferation of cable television in the United States since the mid-1970s has led to a variety of news channels and India is also not far away. Today, one won't find any field in which broadcast media has not touched for its news. As with print journalism, television journalism ranges from sensational, 'tabloid' news shows to the extensive journalistic coverages and interviews with government figures. The Devil's Advocate show by Karan Thapar, Apaki Addalat by Rajat Sharma, and Big Fight on NDTV are some of prominent TV shows which have their impact on masses. Radio journalism is similar to storytelling. It is conversational in style. The sentences should be short and uncomplicated. Use very few adjectives and stay away from quotes. Avoid the negative and lengthy sentences.

Civic Journalism

Civic journalism is an effort to reach out to the public more aggressively in the reporting process, to listen to how citizens frame their problems and what citizens see as solutions to those problems and then to use that information to enrich news stories. It is an organic conception of news that considers community members to be participants rather than objects of public communication that has aroused both admiration and suspicion since its emergence from a number of eclectic sources in the early 1990's. It has been promoted by supporters as a tonic to our well documented civic malaise and pilloried by critics as a subversive scheme to destroy journalistic independence. It is practiced by Newspapers, Radio and TV stations in many parts of the United States and around the world[46].

Investigative Journalism

"Investigative journalism is a kind of journalism in which reporters deeply investigate a topic of interest, often related to crime, scandals, government corruption, or white-collar crime."[47] Whereas a typical daily or weekly news reporter writes items concerning immediately available news, an investigative Journalist might spend months or years on a particular report. Newspapers and wire services do most investigative journalism. The investigation will often require an extensive number of interviews and travel, other instances might call for the reporter to make use of activities such as: surveillance techniques, tedious analysis of documents, investigations of the performance of any kind of equipment involved in an accident, patent medicine, scientific analysis, social and legal issues, and the like. In short, investigative journalism requires a lot of scrutiny of detailed fact-finding and physical effort. An investigative journalist must have an analytical and incisive mind with strong self-motivation to move on when all doors are closed, when facts are being covered up or falsified and so on. It got a boost after Pristine and Woodward broke the Watergate scandal in USA due to which President Nixon had to resign.

Advocacy Journalism

Advocacy Journalism is a 21st century genre of Journalism which is strongly fact-based, but may seek to support a point of view in some public or private sector issue. It is particularly common in Europe and the United States. Corporate crime, government criticism, corruption and social issues are frequent topics of interest. In this way, advocacy journalists serve the public interest in a similar way to muckrakers.[48] Advocacy journalism criticizes the objectivity ideal of mainstream press as an ideological dissimulation of class bias, and underlines the fact that political censorship can easily be replaced by economical censorship. Media outlets may employ political figures as part of their staff. If the media outlet tends to draw from one political viewpoint to the exclusion of other, this would serve as an example of Advocacy journalism. It presents suggestion of fairness and neutrality while actually following an agenda.

Online Journalism

Online journalism[49] is defined as the reporting of facts produced and distributed via the Internet. Many news organizations based on other media also distribute news online, but the amount they use of the new medium varies across the board. Some news organizations use the Web exclusively or as a secondary outlet for their content. The Internet challenges traditional news organizations in several ways. Newspapers may lose classified advertising to websites, which are often targeted by interest instead of Geography. These organizations are concerned about real and perceived loss of viewers and circulation to the Internet. However, the revenue gained with advertising on news websites is sometimes too small to support the site. Even before the Internet, technology and other factors were dividing people's attention, leading to more but narrower media outlets. Bloggers write on web logs or blogs. Traditional journalists often do not consider bloggers to automatically be journalists. This has more to do with standards and professional practices than the medium. But, as of 2005, blogging has generally gained at least more attention and has led to some effects on mainstream journalism, such as exposing problems related to a television piece about any topic which concerned the large section of the people.

Other significant tools of on-line journalism are Internet forums, discussion boards and chats, especially those representing the Internet version of official media. The widespread use of the Internet all over the world has created a unique opportunity to create a meeting place for both sides in many conflicts, such as the Israeli-Palestinian conflict and the Russian-Chechen War. Often, this gives a unique chance to find new, alternative solutions to the conflict, but often-contradicting panics creating endless 'online battles' turn the Internet into the battlefield. Most Internet users agree that on-line sources are often less biased and more informative than the official media. This claim is often backed with the belief that on-line journalists are merely volunteers and freelancers who are not paid for their activity, and, therefore, are free from corporate ethics. Bur recently, many Internet forums began to moderate their boards because of threat of vandalism, which many users see as a form of censorship.

Yellow Journalism

It is a term given to any widespread tendencies or practices within media organizations that are detrimental to, or substandard from the point of view of journalistic integrity. 'Yellow journalism'[50] may, for example, refer to sensationalized news reporting that bears only a superficial resemblance to journalism. Journalistic professionalism, as now understood, is the supposed antidote. Today, the phrase 'media bias' is often used instead of 'yellow journalism', with similar but subtly different meaning. The term, as it commonly applies, refers to news organizations for whom sensationalism, profiteering, and in some cases propaganda and jingoism, take dominance over factual reporting. Most cases tend to be related to journalistic bias and the endemic practices of particular organizations to operate as mouthpieces, for rather limited and particular allegiances, rather than for the public trust. Yellow has been a primary colour in our language for thousands of years. But this yellow was in a new place, in comic strips, as one toothless Little Yellow Kid, on the front page of some of New York's Sunday newspapers. And the newspapers were fighting the fiercest circulation war in American history by clamouring for real war against spam. In disgust, rival editors called it yellow journalism.

Environmental Journalism

Environmental journalism[51] is the collection, verification, production, distribution and exhibition of information regarding current events, trends, issues and people that are associated with the non-human world with which humans necessarily interact. To be an environmental journalist, one must have an understanding of scientific language and practice, knowledge of historical environmental events, the ability to keep abreast of environmental policy decisions and the work of environmental organizations, a general understanding of current environmental concerns, and the ability to communicate all the information to the public in such a way that it can be easily understood, despite its complexity. Environmental journalism falls within the scope of environmental communication, and its roots can be traced to nature writing. One key controversy in environmental journalism is a continuing disagreement over how to distinguish it from its allied genres and disciplines.

Literary Journalism

Creativity and literature are inseparable from Journalism and so is the part of it, which uses literary skills in the writing of non-fiction. A work of creative non-fiction, if well written, contains accurate and well-researched information and also holds the interest of the reader. Creative non-fiction is contrasted to 'research non-fiction' which may contain accurate information, but may not be particularly well written and may not hold the attention of the reader very well. Forms of creative non-fiction can include essays, diaries, autobiography, biographies, magazine writing, travel writing, nature writing, science writing, histories, journalism, and the memoirs. Narrative non-fiction is a type of creative non-fiction which tells a story.

Sports Journalism

Sports journalism[52] covers many aspects of human athletic competitions and is an integral part of most journalism products, including newspapers, magazines, radio and television news broadcasts. While some critics don't consider sports journalism to be true journalism, the prominence of sports in western culture has justified the attention of journalists to not just the competitive events of sports, but also to athletes and the business of sport.

Fashion Journalism

Fashion journalists, with training in news gathering and reporting, write about fashion trends, fashion shows, fashion collections and exclusively cover newsmakers in the field. They may also be asked to provide photo features of the particular area they cover. A fashion photographer has to have an eye for aesthetics and no amount of technical training can make up for that inherent quality.

JOURNALIST

As per Oxford dictionary, "A journalist is one who earns his living by editing or writing for a public journal or journals."[53] T.H. Escott says, "A fair working definition of a journalist would be a man who seeks to influence public opinion in a given direction by periodical writings published at short intervals"[54]. It has been a fashion in some quarters to describe 'Narada' as the first journalist of the world. One would not take this observation seriously for the simple reason that the context is not strictly relevant in a scientific discussion. In any case Narada's Penchant for 'carrying tales' is not what activates a serious minded journalist. Then there are people who would describe the medieval chroniclers (bakhornavisas) as the harbingers of modern journalism. Their job was to send detailed reports of important events to their masters. But a modern journalist is not a chronicler of this type. A journal is, of course, a chronicle of events, but of those events that have a public significance and are meant for public consumption. A newspaper man is interested in events which concern the people, events which affect the interests of the people at large and for some reason, whatsoever be, interested.[55]

Journalists are, therefore, supposed to possess a good deal of intelligence, knowledge and experience as well as natural and trained powers of observation and reasoning. Ultimately, the Indian journalists can draw inspiration from the glorious history of their profession. The Indian journalists and newspapers had taken a leading part in the fight for the country's freedom. There were a few rulers like Sir Charles Metcalfe, who religiously believed in the freedom of the press and even sacrificed his post as Governor General of India for this staunch belief. On the other hand, India had to face Lord Lytton's and Lord Curzon's who delighted in imposing restrictions on the press but the freedom fighting journalists of India stood against them and made effective contributions to the freedom struggle. It was no accident that men like Tilak, Gandhi, Rajagopalachary and Chandersekhar Azad were successful journalists who helped the masses to get educated for their rights and mobilized them against the tyrannical rule of the Britishers.[56] Thus India carries a legacy of having had successful leaders as journalists and vice-versa.

Every journalist, sooner or later, encounters the reader who passionately objects to something he has written. Persistence is a necessary quality for a good journalist. This does not mean offensiveness. Good journalism consists of the intelligent assembly of relevant facts. Get the facts, that is the key to news reporting. Good reporting is the discovery of as many important facts as possible and their selection and presentation so that they make a comprehensive story. An Indian journalist, Arun Shourie says, "Today's journalism in India is a matter of contacts. The journalist's primary subject is government, their primary source of information is government and their primary audience is government. A good journalist—the envy of his peers—is one who has better contacts so that he can get the government handout earlier than his colleagues[57]. A journalist has the same obligations as a teacher or interpreter or an educationist has. A journalist who misuses his power for any selfish or unworthy purpose is faithless to a high trust. While the freedom of the press needs to be guarded as a vital right of mankind, it has to suffer certain explicit restrictions to sub-serve social needs. Freedom of the press does not imply promotion of any private interest of the journalist contrary to the general welfare. Even when there is no legal authority to enforce these cannons, journalism, as a profession, is supposed to put deliberate ponderings to personal instinct, which may encounter effective public disapproval.

Ramsay MacDonald, the labour Prime Minister in United Kingdom says in 1924, "Journalists belong to a great and honourable profession. The journalist is a man whose craft means, that by instinctive ability, he can gather together and coordinate all those feelings that go is the making of public opinion, who has got an instinctive sense of what the interests of the people are, and who, with skill and mastery, can sit down and under the most trying and impossible conditions to produce the finished article."[58]

Success journalism is not necessarily good journalism but good journalism needs to be successful journalism as well. The primary purpose of a journalist is to communicate and a journal that does not sell is a journal that fails of its primary purpose. There was a time when it used to be said that a journalist is born, not made, that you could not push a man through a journalism school and he would emerge at the other end as a journalist. Mahatma Gandhi was never sent to a journalism school nor was B.G. Tilak. Yet, they were men who were considered as great pioneers of Indian journalist fraternity[59]. Today, the sources of information have become amazingly quick and manifold. Their processing requires great skill and capacity. The present day journalists have to be proved. But to match this growth of information, there is a subject of temptations that easily compromise the capacity to deal with this plethora of information and opinions. These temptations and percussions not only manage to keep the journalist on the right side of the powers that be but, what is worse, reinforce him with the belief that he is simply doing his duty in this. These temptations range from a foreign trip to foreign whiskeys. It requires great inner control to spurn these temptations especially at a time when the craze for such things is the ruling fashion of society. These temptations not only affect the journalist but also the reader.

A good education, good health, considerable patience and determination are some of the essentials shared by journalism with other professions. But the journalist, besides possessing these endowments, must primarily have that instinct of discreet value for information, that "nose for news", as it has been aptly expressed, without which he may be pursuing a calling for which he is not meant. He should be the man, who can read sermons in stones; who sees the dullest incidents and topics, can see first-rate copy lurking in unsuspected places. That is the first of all qualifications, which he should possess. Then, he must be a person who can put his whole personality in the assignment he is called upon to perform. Thus, the journalist must not only have the instinct for finding news, but he must also know which news to keep and which to throw away and having finally selected his news, he must know the value of each and how to treat it. According to James Lewis, "one of the duties of a newspaper is to build a sense of community of nationhood.

That, to my mind, can only be done successfully by recording the lives and activities of the people who form the community or the nation—at all levels rather than the merely political. It is easy to point out shortcomings without mentioning the difficulties—newsprint shortages, long distances, slowness of communications, language problems, inadequate staffing, and the need to cater for many local, or minority interests, which otherwise would not be served at all."[60]

Wickham Steed says, "The ideal journalist would be one who having mastered and assimilated the wisdom of the ancients, the philosophers of the more modern, the knowledge of the scientists, the mechanics of engineers, the history of his own and of other times and the chief factors in economic, social and political life, should be able to hide all these things in his bosom, and to supply as much of them as might be really digested, to his millions of readers in proportion as he divined their desire for them"[61].

MASS MEDIA

Mass Media is a term used to denote a section of the media specifically envisioned and designed to reach a very large audience such as the population of a nation-state. The term was coined in the 1920's with the advent of nationwide radio networks, then applied to mass circulation of newspapers and magazines, although mass media was present centuries before the term became common. The concept of mass media is connected to internet media, as now individuals have a means of potential exposure on a large scale comparable to what was previously restricted to selected group of mass media producers. The term 'Mass Media' refers to the means of public communication reaching a large audience. When the members of the general public refer to the media, they are usually referring to the mass media, or to the news media, which is a section of the mass media[62].

The nation's leaders depend upon the mass media not merely to inform the people, rather they are themselves informed by the media. In many cases, the media sets the agenda that captures attention. Journalists often decide what will be discussed, debated or acted upon simply by deciding what to highlight and what to ignore in their reports. The information is supplied by media but that does not mean that it is entirely responsible for shaping our opinion. We have developed mental process that enables us to reject information that does not square with our individual views of the world. The fact is that public reaction to information is so unpredictable that the mass media often create opinion quite by accident. Quite a bit of it is due to the high volume growth and high visibility of the various masses. But there is some truth behind some of the criticism levelled against the mass media. The practices of the mass media have not always been ethical. All is not well with the present day journalism: sometimes, people's expectations are not responded and sometimes moral values and values of life are abused for personal behavioural aberrations.

Life, of course, is not a stationary thing. Life is a continuing development with a 'before' and an 'after'. The media catch aspects of life in midair and fire them as rigidly as a posed smile in a photograph. The very mechanics of the process is made for distortion. By exercising their legitimate function of revealing something that someone doesn't want known, the press and television lay themselves open to this criticism. There is a running conflict between politicians and the media. But the problem is accentuated today because the politicians need the media so desperately. It is now a serious quality of a public figure that he/she should come across well on public debate or on television. The press is always a means of increasing and deepening communication. As such, it was regarded as dangerous and subversive by many in authority. The history of the press has always been that of a battle for freedom against those who would stifle the open expression of opinion.

The entertainment media are anything but neutral in terms of the effects. The reporters do not exercise objectivity in their reporting. It is the type of media they work for, which often determines what will be covered, how it will be covered, what effect that coverage will have on the viewers or readers. Historian Elizabeth Eisenstein notes, "History bears witness to the cataclysmic effect on society of inventions of new media for the transmission of information among persons. The development of writing and later the development of printing are example. By its very nature, a reading public is not only more dispersed, it is also more atomistic and individualistic than a hearing one."[63]

A press, however free from governmental direction or control, is not really free if it submits to other controls. In return for what they have granted, the people have the right to insist that freedom of the press should mean freedom from any deleterious influence, whether imposed by interests too strong for the publisher to resist, or self-imposed for benefits received or hoped for. Too often, the position taken by the press on questions involving social reform and the fundamental human rights of the great mass of the people is dictated by narrow financial, rather than by public consideration.[64] The fact that the press is privately owned and operated for profit is an assurance that the newspaper must present enough news to attract readers, very few newspapers distort the news they publish. Some papers still prefer to be party organs, but they are few. Their competition is such that they generally supply reliable news. They may denounce in the editorial columns what they have printed in their news columns, but, nevertheless, they print news.

ELECTRONIC MEDIA

Radio and TV are novel gifts of the twentieth century to humanity. The development of these media of mass communication, however, cannot be attributed to any single man and nation. Radio, Internet and TV are primarily useful in signaling events, providing the immediate and usually sketchy reports that announce happenings. The limitations of the electronic media leave an important role for newspaper. The latter cannot compete with radio and TV for rapid transmission and they can't compete with TV in the shear impact of seeing and hearing news in the making. But a newspaper is available at any time and it can provide a vast range of information on many subjects. Both Radio and TV fight for the same cause. One opens ear while the other your eye. Radio is a medium which you have to hear, TV is both to be heard and seen and the printed medium only to be read. In the newscasts of the visual medium, the words spoken by the news presenter, the visuals, the captions, and the personality of the presenter, to an extent, form the part of the total newscast. Words, however, have a significant, if not a major, role to play. Thus, both in Radio and TV, the spoken word is of great consequence. The news is brought to you in the spoken word in its entirety by a faceless news reader in one case and by a presenter, appearing on the screen, in his or her words, aided by visuals, in the other. The spoken word idiom is basically different from the one employed by the print media[65]. Just as radio news writing evolved from newspaper writing, so television news writing evolved form radio news. If a television news item has no pictures, the story is dry and the news reader in vision or on camera also appeares dull. Such stories are not different from radio news items. But with the visuals, things change. The news script should supplement the picture giving additional relevant information. The basic and fundamental principle is that the words and pictures should go together, the news copy should match the picture. The television news writer has to make sure that he uses words to tell the story with the help of the visuals[66].

The internet means an international network where innumerable computers are connected to each other. The internet is a major communication medium that helps people to communicate with each other from any part of the world. They can pass information between each other in a fraction of a second. Millions of people throughout the world use the internet to share information and ideas and search for information on any topic. In 1969, the Department of Defence of the United States of America set-up a network called ARPANET (Advanced Research Projects Agency Network).[67] The network connected one computer in California with three in Utah. Later, the Department of Defence allowed universities to join the network for sharing the hardware and software resources. In this way, it grew bigger and finally gave birth to the present day popular internet. Every means of public communication goes through a series of phases and is eventually superseded. In the last century and a half, politicians have had to come to terms with the platform, the loudspeaker, the mass press, the poster, a local press, radio, cinema and then television. No technology has eradicated any predecessor, rather they have all accumulated, each demanding fresh communicative skills and each somehow managing to impose its nature upon the process it was intended to assist[68].

Radio broadcasting began in India in 1927, with two privately owned transmitters at Mumbai and Kolkata. These were nationalized in 1930 and operated under the name Indian Broadcasting Service until 1936, when it was renamed All India Radio (AIR). Although officially renamed again to Akashwani in 1957, it is still popularly known as All India Radio. It is still the most sought after media, considering the fact that it is accessible even in the remotest parts of our country where any other media like TV or newspapers cannot reach. When India attained independence in 1947, AIR had a network of six stations and a complement of 18 transmitters. Today, it has network of 223 broadcasting centres with 143 medium frequency, 54 high frequency and 161 FM transmitters. The coverage is 91.42% of the area, serving 99.13% of the people in the largest democracy of the world[69].

Indian television started off in 1959 in New Delhi with tests for educational telecasts. Indian small screen programming started off in the early 1980's. At that time, there was only one national channel, Doordarshan, which was government owned. After "Humlog", the Ramayana and the Mahabharata were the first major television series produced. In 1992, the government liberated its markets, opening them up to cable television. Five new channels belonged to Hong Kong based STAR TV which gave Indians a fresh breath of life. MTV, Star Plus, BBC, Prime Sports and STAR Chinese channel were the 5 channels. Zee TV was the first private owned Indian channel to broadcast over cable. Further, regional channels flourished along with a multitude of Hindi channels and a few English channels.[70]

ELECTRONIC MEDIA GIANTS

TV Today and Aajtak

TV Today Network Limited (TVTN) was incorporated on December 28, 1999 as a Company with a limited liability, under the Companies Act, 1956. TVTN received the certificate of commencement of business on February 7, 2000. Living Media India Limited (LMIL), its holding Company, promoted TVTN; LM1L had been conducting News Broadcasting business through one of its divisions, 'TV Today Division' since 1994. TV Today Division has been transferred to TVTN by Business Transfer Agreement executed between LMIL and TVTN. Presently, TVTN runs two 24-hour News and Current Affairs channels, namely, 'Aaj Tak' in Hindi and 'Headlines Today' in English. India Today Group's foray into the audiovisual media began with Newstrack, a video news magazine that shook up the establishment. By 1995, TV Today Network had evolved to produce one of the most influential current affairs programmes, Aaj Tak telecast on the television network and it enjoyed a strong nationwide viewership. Because of its popularity, the group launched a 24-hour Hindi news channel, Aaj Tak, in December 2000, which covers India with insight, courage and plenty of local flavours. Within six months of its launch, Aaj Tak emerged as India's number one news channel. Due to its success in Hindi journalism, the TV Today Group launched its second most popular channel, Headlines Today, in English to have a greater share of the market in viewership.

NDTV

New Delhi Television Ltd. (NDTV Ltd.) founded in 1988, is India's first and largest private producer of news, current affairs and entertainment television. NDTV is home to the country's best and brightest reporters, anchors and producers which includes twenty-three offices and studios across the country and also host to India's most modern and sophisticated production and newsgathering facilities. On April 14th, 2003, NDTV simultaneously launched two 24-hour news channels, NDTV 24x7 in English, and NDTV India in Hindi. Since its inception, NDTV has made its own market and its programes are widely appreciated.

CNN News

CNN was launched on June 1, 1980. The network has forty-two bureau around the world and more than nine hundred affiliate offices worldwide. CNN has launched many regional and foreign language networks around the world. CNN was the first to launch its news website CNN.com and its global reputation was greatly enhanced in 1991 during the Gulf War, where its live war coverage was carried across the world. However, controversy arose years later when Eason Jordan, chief news executive of CNN, admitted that CNN had kept quiet about some of Saddam Hussein's atrocities and threats in order to keep its Baghdad Bureau open. CNN's integrity and bias came under fire during the 2004 U.S. Presidential Election, when two of Presidential candidate, John Kerry's advisors, Paul Begala and James Carville, were allowed to host CNN's Crossfire show during the election. In an effort to quell another blossoming controversy, Eason Jordan resigned from CNN on February 11, 2005, after making defamatory innuendo suggesting that the United States military was 'targeting' journalists in Iraq. A television movie, Live from Baghdad, was later made about the network's coverage of the war. Coverage of this and other conflicts and crises of the early 1990s led twenty-four hour news coverage and had influenced the decision-making processes of the American government. CNN International, now provides regional editions of its news service in response to foreign demand for less United States centric news coverage and set a rivaling tone with British Broadcasting Company. CNN International uses local reporters in many of its news-gathering centres, though they cover stories from an international perspective. On September 11, 2001, CNN was the first network to break news of what made as history the infamous September 11 attacks. It's a channel which is leading the international media of contemporary times.

BBC News

The British Broadcasting Company (BBC) broadcasted first radio bulletin on November 14, 1922. On July 5, 1954, the first television news bulletin was broadcasted. The BBC television service originally carried news in the form of images with a newsreader narrating off the camera, but later decided that a newsreader on screen would attract more viewers and thus changed the old tradition. In 2008, the News Centre moved to BBC Radio's headquarters, BBC Broadcasting House at Portland Place in Central London. The News department consists of 3,500 staff, of which 2,000 are journalists. The annual budget of BBC News is £350 million. BBC News output has won critical acclaim worldwide and praise for its unbiased and balanced reporting. These days, it is, however, not free from controversies, the most recent being the Hurton Report which led to a shook up of the corporation's operations. Despite this controversy, some commentators, particularly those from the centre right have accused the corporation and its news coverage of bias. The Television News section of BBC News is responsible for the main news bulletins on BBC One and BBC Two, news output on BBC Three and BBC Four.

The media have used their great power to promote the interest of their owners. The owners have propagated their own views, especially in political and economic spheres. The media have been the tool of big business generally. At times, advertisers have controlled policies and content. The media have resisted social change. They have perpetuated the status quo. Media in reporting current happenings, have generally been more concerned with the specific and the sensational than with the significant. In providing entertainment, they have been nearly rated with lacking substance or artistic merit. They have endangered public morals. The media without good cause have violated the privacy and debased the dignity of the individuals. The media have been controlled by individuals of a socio-economic class, the business class and newspapers have difficultly starting new communication enterprises. Further more, control is in the hands of very few people. As a result, the free and open market of information and ideas has been endangered. The media have helped to make the people, a nation of spectators rather than doers. The really serious situation arises when a dispute occurs with the rulers who wield enormous power and are not above misusing it. They are wary about the newspapers because power recognizes power and they are

afraid of the power of the newspapers which can influence the public and instigate them against the rulers. We have seen various ways in which the democratic government tries to influence and mislead public opinion, but the forceful press would naturally try to educate the public.
Therefore, the government is tempted to buy up the press and harass it if it cannot buy it. And the one way of doing it is the very use of government advertising, with the increasing size being given only to those newspapers that are pro government policies. And the influence of the public sector as an advertiser is increasing and few governments are above misusing it. Further, the government has enormous patronage at its disposal with which it can simply buy up chosen journalists and through them corrupt their bosses and other media barons.

The favourite newspaper men are given choicest living apartments at favourable rents, chosen as delegates at various intellectual and cultural conferences at home and aboard, taken along on foreign trips, included as delegates visiting foreign countries and treated favourably in cases such as leaking inside news. If the government power fails to win over the press, it will try to brow-beat it. It can harass the press in numerous ways. In India, a newspaper has to have a government license to publish. A printing press cannot be established without the previous permission of the government. But most importantly, the press has to depend on the government for the supply of the sheet of newspaper on which the government can have its control. It can temper skillfully with the newsprint assigned to a newspaper and manage to delay its supply. But besides all this, the government can indulge in several petty and minor harassments, i.e. suddenly the power supply of the printing press may be discontinued at regular interval. But the governmental power is not the only power with which the press has to cope, though it can be the most dangerous. There are parties and groups. There are trade union centres. They operate hopefully in the interest of the people, but actually, they hold the society or some of its sections at ransom by their unsavoury acts in India, like the necessary 'band'. A newspaper has to deal with such organizations and inform people about their true character. For this purpose, the newspaper must use its news, comments and views of correspondents to correct the aberrations of democratic society.

The International Commission for the study of communication problems, appointed by UNESCO, pointed out that professional ethical norms have been codified in all regions of the world. They vary considerably both in their form and scope. In some countries, different codes govern the press, broadcasting and the cinema. These codes are formulated and adopted voluntarily by the professionals and their associations; in other cases, however, the law of the land imposes them. Moreover, principles such as objectivity, impartiality, truthfulness and freedom of/right to information are frequently formulated in rather vague and ambiguous terms. Most such codes refer to such important concepts as safeguarding freedom of information, freedom of access to information sources. These also refer to matters like objectivity, accuracy, truthfulness or no misrepresentation of facts, responsibility vis-à-vis the public rights and interests and in relation to national, racial and religious communities, the nation, the state and maintenance of peace, unfounded accusations, violation of privacy, right of reply, etc. In such a scenario, it is imperative for a student or researcher to study the various aspects of media ethics, its ramifications, its uses and abuses, etc. and more particularly in the context of secularization of media under the concept of sharing news, views, knowledge, research results, and opinions.

Diverse cultures have existed in the world, in each country for that matter, based on the social and cultural milieu, as a result of millions of years of human effort in different pockets of this planet. Whether under the compulsive environment of enforcing uniformity, we are steadily losing cultural differences, which ever represented colourful disposition and peculiar behaviour of the tribes, groups, organisations, etc. reflected through the various institutions and folkways, is a serious question.

It is the innate desire or inspiration, which drives men to this profession. Therefore, Journalism is for one who has a taste for adventure. It attracts those who have a hatred for monotony, who feel a thrill or delight with their fingers. So to speak, at one end of the wire, which brings all the world's news first to him and his colleagues, while other men sleep. There is something really worthwhile in putting up with many inconveniences if only for a short period. In a big newspaper office, there is to be obtained, an education, which not all the public schools, not all the universities, nor all the travel and book-learning can teach one. Some men enter journalism as reporters, rising through good work to doing 'specials', becoming political correspondents, and afterwards being exceptionally fitted through such wide and varied experience in gathering news in many parts of the world, are offered the post of editor.

If the newspaper has a future, it will have that future because it provides a kind of mass communication more satisfactory for some purposes than any other. It will put greater emphasis to balance, and comprehensive news coverage on every level. It will explain, analyze and interpret the news more effectively. It will present it in informal writing, in almost conversational style. It will use pictures to report the news, wherever pictures can tell the news more easily than words. It will have greater visual appeal, avoiding the crowded look that comes from cramming too much copy on a page. It will scorn sensational news and inflammatory editorials, preferring to play up constructive community service, whether the community is local or global.

Notes and References

1. Christopher, C., Dynamics of Journalism (New Delhi: Anmol Publications Private Limited), 1997, p. 1.
2. Bond, F. Fraser, An Introduction to Journalism (USA: McGrew-Hill Book Company), 1989, p. 4.
3. Pant, K.C., Modern Journalism (New Delhi: Kanishka Publications), 2004, p. 5.
4. Wain Wright, David, Journalism Made Simple (London: Allen & Allen Company Limited) 1972, pp. 26-27.
5. Pant, K.C., Modern Journalism, *op. cit.*, p. 64.
6. Keeble, Richard (ed.), Print Journalism: A Critical Introduction (New York: Rutledge Taylor), 2005, p. 75.

7. Parathasarathy, Rangaswami, Basic Journalism (New Delhi: Macmillan India Ltd.), 1984, p. 21.
8. Jones, John Paul, Gathering and Writing the News (Chicago: Nelson Hall Inc.), 1976, p. 16.
9. Padhya, Prabhakar, Principles of Journalism (Bombay: Popular Prakashan), 2004, p. 15.
10. Johnson, Stanley and Harriss Julian, The Complete Reporter (New York: The Macmillan Company), 1958, p. 19.
11. Keeble, Richard (ed.), Print Journalism: A Critical Introduction, *op. cit.*, p. 76.
12. Christopher, C., Dynamics of Journalism (New Delhi: Anmol Publications Private Limited), 1997, p. 118.
13. Parthasarthy, Rangaswami, Basic Journalism, *op. cit.*, p. 12.
14. Wain Wright, David, Journalism Made Simple, *op. cit.*, p. 56.
15. Chenery William L., Freedom of the Press (New York: Harcourt, Brace and Company), 1955, p. 34.
16. Bond, F. Fraser, An Introduction to Journalism, *op. cit.*, p. 4.
17 Parathasarathy, Rangaswami, Journalism in India, *op. cit.*, p. 257.
18. Basu, Bishwas, Your Guide to Journalism (Chandigarh: Abhishek Publications), 2006, p.196.
19. Wadhwa, Priyanka, Development of Journalism (New Delhi: Murari Lal and Sons), 2007, p. 212.
20. *Ibid.*, pp. 212-13.
21. *Ibid.*
22. Basu, Bishwas, Your Guide to Journalism, *op. cit.*, 2006, p. 200.
23. Wadhwa, Priyanka, Development of Journalism, *op. cit.*, p. 231.
24. Datta, K. Vishnu (ed.), Journalism Today (New Delhi: Akansha Publishing House), 2006, p. 1.
25. Hargreaves, Ian, Journalism: Truth or Dare (London: Oxford University Press), 2003, p. 2.
26. Keeble, Richard (ed.), Print Journalism: A Critical Introduction, *op. cit.*, p. 8.
27. *Ibid.*, pp. 26-31.
28. Pant, K. C., Modern Journalism, *op. cit.*, p. 5.
29. Miller, Corl G., Journalism (New York: Holt, Rinehart & Winston, Inc.), 2001, pp. 18-21.
30. Smith, K., The Mass Media: Reporting, Writing (New York: Harper Row Publishers), 1999, p. 551.
31. Bond, F. Fraser, An Introduction to Journalism, *op. cit.*, p. 3.
32. *Ibid.*, p. 26.
33. Raghavan, G.N.S., The Press in India: A New History (New Delhi: Gyan Publishing House), 1994, p. 4.
34. Basu, Bishwas, Your Guide to Journalism, *op. cit.*, 2006, p. 158.
35. Parthasarathy, Rangaswami, Journalism in India (New Delhi: Sterling Publishers Private Limited), 1989, p. 27.

36. Wadhwa, Priyanka, Development of Journalism (New Delhi: Murari Lal and Sons), 2007, p. 29.
37. Parathasarthy, Rangaswami, Journalism in India, *op. cit.*, p. 62.
38. Wadhwa, Priyanka, Development of Journalism, *op. cit.*, p. 181.
39. Parathasarthy, Rangaswami, Journalism in India, *op. cit.*, p. 289.
40. Wadhwa, Priyanka, Development of Journalism, *op. cit.*, p. 199.
41. Basu, Bishwas, Your Guide to Journalism, *op. cit.*, 2006, p. 177.
42. *Ibid.*
43. Choudhary, J.C., Introduction to Journalism and Mass Communication, *op. cit.*, p. 10.
44. Basu, Bishwas, Your Guide to Journalism, *op. cit.*, p. 73.
45. *Ibid.*, p. 74.
46. Prabhakar, Naval and Basu, Narendra, Journalism and Mass Communication (New Delhi: Commonwealth Publishers), 2007, p. 55.
47. Basu, Bishwas, Your Guide to Journalism, *op. cit.*, p. 79.
48. Choudhary, J.C., Introduction to Journalism and Mass Communication, *op. cit.*, pp. 26-27.
49. *Ibid.*, p. 11.
50. Basu, Bishwas, Your Guide to Journalism (Chandigarh: Abhishek Publications), 2006, p. 68.
51. Basu, Bishwas, Your Guide to Journalism, *op. cit.*, p. 80.
52. Choudhary, J.C., Introduction to Journalism and Mass Communication, *op. cit.*, p. 13.
53. Mansfield, F.J., The Complete Journalist (London: Sir Issac Pitman and Sons Limited), 1944, p. 2.
54. *Ibid.*
55. Padhya, Prabhakar, Principles of Journalism, *op. cit.*, p. 14.
56. *Ibid.*, p. 556.
57. Parthasarathy, Rangaswami, Basic Journalism, *op. cit.*, p. 22.
58. Mansfield, F.J., The Complete Journalist, *op. cit.*, p. 6.
59. Singh, J.K., Media and Journalism (New Delhi: APH Publishing Corporation), 2007, pp. 1-5.
60. Hargreaves, Ian, Journalism: Truth or Dare (London: Oxford University Press), 2003, pp. 18-20
61. Mansfield, F.J., The Complete Journalist, *op. cit.*, p. 2.
62. Choudhary, J.C., Introduction to Journalism and Mass Communication (New Delhi: Authorspress), 2007, pp. 131-132.
63. Shukla, A.S., Handbook of Journalism and Mass Communication (New Delhi: Rajat Publication), 2008, pp. 50-51.
64. Chenery, William L., Freedom of the Press (New York: Harcourt, Brace and Company), 1955, p. 159.
65. Rajsekhar, T. (ed.), Modern Media and Television Journalism (New Delhi: Sonali Publications), 2007, p. 121.
66. Shrivastava, K.M., Radio and TV Journalism (Bangalore: Sterling Publishers Private Limited), 1989, p. 132.

67. Pant, K.C., Modern Journalism, *op. cit.*, p. 200.
68. Rajsekhar, T. (ed.), Modern Media and Television Journalism, *op. cit.*, p. 3.
69. Singh, Manorma, History of Journalism (New Delhi: Discovery Publishing House), 2007, p. 232.
70. *Ibid.*, pp. 258-259.

2

Media in Indian Perspective: The Gandhian Era

Media considered as fourth estate in hierarchy after Legislative, Executive and Judiciary, has been putting its marks on every aspect of human being's life irrespective of place, religion, caste and creed. Its aim is to unfold the mystery of society on each account without bothering whether such writings are legally or socially permissible in contemporary times or not. Mohandas Karamchand Gandhi, popularly and reverently known as Mahatma Gandhi, was the one and only immortal soul whose ideas continue to evoke interest in every human being's mind and impactivily thought even several decades after his death in 1948. Gandhi always set high standards for printing words and was of the view that it is the only platform where you can address the mass society in one go and educate them for their legal rights. The most potent weapon to revolutionize the society, Gandhi visualized its importance in early stage of his life, embraced it and made it a part and parcel of his plan of action. Journalism, which is a discipline of gathering, writing and reporting news and broadly includes the process of editing as also publishing the news articles, fascinating, entertaining and informing everyone; thus the man of the millennium, Mohandas Karamchand Gandhi, was no exception. The power of his communication was so forceful that whatever he said and wrote, made an everlasting mark on reader's mind and his approach to journalism was totally devoid of any self-interest. None of his contemporaries or afterwards ever used the media so forcefully to ponder over the general issues that concerned the society as he did. He knew the importance of communication and used it to shape the opinions and mobilzing the people.

In the coast of Kathiawad in western India, Mohandas Gandhi was born on October 2, 1869 to his parents, Karamchand Gandhi and Putlibai. He was skinny and dark, yet he was no ordinary child. He was born by divine design to fight and reduce a great empire and without taking to arms set his country free. He was to be called the 'Mahatma' or the 'Great Soul'. Having led his people to freedom, he was to lay down his life for their sake. At the age of seven, he was sent to a primary school. He was shy, books were his sole companions. Mohandas was only 13 when he was told that he was soon to be married. His parents had already chosen his bride, Kasturba. After passing his high school examination, Mohandas was sent to England to study law and become a lawyer. On September 4, 1888, Mohandas left Mumbai for England. In London, young Gandhi found everything around him strange. His efforts to be an Englishman lasted only about three months; then he gave up the idea. He soon became a serious student, and concentrated very hard on his studies. On June 10, 1891, he was called to the bar. Gandhi was admitted as a lawyer and the next day he formally enrolled in the High Court. The following day, June 12, he sailed for India. Gandhi, after returning to India, set-up his practice as a lawyer in Rajkot. Soon, however, he was disgusted with the greed and the pettiness that he found among the lawyers. Gandhi realised that it was difficult for the poor and the humble to get away from such things. It was then that an offer came to him to go to South Africa on behalf of Dada Abdullah & Co. The opportunity to see a new country and a new people excited Gandhi and he accepted the offer. In April 1893, he left Mumbai for South Africa. Gandhi approached the port of Natal towards the end of May

1893. The first thing he noticed was that the Indians there were treated with very little respect. Gandhi spent three years in South Africa meeting the Indians and talking about social injustices. He was now a well known figure; everyone recognized his frockcoat and turban. His practice was going very well and he knew that the people there wanted him with them. At this time, Gandhi was becoming more and more involved in public activities, and his way of life became simpler. It was in 1901, six years after Gandhi brought his family to Durban when he felt that his future activity lay not in South Africa but in India.

Since communication means reaching out to the other person or persons, the process can be verbal or non-verbal, intentional or unintentional, provided the goal is achieved and one man who can fit in this communication theory exactly is none other than Mahatma Gandhi.[1] Taking the centre stage after returning from South Africa, he led from front and put forward his own opinion. Gandhi always set high standards for printing words and was of the view that it is the only platform where you can address the mass society in one go and educate them for their legal rights. In his autobiography, he wrote, "The sole aim of journalism should be the service of nation and people. The newspapers are a great power, but just as unchained torrent of water submerges whole countryside and devastated crops, even so an uncontrolled pen serves to destroy. If the control is from without, it proves more poisonous than want of control. It can be profitable only when experienced from within."[2]

Bhikhu Parekh has candidly summed up this aspect of Gandhi's communication skills in the following words: After a long reflection and experimentation, he evolved a distinct mode of discourse that was also a form of praxis. Convinced that human actions derived their emotional energy from heart which could only be addressed and activated by a judiciously selected language of symbols and recognizing that Hindu culture was deeply symbolic, he evolved a powerful cluster of culturally evocative symbols including such things as the spinning wheel, the khadi, the cow and the Gandhi cap partly by conscious design and partly as spontaneous expressions of his own way of life—his dress, language, mode of speaking, food, bodily gestures, ways of sitting, walking and talking, humour and staff, became a symbol of a specific way of life. Each evoked deep cultural memories, spoke volumes and conveyed highly complex messages[3]. Communication happens at many levels (even for one single action), in many different ways and for most beings, as well as certain machines. Several, if not all, fields of study dedicate a portion of attention to communication, so when speaking about communication, it is very important to be sure about what aspects of communication one is talking about.

Definitions of communication range widely, some recognizing that animals can communicate with each other as well as human beings, and some are narrower, only including human beings within the parameters of human symbolic interaction. "What is really needed to make democracy to function is not the knowledge of facts, but right education. And the true function of journalism is to educate the public mind, not to stock the public mind with wanted and unwanted impressions. A journalist has, therefore, to use his discretion as to what to report and when. As it is, journalists are not content to stick to the facts alone. Journalism has become the art of intelligent anticipation of events."[4] The renowned personality of mass media and probably the greatest journalist of all time, Mahatma Gandhi reached out to millions of people across the world through his communication skills and journalistic approach and then put an ever lasting impact on Indian National Movement and waged a battle single handedly against the mighty Britishers. He took to journalism as a medium to educate the common masses as well as to install patriotic feelings in their hearts for the cause of others. In his journalistic career, which spanned roughly four decades, he wrote articles on various topics, simple and clear, with passion and burning indignation. Gandhi was not a journalist in the popular sense of the term. His life and writing had a symbiotic relationship with each other. Gandhi wrote with a purpose. Writing for him, was not a writer's pursuit for creativity for a role, it was a duty, bound to be performed. Neither was writing a proselytizing mission with him. Writing satisfied his need to share his ideas with others, a two-way dialogue, between him and his readers on a joint journey on the path leading to the truth[5].

Newspapers were not only informative and entertaining to Gandhi but also made him ambitious and he started thinking to write for them. The desire is latent in human beings as everyone wants to see his name and article in print and it was that temptation which could not be resisted. His friendship with the members of London Vegetarian Society provided him a necessary launching pad to write for its organ, "The Vegetarian", and those were his earliest writings on the record. A struggling barrister of Mumbai that he was at that time, he had to do something more tangible than indulging in non-remunerative journalism. South Africa not only shaped many of the ideas and traits of Gandhiji, but also made him an out-and-out journalist as well. If London Vegetarian Society afforded him a forum to write and speak, the political situation in South Africa chiseled him into a conscientious journalist. While fighting incessantly against all disabilities imposed on Indians, through representation, petition, memorandum etc, he did not, for a moment, minimize the great role of newspapers. He would scan through all local papers and reply suitably to any queries or distortion of facts. In a letter to the editor of The Times of India, he wrote, "Publicity is our best and perhaps the only weapon of defense"[6]. Gandhi considered journalism as a selfless service to the society. He advocated that journalism should never be prostituted for selfish ends for amassing money. As an operation in ideas, journalism should be as free as possible from the limitations of industrialism. Using print media for the dissemination of his ideas was part of a clear strategy with Gandhi. He was a prolific writer who left behind a vast body of articles and books.

Gandhi's first major essay in journalism was the 'Green Pamphlet', describing the conditions of Indians in South Africa. Gandhi wrote the piece while he had come home to Rajkot on a brief visit from South Africa (1901). The success of the pamphlet made Gandhi more confident of the efficacy and publicity value of print media. The Hindu, The Statesman, The Times of India and The Englishman vied with each other in publishing Gandhi. By that time, Gandhi had made name for himself in the arena of Journalism. By 1903, Gandhi had realized that occasional writing and open letters or articles in newspapers were inadequate to meet the great campaign strategy that he had in his mind. This realization led to Gandhi taking over the editorship of the Indian Opinion, a weekly published from South Africa, which established Gandhi as a journalist. On one hand, the readers were given lessons in hygiene and sanitation and on the other, they were reminded of their rich culture and civilization. In short, the journal addressed itself to the whole gamut of Gandhi's concerns that were communicated in the most straightforward and lucid manner. Care was taken to make the whole exercise of communication come to the level of the dialogue between the readers and the writer. Through judicious use of print media, Gandhi was able to highlight the plight of Indians in South Africa, publicize the discriminatory laws and actions they were subjected to, and finally, to organize Satyagraha to streamline the things. Another great quality of Gandhi, the editor, was his direct and forthright manner in conveying the things. Direct presentation was the beauty of all his writings. He had a clear thinking and knew well what he was going to say. He would put forth his ideas and arguments in crisp short sentences.

Gandhi attempted to realize his dream through effective use of his writings and was fairly hopeful of doing so. Gandhi used the print media actively during his stay in South Africa and highlighted the plight of Indians in his columns. He continued to follow the standards of journalism even in the later part of his life that he set for himself and his staff during the initial struggle in South Africa. Similarly, his ornamental style of writing and his restraint were emulated by the upcoming journalists of the contemporary times. About impact of his writing during that period, one can safely say that he was at least able to make the Indian community aware of their rights in the colony. Gandhi used very dignified language to put across his ideas, which were in the nature of educating the Indians and others. His attitude, as revealed from his writings, never had a tone of confrontation or challenge; rather Gandhi was developing a new technique and style of appealing to the fairness for which the British were known. Mahatma Gandhi's life, attitude and political action were informed by the highest moral principles and compassion. Uniquely among public men, he sought to analyze and explain events and his own reaction in terms of these principles through his talks, statements, writings and interviews. The moral force that he brought to bear on the political discourse was compelling and inspired large section to take up the cause of freedom.

Gandhi, in fact, brought in many new elements, which introduced fresh life in the field of journalism. "As a result of his wide interest, his genius for simplification, his eagerness to reach the largest number of people and startling nature of his activities, there was a quickening of life in journalism. Many of his followers were moved to write and publish in the Indian languages and in imitation of his own direct style, they wrote a simple prose. Regional journalism began to acquire an importance and there was hardly an area of the country which did not have its newspapers."[7] Undoubtedly, Gandhi introduced a new and a noble element in the field of journalism. It was his approach—his human approach—which gave his writings a character. He never looked upon the reading public as target for propaganda. He belonged to the people by identifying himself with them and wrote about their feelings and aspirations. For Gandhi, neither subject was too big nor too small. Louis Fisher once said that Gandhi would attach equal importance to a letter written to President Roosevelt as much to an article on the subject of individual rights. Gandhi was very much laconic in speech. He seldom used a superfluous word. Each coma or colon conveyed something or the other. Moreover, his expression was much less than his profound thinking on the subject. He had suggestions to give on each item published in the journal.

Gandhi, as an edito, would correct himself publicly if he found that some untruth had crept in his writings. To cite an example, he compared the Jalianwala Bagh massacre to that of Glenco. A correspondent drew his attention saying that the latter was more horrible. In the next issue of the Young India, Gandhi corrected his statement. Newspapers or view papers is a social institution. Its success depends on how they produce materials in their columns. It is also judged by the readers whom they are going to address through their writings. Unfortunately, papers mostly cater to the lower taste of the readers, through sensation mongering rather than educating them for better citizenship. Some times, the monetary benefits pushed back the ethics in journalism and yellow journalism and page 3 stories occupied the main attention. To whom the journalist is loyal? To the proprietor, to one's own self or to the particular class he belongs to? As per Gandhiji, 'readers' were the most important. A journalist may be a patriot, a party member or a faithful employee but his loyalty ought to be primarily associated with his readers. Public has the right to know the truth. He must be informed objectively as to what is happening. His stories neither are hampered by partiality nor by loose connectivity. If the paper loses confidence of its readers, it has lost all that is worth in journalism. Gandhi interpreted that the writer alone is in a position to link up with the very sources of life on important event, be it political, social or economic and bring it strictly into human domain that is accessible to all.

Personally, Gandhiji did not like to write much in English, though he loved the language and developed a style of his own. He knew English could not be the national language of India. But as long as the national language, Hindustani, was not developed, he had to choose a medium through which his message could be reached to the four corners of the country. As a nationalist, he wanted a common language for the country and though aware of the richness of the Gujarati literature, did not hesitate to support and foster the claim of Hindustani for this honour. He made all efforts to make the language acceptable all over India. On his writing skills, J.H. Holmes wrote, "Gandhiji's literary achievement is more remarkable in view of the fact that he was never, in any sense of the phrase, a literary man. Unlike his great contemporary, Rabindra Nath Tagore and his accomplished successor Pandit Nehru, the Mahatma had no special grace of style. Seldom, in his writings, did he rise to heights of eloquence and beauty. Gandhiji interests were never aesthetic rather pragmatic. He had no desire or ambition, no time to be an artist. His own thought was of his own people and his struggle to make them free. So, he wrote with disciplined simplicity, seeking only to make himself clearly understood. The result was the one most important quality of literary art, namely clarity. I doubt if, in all his works, Gandhi ever wrote a sentence, which failed to express with utter precision the thought he had in mind to convey. He wrote in a style that was perfect for his purpose of communication. To read his writings is to think of the contents and not of the style, which means a triumph in the adoption of means to ends."[8]

His articulation is not only clear and simple but also meaningful, taken in the context of his leadership of the most gigantic nationalist struggle of the twentieth century. He wrote extensively in Young India and Harijan, the leading voice of the era presenting various contemporary issues and forces readers to give it a thought. Writing for ordinary folk, he usually employed various metaphors to realize Indians about their abilities and rich traditions. Gandhi was not merely a leader; he also became a part of the masses. His simple attire, use of colloquial language, reference to the popular allegory of Ramrajya had made him comprehensible to the common people. Gandhiji introduced a new lively tone in his correspondence. Unlike the formal artificial letters in an average newspaper office, his was couched in simple and direct language. It was fashioned to suit the needs of the occasion. When he was away from the scene of action, he would make sure, through letters, etc. to keep in constant touch with them. Gandhi was very methodical in whatever subject he laid his hands on. He knew that mere good writing was not enough. He must see that the paper was published and dispatched in time and that proper account was maintained. He used to take the best out of his associates in running the paper. In his first meeting with Gandhi, Lord Reading, the then Viceroy, expressed surprise at his growing popularity among the Indians by saying, "There is nothing striking about his appearance. He came to visit me in a dhoti and cap, woven on a spinning wheel, with bare feet and legs and my first impression on seeing him ushered into my room was that there was nothing to arrest attention in his appearance and that I should have passed him by in the street without a second look at him. When he talks, the impression is different."[9]

When Gandhiji arrived in India on January 9, 1915, journalism did not establish itself as a profession, excepting in case of Anglo-Indian press. Advertisement did not play that important role as it plays today. By and large, people had to depend on sales promotion and more importantly on monetary help from individuals. Moreover, advertisement was meant for the capture of a section of the society whereas in modern times, it's catering to influence all strata of life. Gandhiji's objection to advertisement was more on moral and ethical grounds. It becomes difficult to draw a line between what is bad and beneficial advertisement. Once a newspaper agreed to take advertisement, there was no limit to that. In their quest for money, they published indecent and harmful advertisement. This was, according to him, not the objective of journalism. Rather than serving the community, such action would run to the detriment of its interest. Gandhi, commenting on Hind Swaraj in 1921, elaborated the purpose behind the book. He says, "It was written in answer to the Indian school of violence and its prototype in South Africa. I came in contact with every known Indian anarchist in London. Their bravery impressed me, but I feel that their zeal was misguided. I felt that violence was no remedy for India's ills and that her civilization required the use of a different and higher weapon for self-protection. The Satyagraha of South Africa was still an infant hardly two years old. But it had developed sufficiently to permit me to write of it with some degree of confidence. Hind Swaraj teaches the gospel of love in the place of that of hate. It replaces violence with self-sacrifice. It puts soul force against brute force."[10]

Gandhiji was great advocate for the freedom of press. In the Young India of January 12, 1922, he wrote on the liberty of press, "Liberty of speech means that it is not gagged even when the speech hurts, liberty of the press can be said to be truly respected only when the press can comment in the severest terms upon an even misrepresented matters, broken against misrepresentation or violence being secured not by and administrative gagging order, not by closing down the press but punishing the real offender, leaving the press itself unrestricted. Freedom of association is truly respected when assemblies of people can discuss even revolutionary projects, the state relying upon the force of public opinion and the civil policy, not the savage military at its disposal, to crush any actual outbreak of revolution that is designed to confound public opinion and the state representing it."[11] Gandhi further put forward his views on nation, nationalism and national identity in Harijan. He rarely used the term nation except when forced to do so under circumstances in which Jinnah defended the 'Two Nation Theory'. In opposition to Jinnah, he argued that the language of nationalism was both incompatible with the Indian situation and inherently absurd. India was not a nation but a civilization, which had benefitted from the contribution of different races and religions over the centuries. Challenging the basis of two-nation theory, Gandhi, therefore, asked, "Is India composed of two nations? Are not Christians a third, Parsis a fourth and so on? How are the Muslims of Punjab different from the Hindus and Sikhs? Are they not all Punjabis drinking the same water, breathing the same air and deriving the sustenance from the same soul"?[12]

Although Gandhi's responses in Harijan were issue based, they largely followed the theoretical conceptualizations that he articulated in the Hind Swaraj, one of the most important treatises that he wrote to clarify his views to readers. While writing in Hind Swaraj, Gandhi was influenced by leading western thinkers of the contemporary times. As he himself admitted, "Whilst the views expressed in Hind Swaraj are held by me, I have but endeavored humbly to follow Tolstoy, Ruskin, Thoreau, Emerson and other writers besides the masters of the Indian philosophy."[13] The Mahatma was perhaps the first to have realized the political inadequacies of the urban-centric national movement in a diverse society like India. In addition to article written by Gandhi, a regular section in Harijan was the 'Question Box', where Gandhi responded to questions on various issues of contemporary relevance. Questions generally structured around what the Mahatma had written in the weekly and elsewhere. Since the question box ensured a dialogue with those seeking to grapple with his views, Gandhi was always favourably disposed towards the section. Harijan was important in another aspect, as the forum where Gandhi generally dealt with the criticism of his published views. Gandhi differentiated between news and journalists' impression of coming events. He would not like interpretative news, which to him, was journalistic kite flying. He would advise journalists to print authentic news with no fear of contradiction. He would ask them to withhold news as long as it could not be verified. The readers in the west were not only getting the news but speculative news with particular slant or with different interpretations, so as to create a public opinion that the paper desired.

The tendency of the journalists to pick up the bits from here and there and dish them up for the purpose of creating sensation was, according to him, back door journalism. Such type of journalism misled the public and harmed the genuine cause. Calling them bad examples of foreign journalists, he requested his Indian counterparts to desist from such cheap performance. The main aim of the journalist would be to strengthen the society along with unbiased reporting. During the Quit India movement, he appealed to princes, to Government servants, to soldiers and to students with the request to help the struggle. But Hiren Mukherjee, Deputy leader of the Communist Party in the parliament criticized him at that time saying, "No particular role was allotted to the workers and peasants and though they formed the overwhelming majority of the people, they were expected simply to line up in the manner directed by their superiors. The priorities given to journalists in Gandhi's order of appeal were perhaps not entirely accidental. The Mahatma, with all his great courage and occasional sublimity, had throughout his life, had a shrewd eye to publicity whatever he thought and did."[14]

Gandhi had of late, been greatly distressed at the general fall in the standard of the press. He hated speculation. This was sometimes mischievous and often misleading. He hated fabrication on facts and news. He did not believe in so called journalistic 'scoop'. As one who believed in the service to the community, he would advise against publication of doubtful news. Due to the charismatic personality and his journalistic qualities, the journalists of contemporary times began to imitate him. They went to the field and collected stories about the common man—his thought and feeling, his desire and ambition. Whether it was a political, economic or social article, it invariably moves around the masses. The modern media is still taking a leaf out of the books of Mahatma Gandhi regarding moral and ethics in journalism but due to the cutthroat competition in this field, few are the buyers of Gandhi's journalism. Media, in contemporary times, has become so powerful that it can mould the society and change the viewpoint of common masses towards any general issues that come across its way. Thus he was a man of thought and action, a rare combination. As a man of thought, he was highly critical of the madness of modernity and articulated an alternative vision, the best insights of both, the pre-modern and modern worldviews while avoiding the naive individualism and moral vacuum of the currently fashionable post modernism.[15] As a man of action, he led from the front the nationalist struggle of freedom on the basis of what he thought was morally acceptable. Without compromising his integrity, he also demonstrated how to build a strong political platform drawing upon the moral strength of Satyagrahis.

GANDHI'S JOURNEY TO JOURNALISM

To explore the journalist hidden in Gandhi is no easy exercise, for he was versatile, meticulous and authentic in his writings as in his speeches and actions. No wonder he produced about two million English words alone, the estimate for Hindi and Gujarati being not known. Starting in South Africa as a free-lance Journalist, Gandhi went on to become one of the finest journalists, producing some of the best journals in the history of Indian journalism. Indian Opinion, Young India, Harijan and Navajivan were the important journals that were edited by Gandhi. Additionally, he was associated with lots of other publications during the peak of India's freedom struggle.

Gandhi's sojourn with journalism began first with the

Indian Opinion which was launched in South Africa, with a view to ventilate the grievances of Indians and mobilize public opinion in their favour. For this, Gandhi started writing in and giving interviews to newspapers. He maintained a list of friendly papers, which gave him wholehearted support. He focused on open letters and letters to the editor, but soon perceived that occasional writings and the hospitality of newspapers were not adequate for the political campaign he had launched. Gandhi had all the qualities of a good Journalist. Gandhi made known the ideals he had set before himself as a journalist in his autobiography. The genesis of Gandhi's reliance on mass media and his usage of newspapers, Journals to generate public opinion and initiate political mobilization can be traced back to his struggle in South Africa. The Indian labourers who had gone to South Africa and the merchants who followed them were denied the right to vote. They had to register and pay toll tax. They could not reside barring in prescribed locations which were dirty and congested. Gandhi soon became the leader of the struggle against these conditions and during 1893-94, was engaged in a heroic though unequal struggle against the racist authorities of South Africa. It was during this long struggle, lasting about two decades, that Gandhi developed the technique of Satyagraha based on truth and non-violence. As early as 1896, the roots of the Satyagraha took shape in Gandhi's mind. In the 'Green Pamphlet'[16] he pointed out that his method in South Africa was to conquer "hatred by love." In 1899, Gandhi held out the hope: "victory must be ours, for our case has been universally regarded as just, our methods moderate and without reproach."[17] And to achieve this victory, Gandhi resorted to Satyagraha. When the Satyagraha struggle started, Gandhi became involved in the publication of the weekly journal, Indian Opinion, published in English and Gujarati. It made a significant contribution in educating Indians and instilling in them the courage to resist injustice. Satyagraha in South Africa would perhaps have been impossible without it. According to Gandhi, through the "medium of this paper, we could very well disseminate the news of the week among the community. The English section kept those Indians informed about the movement who did not know Gujarati and for Englishmen in India, England and South Africa, Indian Opinion served the objective of a weekly newsletter." Gandhi considered Indian Opinion as an effective instrument for mass mobilization against the mighty Britishers.

Gandhi also regularly wrote for the local white press to clarify the Indian stand and expose the partisan and anti-Indian policies of the South African Government. In a letter published in Rand Daily Main on 6th August, 1910, Gandhi wrote: "Will you permit me to correct some statements made in your leading article on Lord Ampthills' action in the House of Lords on the passive resistance struggle. May I remind you that passive resistance started in 1907 when the question of priests, doctors and lawyers had not come up for public discussion, and when it did arise, it simply arose with a view to forcibly illustrate the injustice that had been done by the Government in not conceding the demands of the community. Passive resisters who are not criminals in the ordinary sense of the term have been sent to a penal settlement, like Diepkloof, where the ordinary privileges of prisoners are withheld."[18] In his opinion, this was undoubtedly a glaring example of mistreatment. This reflects Gandhi's concern for highlighting issues through the press. In fact, the files of Indian Opinion reflect the steady growth of the Gandhian spirit. The early issues carried petitions and prayers. There was appeal to reason and expostulation. The significant bulk of editorials of Indian Opinion contained a mild protest against racial segregation. For, at this stage, Gandhi had firm faith in the British Constitution. However, with the passage of time, the harshness of the Empire, Gandhi had to change his stand. "Is this monstrous; injustice to be really done, he asked, in regard to the anti-Indian regulations which were steadily growing in number? Even at the eleventh hour, we cannot abandon expectation that the better nature, the truer self, of our white brokers will yet assert itself." He kept on repeating this expectation in several editorials until at last exasperated, he said, "Perhaps in the Transvaal, people are living in the Middle Ages. He had already alerted every Indian in South Africa to be ready for self-sacrifice for the sake of the whole community whose fate was hanging in the balance. He appealed; Individual differences must be sunk in the face of common danger. The slightest deviation would bring us down the precipice, because of the opposition established against us is overwhelming. After moving its office and printing press to Phoenix, Indian Opinion continuously carried a vivid portrayal of the sufferings of the Indian community in South Africa. It made effort to educate public opinion and to gather with indicated line of duty that every Indian must follow in order to win his elementary human rights. Close communion linked the editorial office with the readers of the journal. The correspondence columns were a good training ground for Gandhi himself. It was as though the whole community of the Indians thought audibly with him through the piles of letters the mails brought. Indian Opinion hardly ever had more than 1,100 subscribers but each copy had a group of eager readers and passed from hand to hand. In fact, Gandhi adopted this style in all his future journalistic efforts.

Gandhi came back to India in 1915 at the age of 46. He was keen to serve his country and his people. He first decided to study Indian conditions before deciding the field of his work. He found the ground ready for action in 1919 that was a watershed year in Indian history. Discontentment was brewing all over the country for several reasons. The Rowlatt Act, the Jallianwala Bagh massacre and martial law in Punjab had belied all the generous wartime promises of the British. The Montague-Chelmsford Reforms that were announced towards the end of 1919, with their ill-considered scheme of diarchy, satisfied few. The Indian Muslims too were angry when they discovered that their loyalty had been purchased during the war by assurances of generous treatment of Turkey after the war, a promise which the British statesman had no intention of fulfilling. Gandhi was in close touch with the Khilafat leaders for some time. He was sympathetic to the Khilafat cause as he felt that the British had committed a breach of faith by making promises which it had no intention of keeping. In February 1920, Gandhiji suggested to the Khilafat Committee to adopt a programme of non-violent non-cooperation to protest the government's behaviour. On June 9, 1920, the Khilafat Committee at

Allahabad unanimously accepted the suggestion of non-cooperation and asked Gandhiji to lead the movement. Prior to this, in May 1920, the All India Congress Committee, in a meeting, decided to convene a special session in September to enable the Congress to decide on its course of action.

USE OF PRINT MEDIA

Non-cooperation Movement

The beginning of the civil defence movement against the Rowlatt Bill was made at a meeting held at the Sabarmati Ashram where, on 24.2.1919, a pledge drafted by Gandhi was signed by those present at the meeting. The pledge read as follows: "Being conscientiously of the opinion that the Bills known as the Indian Criminal Law Bill No. 1 of 1919 and the Criminal Law Bill No. II of 1919 are unjust, subversive of the principles of liberty and justice and destructive of the elementary rights of individuals on which the safety of the community and the State itself is based, we solemnly affirm that in the event of these Bills becoming law and until they are withdrawn, we shall refuse civilly to obey these laws and such other laws as a Committee to be hereafter appointed may think fit and we further affirm that in this struggle we will faithfully follow truth and refrain from violence to life, person and property."[19]

Meanwhile, the non-cooperation movement was launched formally on August 1, 1920, after the expiry of the notice that Gandhiji had sent to the Viceroy in his letter of 22 June in which he had asserted the right recognized "from time immemorial of the subject to refuse to help a ruler who misrules." The Congress accepted non-cooperation as its own programme of action in its special session of September. The Non-Cooperation programme proposed by Gandhi comprised surrendering of titles and honours, refusal to attend government functions, boycott of government-affiliated schools and colleges, gradual boycott of courts, refusal of military to serve in Mesopotamia, a complete boycott of the reformed council and boycott of foreign goods, besides others. Gandhi promised that if the programme was fully implemented, Swaraj would be ushered in within a year. The

Nagpur session of the Congress in December 1920, where the non-cooperation resolution was passed, thus committed the Congress to a programme of extra-constitutional mass action. Several revolutionary terrorist groups also pledged support to the movement. In order for the Congress to fulfill its new commitment, significant changes were introduced in its creed and its organizational structure. The goal of the Congress was changed from the attainment of self-government by constitutional and legal means to the attainment of Swaraj by peaceful and legitimate means. The new Constitution of the Congress, the handiwork of Gandhiji, introduced other great changes among them, the working committee was reconstituted with 15 members; Provincial Congress Committees were to be organized on a linguistic basis; membership was reduced to four annas per year.

Gandhi's response to Non-cooperation was, "rejection is as much an ideal as the acceptance of a thing. It is necessary to reject untruth to accept truth..... we have lost the power of saying no.... this deliberate refusal to co-operate is like a weeding process that a cultivator has to resort before he sows. Non-cooperation is the nation's notice that is no longer satisfied to be in tutelage. An India prostrate at the feet of Europe can give no hope to humanity. An India awakened and free has a message of peace and goodwill to a groaning world. Non-cooperation is designed to supply her with a platform from which she will preach the message[20].

The adoption of the Non-Cooperation Movement by the Congress, which was started earlier by the Khilafat Conference, provided it a new energy and from January 1921, it began to register considerable success all over the country. After having conceived the programme of non-cooperation, Gandhi took a whirlwind tour of the country to popularize his ideas of non-cooperation. He addressed hundreds of meetings and met a large number of political workers. Along with this, he strategically utilized the press to add impetus to the movement. He had also taken over the editorship of the journals, Young India and Navajivan by then. Introducing the two journals to his readers, Gandhi wrote: "With much striving, I have formulated some principles for my life and put them into practice, it is my sincere aspiration to place these principles before India and share my happiness with her; a newspaper is one means to that end. The agitation against the Rowlatt Act was an object lesson in Satyagraha. Hence Navajivan will keep it alive before the public."[21] In these journals, Gandhi freely ventilated his views and also used them to educate the public on Satyagraha. Gandhi used these journals to inform the masses on various aspects during the non-cooperation movement. For instance, in an article, 'The Doctrine of the Sword' in the Young India, Gandhi wrote: "Non-violence is the law of our species as violence is law of the brute. I have, therefore, returned to place before India the ancient law of self-sacrifice. For Satyagraha and its offshoots, non-cooperation and civil resistance are nothing but new names for the law of suffering"[22].

A large number of lawyers and judges believed that if they non-cooperated, the plight of common man would be worse off with no one to defend his rights. Gandhi answered all these criticisms through the columns of Young India and Navajivan. He generated public discussion on all these issues and presented the arguments put forward by both the parties so that the public could come to an independent judgement and freely follow the dictates of conscience. Some selections from Gandhi's arguments in defence of his unconventional ideas as excerpted from his journals are given below: "when Government does not represent the will of the people, when it supports dishonesty or terrorism, the judges and executive officials by retaining office become instruments of dishonesty and terrorism. I would submit to our distinguished countrymen who occupy high offices that their giving up their offices will bring the struggle to a speedy end and would probably obviate the danger attendant upon the masses being called upon to signify their disapproval by withdrawing cooperation."[23]

In speech after speech and in editorial after editorial, Gandhi explained ceaselessly and untiringly the nature of this movement. The movement of non-cooperation is nothing but an attempt to isolate the brute force of the British from all the trappings under which it is hidden and to show that brute force by itself cannot for one single moment hold India. Thus Gandhi adopted different techniques for mobilizing the masses such as extensive tours and padyatra, speeches at public meetings, effective journalism, prayers and bhajans, fasts, brahmcharya and swadeshi and fighting for the rights of minorities and especially untouchables. Gandhi touched every heart and every aspect of Indian life. He mobilized the masses and directed their struggle for complete freedom and reconstruction of the society. Gandhi's writings were very forceful and were written with conviction. They left a great impression on his readers. Thus he wrote once in the context of non-cooperation in the Young India: "Our non-cooperation is neither with the English nor with the West. Our non-cooperation is with the system the English have established, with the material civilization and its attendant greed and exploitation of the weak. Our non-cooperation is refusal to cooperate with the English administrators on their own terms. He asked the English: Come and cooperate with us on our terms, and it will be well for us, for you and the world. However, Gandhi was aware of the mood of the masses and the sentiments that prevailed. He was quick to warn his countrymen about any form of violence through his journal. Violent resistance is itself non-cooperation and it is immoral because of its violence. It becomes moral when it is non-violent. Non-cooperation with evil is a sacred duty."[24] Gandhi supported non-cooperation based on nonviolence. The active state in you requires you to resist the wrong doer. Gandhi was quick to respond to the various forms of participation by various sections of the society during the peak of the non-cooperation movement. The 19th January, 1921 issue of Young India, for instance, had the following item as a flier (the top news): "Students strike in Calcutta. The latest information to hand about the great students' strike of Calcutta is that nearly 8,000 college students are on strike. The following colleges are affected some wholly, others partially, Bangabasi and Ripon. This was not merely a great moral booster for the students' struggle in Bengal but also inspired students' groups in other parts of the country."[25]

This caption was followed by a long letter titled 'To Young Bengal' written by Gandhi himself that was carried over in the second page. Gandhi wrote, "I have just read an account of your response to the nation's calls. I had expected no less; 1 certainly expect still more. You have taken the step. You will not recede. We cannot get Swaraj if not one class in the country is prepared to work and sacrifice for it. The Government will yield not to the logic of words. It knows no logic but that of brave and true deeds. You dare not go back without hurting yourselves and the cause. Intolerance is a species of violence and therefore against our creed. Non-violent non-cooperation is an object lesson in democracy. The moment we are able to ensure non-violence, even under circumstances the most provoking, that moment we have achieved our end, because that is the moment when we can offer complete non-cooperation."[26] The next issue of the Young India had a one and a quarter column report titled 'The Student Movement in Calcutta' on the front page. It was basically a news report and contained all the facts and figures about the protest movement, apart from explaining the style and method of the students' struggle. This was certain to inspire and train other such movements in other parts of the country. As the non-cooperation movement progressed, cases of assault on people increased."[27] Gandhi would immediately know the significance of publishing something like brutalities of the British administrators on the freedom fighters. Thus the January 12, 1922 issue of Young India had an item titled 'Summary of Reports of Repression'. Besides the news of 'Cases of assault at Secunderabad' on volunteers, brave tales of 'Two Wives' of the Secretary of Sitapur District Congress Committee and beating up of two reputed Zamindars of Hajipur in Bihar, the summary contained details like number of workers sent to jails from Chittagong.[28]

Gandhiji used to write sometimes for the English daily, the Bombay Chronicle, which was started by Sir Pherozshah Mehta and was edited by B.G. Horniman. He also occasionally contributed to the English monthly, Young India, with which Jamnadas Dwarkadas, Umar Shobhani and Shankerlal Banker were associated. Articles by Gandhiji were published in the Hindustan of Ranchhoddas Bhavan Lotwala as well as in the Gujarati monthly Navajivan and Satya edited by Indulal Yagnik. After Gandhiji had settled in Gujarat and after his participation in different public activities, he felt the need of a Gujarati journal to publish his views elaborately and extensively. He put the proposal before Shankerlal Banker and Indulal Yagnik. Both were associated with the Navajivan and Satya. They took up Gandhiji's proposal and decided to convert their monthly into a weekly. It was decided to publish the proposed weekly under a new name Navajivan from Ahmedabad under the editorship of Gandhiji.

Again, in November and December 1920, the weekly contained articles written by Gandhiji, each one of them explaining the Non-cooperation movement that was contemplated. These aimed at clarifying Gandhiji's stand on the movement and the programmes suggested by him. Its issue dated 22nd December, 1920 was full of information about the 35th session of the Indian National Congress due to meet at Nagpur that year. When the Congress was in session, arrangements were made to procure telegraphically the news about the business transacted at Nagpur. The Navajivan, during January 1921, was full of details about the resolutions made and the speeches delivered at the Nagpur session. When that body held its 36th session at Ahmedabad during December 1921, a whole issue of the Navajivan was devoted to news about it with full texts of the speeches of the participants in the discussions of the resolutions moved and adopted. It appears from some notices appearing in the Navajivan during those days that arrangements were made to sell single copies of the weekly through hawkers in the city of Ahmedabad and that as these copies were soon exhausted, reprints had to be issued to meet the demand.

Gandhiji was running English weekly the, 'Young India', at that time. Some articles written for that journal were published in Gujarati Weekly, Navajivan. Gandhiji had written an article 'Tampering with Loyalty' in September 1921. That article was published in the Gujarati Weekly, Navajivan, dated 2nd October, 1921, under the caption 'Rajdroha' (Rajdroha means sedition in Gujarati). Again, Gandhiji had written an English article, 'The Puzzle and its Solution' in the Young India in December 1921. That was published in Gujarati in the Navajivan dated 15th December 1921, under the heading 'Viceroy in Munzvan' (The Dilemma before the Viceroy). The third article appeared in the Young

India during February, 1922, under the title 'Shaking of the Manes'. It appeared in the Navajivan dated 26th February 1922, as 'Hoonkar' (Roaring of the Lion). The Government which was watching these writings of Gandhiji decided to launch prosecutions against him as the editor and against Shankerlal Banker, the publisher of Young India, for what the Government termed 'seditious' writings. Subsequently, Gandhiji and Banker were arrested, in the second week of March 1922. They were charged with contravening section 124-A. of the Indian Penal Code, later convicted and sentenced. Gandhiji was released in 1924 on health grounds. He assumed the editorial responsibility of Navajivan and Young India in the first week of April that year. He continued to review the political situation in the country and to spread his views through these journals. The Gujarati press was coming more and more under his influence. This is evidenced not only by the increasing space devoted by it to Gandhiji's views and activities, but also by the reports of the two conferences that Gujarati Journalists held (December 1925 and December 1927, both in Ahmedabad). It was declared that the press corps in Gujarat were under the total influence of Gandhiji and that the call of the nation had become the life and blood of the Gujarati press. At the beginning of the year 1928, the Government of Bombay proposed to raise the land revenue assessment in the Bardoli area of the Surat District by 22 per cent. The landholders of that area disapproved of this increase; they approached Gandhiji and told him their grievances. Gandhiji agreed to help organize a no-tax campaign in that area. He addressed an appeal to the peasants of Bardoli on 5th February, 1928, in which he said that the name of the Bardoli connotes Swaraj and vice versa. He advised the peasants to show their strength in the resistance movement and named Vallabhbhai Patel as their Sardar (leader) for the conduct of the movement. Navajivan had been reporting the progress of the movement, and Gandhiji devoted one whole issue of his weekly to Bardoli matters.

He published in it the full text of the letters exchanged between Vallabhbhai Patel and the Governor of Bombay. The Gujarati press had already started reporting news about the activities in Bardoli. The Bombay Samachar commenting upon the issue, blamed the Bombay Government for what it termed as an unjust levy. The Sanj Vartaman quoted the arguments of Vallabhbhai; the Gujarat said that 'Bardoli was agog with activities'. The Jame Jamshed exhorted the people of Bardoli to keep up their pledge, the Sanj Vartman reiterated Gandhiji's advice to the Satyagrahis of Bardoli. The Gujarat said that the demand of the people of Bardoli was just and hence 'victory will undoubtedly come to the people'. Some papers advised the Bombay Government to act judiciously and wisely; some emphasised the demand of the Satyagrahis to set-up an inquiry into the matters. The Government made arrangements to confiscate the properties of those who did not pay their revenue dues. They had deployed a special police force for the purpose. Government had also set-up a publicity bureau to publish hand-outs from time to time. In these hand outs, the Government gave its own version of the revenue assessment issue. The Congress workers had also set-up their information office from which they issued daily Patrikas (leaflets).These they distributed all over the District and sent some to the newspapers in Surat, Broach, Bombay, and Ahmedabad. It is reported that more than 10,000 leaflets were distributed everyday. The Government started taking action against those who did not pay up their revenue as per the Government assessment. By May 1928, the number of confiscations of property had increased and many peasants' properties were taken over by the Government. Vallabhbhai then addressed an appeal to the people to raise funds for rendering monetary assistance to the Bardoli Satyagrahis.

Gandhiji was very benovelent and thus he readily reiterated that appeal through the Navajivan. He said, the present Satyagraha is a Yajna a sacrifice which needs offerings. He called upon the people to donate to what he termed the 'Satyagraha Fund'. This appeal was published and supported by journals throughout Gujarat. The Prajabandhu and the Navajivan opened a 'Bardoli Satyagraha Fund' and started collecting contributions. They also devoted special columns to the publication of the periodical collections received for the fund. It was reported by these journals that Rs.1, 99,857 had been collected by June 1928 and that the figure surpassed four lakhs of rupees by August that year. After some negotiations, the Government agreed to set-up an inquiry into the revenue assessments and the Satyagraha was called off in August 1928. The announcement was carried by all the Gujarati dailies and weeklies and was praised profusely with comments. Other Journals such as the Deshbhakta, the Nootan Gujarat, the Sanj Vartman and the Gujarati paid tributes to the Satyagrahis, the Government and to Vallabhbhai whom they all believed to have emerged as a true Sardar (leader) of the people of Gujarat. Gandhiji had brought out one whole issue of the Navajivan called the 'Bardoli Ank-the Bardoli Special Number' in which he paid tributes to the people of Gujarat for the support that they had given to the movement. The Sanj Vartman, the Bombay Samachar and the Gujarati published photographs depicting the different stages during the Bardoli Satyagraha movement.

Civil Disobedience Movement

The 44th session of the Indian National Congress met at Lahore during the last week of December 1929, resolved to change the creed of the Congress organization by construing the word 'Swaraj' in article to mean "complete independence—Purna Swaraj." That resolution had authorized the All India Congress Committee to launch upon a programme of Civil Disobedience including non-payment of taxes. This became a starting point of a series of events culminating in a movement against the Government. When the Congress session met at Lahore, the Gujarati dailies and weeklies were full of reports about it. Independence resolution of the Congress was more than that pertaining to any other subject. The main topic of discussion was the interpretation of the term Swaraj with reference to dominion status. Commenting upon this in the Navajivan dated 5th January, 1930, Gandhiji had explained that the word Swaraj meant 'absence of dependence of India on anyone in any matter'. The Bombay Samachar thereupon published the following words in bold type on its front page in its issue dated 9th January, 1930. Gandhiji wrote again on the Independence resolution in the Navajivan dated 12th January. In that issue, he also reported his speech before students of the Ashram in which he said, "I do not know what form the Civil Disobedience movement will take but I am desperately in search of some effective formula however."[29]

The subsequent issues of some of the dailies were full of hints that Gandhiji might be arrested at any time. Some of the press headings were Gandhijini dharpakadna vagata bhankara and Gandhijini dharpakad thavani vaki (both meaning that Gandhijis' arrest was imminent). Gandhiji then wrote to the Government and put out a list of 'demands' (these were even including repeal of the salt tax) which, in an article, he characterised as the soul of independence and a test of true Swaraj. Quoting these words, the Bombay Samachar and the Gujarati wrote editorials on 16th February, 1930 and the Gujarat mitra and Darpan on the 16th while the Prajabandhu had been writing similarly since the 13th of that month. "The responsibility for the current unrest lies entirely with the British Government. But people would not put off their contemplated movement in spite of the steel frame of the bureaucracy", was the message, loud and clear.

Gandhiji worked as a motivating force then and wrote in the Navajivan dated 23rd of that month, saying, 'If 1 am arrested, people must continue the porgramme of Civil Disobedience'. He wrote again on 2nd March in the same journal saying that he proposed to break the salt law in contravention of the Governmental restrictions. He then sent a letter to the Viceroy explaining his stand on the current issues and published the full text of his communication in the Navajivan dated 9th March. He also announced that on the 12th March, he would begin to track on foot a distance of 241 miles from Ahmedabad to Dandi in the Surat District where he proposed to collect natural salt in contravention of the prohibitory regulations with a view to putting Civil Disobedience into action. Gandhiji's letter was published by the Gujarati dailies and weeklies with big headings along with editorial comments. Some of the headings were, Gandhijini Viceroys hradaydravak appeal (A heart moving appeal by Gandhiji to the Viceroy), Gandhiji sarkarne akhrinamu (Gandhiji's ultimatum to the Government). While the editorial comments were, 'still there is time for the Government to act judiciously', 'the present movement', a

Mukti Sangram for Bharat (freedom fight for India) in which Gujarat must make its offerings'. Gujarat will not lag behind this time.

During the Civil Disobedience Movement, the Government passed the Press Act, giving itself numerous powers. Gandhi gave a fitting reply to this ordinance. He asked the press not to be cowed down. His argument was: They may confiscate type and machinery, they will not confiscate pen and still less speech, but recognize that they can succeed in confiscating even these last two. But what they will never succeed in suppressing and what is after all the thing that matters is the thought of the nation and at the present moment, there is hardly a man or woman breathing in India who with every breath does not breathe of disaffection, sedition, disloyalty and whatever other term one may use to describe the mentality of the nation which has set its mind on destroying the existing system of Government.[30]

GANDHI'S COMMUNICATION STRATEGY DURING SALT SATYAGRAHA AND ROUND TABLE CONFERENCE

The Indian National Congress, in its Lahore session in December 1929, passed a resolution proclaiming Complete Independence, Purna Swaraj, as the country's immediate goal and authorized the launching of a Civil disobedience to achieve it. Explaining to a correspondent as to why the prefix 'purna' was used with 'swaraj', Gandhi wrote, "'Swaraj' in the Congress constitution was given a double meaning, it could be within the Empire, if possible; without, if necessary. A word or an expression had, therefore, to be found in order to connote the last meaning only. We could not do without the term 'Swaraj'. Hence the expedience of 'Purna Swaraj'"[31]

Salt Satyagraha by Gandhi

Another earmarking movement led by the Father of Nation was the Salt Satyagraha that started as scheduled on the 12th March with a batch of 78 Satyagrahis. The Bombay Samachar splashed the news on the front page in bigger type. 'Tapasvi Rama Panchavati chhodi Lanka leva vicharechhe'— The ascetic Rama abandoning his hermit abode in Panchavati sets out to take Lanka. So did all the Gujarati Journals. Describing the situation, late Nandalal Bodiwala, founder editor of the Ahmedabad daily, Sandesh and other newspapermen said that ever since the news was in the air that a Civil Disobedience movement was going to be launched, people had been addicted to read the day-to-day political happenings and press comments. Hence, almost all the Gujarati dailies had sent their correspondents to cover the news about Gandhiji's march, as did some English dailies and foreign journals. Bodiwala said that he had brought out special supplements in a bigger size to publish the news about the distance traversed by the marchers, about the manner in which people received the marchers in their respective villages and especially about the utterances made by Gandhiji from time to time. He said that the demand for news had increased so much in Gandhiji that not only dailies but weeklies and fortnightlies had to issue special supplements. He himself had to bring out four and at times six supplements a day. So did the Khedarartman and Pratap from district Kheda and Surat. Popular identification with the movement and their expectations from the press were such that the Journal not supporting the movement met with public condemnation. Ranchhoddas Bhavan Lotwala's journals were writing against the Civil Disobedience movement and were characterizing it as a 'mad' step. It is reported that some people in Bombay had called a meeting to express their disapproval of Lotwala's Journals and subsequently the latter suffered a loss.

Gandhiji reached Dandi on 5th April, 1930. He went to the seashore the next day and picked up natural salt declaring that "everyone was free to prepare and sell salt no matter what the Government did", and that "people throughout the country should break the salt law and should be willing to court arrest if that be the consequence." The newspapers which gave news of Gandhiji's defiance of the salt law also published news about similar acts of defiance from almost all parts of the country. Regarding Gandhi's Dandi march, Anthony R. Deluca wrote: "The march had clearly confirmed Gandhi's status as a prominent international political figure" he also exhibited a profound awareness of international public opinion as he promoted his message of non-violence and issued the following appeal form Dandi at the end of the march, "I want world sympathy in this battle of Right against Might."[32]

The Navajivan which had been publishing the news, about Gandhiji's march and the reports of his speeches since he set out on 12th March, gave information in greater detail about the arrests and lathi charges throughout the country. It was issuing supplements for this purpose. In one of them was published on the front page in bold type a message from Gandhiji congratulating Gujarat "I want still more from the people."[33] Gandhiji then proceeded to Dharasana where the Government salt depot was situated. But he was interrupted and was arrested on 4th May, 1930. That led to a number of demonstrations and arrests in the country. The comments in the Gujarati press from 5th May, 1930, onwards can be summarized as Mahatmaji has contributed his mite: it is up to the people now to show their strength. A fund should be raised to help continue the Satyagraha. People should stick to their pledge; non-violence as preached by Gandhiji should not be abandoned.

While the nature of the news and comment appearing in the Gujarati press regarding the nationalist movement was as has been described, the growth that it had attained by the middle of 1930 was as indicated below. There were 91 Gujarati Journals and dailies, 71 weeklies and 9 fortnightlies with an aggregate of 2,08,125 copies per issue in circulation by that time. Data about the monthlies in circulation during 1930 are not available as in figure of 36,500 copies per issue, while the weeklies had touched a total of 1,62,875 and the fortnightlies that of 8,750 copies per issue in circulation by that time. The Gujarati dailies were published now not only from Mumbai, but in addition from Surat, Nadiad, and Ahmedabad and were very critical of the Government. When the press comments and reports reached such a stage, the Government promulgated an ordinance, the Ordinance of 1930, under Section 72 of the Government of India Act of 1919. That ordinance revived the Indian Press Act of 1910 which had been repealed in 1922. Under the ordinance, which, according to the Government, was meant to 'Provide for the better control of the Press', magistrates were empowered at their discretion to demand securities of not less than Rs. 500 from any person keeping a printing press, it may be recalled that keepers of priming presses were required to make a declaration under Section 4 of the Press and Registration of Books Act. 1867. From the publishers, who were required to make a declaration under section 5 of the 1867 Press Act, Magistrates were also empowered under the

ordinance to demand securities. Powers to declare such securities forfeited were conferred upon the magistrates when it appeared to the local Governments that any matter published was likely to have a tendency, directly or indirectly, whether by inference, suggestion, allusion, metaphor, implication or otherwise, to do certain things which would bring the Government into hatred or contempt. When the ordinance became operative, the Prajabandhu of Ahmedabad suspended publication, as the editors put it, 'before securities were demanded'. The Navajivan also closed down officially but efforts were made to continue publication of a sheet or two of cyclostyled copies of the journal.

Round Table Conference

During this period, a Round Table Conference had been convened in London by the British Government to discuss Indian problems. Subsequently, negotiations took place between Gandhiji and the Government and the Government issued orders to release Gandhiji and the other Congress leaders by the last week of January 1931. The Prajabandhu had resumed publication from 16th November, 1930 and the Navajivan by the middle of March, 1931. Gandhiji went to London to attend the Round Table Con-ference on 29th August, 1931. The news about the proceedings at that conference was supplied to the press by Reuter's news agency and the Sanj Vartman sent its own correspondent to cover the news from London. The press during those days was full of news about the conference proceedings and of comments which exceeded in space which was allotted to the news from London. Gandhiji returned to India by the end of December 1931. He was arrested again on

4th January, 1932. By now, the Indian Press Emergency Powers Act of 1931 was already in operation. The people converged on the office of the Navajivan on 14th January, 1932. The Prajabandhu which had started publication from 16th November, 1930, closed down again on 10th January, 1932. However, the management of those weeklies made arrangements to issue a single-sheet daily newspaper called the Gujarat Samachar from 16th January, 1932. The then editor, Indravadan Thakore states that the management did so to supply the reading public with the latest news about current politics, hence, the daily contained only news and no editorials. It may be noted here that the circulation of the new dailies in Ahmedabad (the Sandesh and the Gujarat Samachar) increased rapidly as did that of the Bombay Samachar in Mumbai. To cope up with the demand, the Bombay Samachar had to be published on a newly purchased rotary printing machine.

The mass movement culminated in the release of Gandhiji and the other Congress leaders. Before these events are recorded, a reference to the Gujarati press as it stood by the end of the year 1932 should be made here. There were in all 207 Gujarati journals of varied periodicity including 2 dailies, one bi-weekly, 68 weeklies, four fortnightlies, in clearer terms. The Congress resolution asked the British Government to indicate the place of India in any order envisaged. The resolution was commented upon by Gandhiji in the English weekly, the Harijan, dated 15th September, 1939 and its Gujarati version was published in the Harijanbandhu the following week. The Congress resolution was published by the Gujarati newspapers with big headings some of which read: Tamari neeti saaf saaf shabdoman janavo' (Declare your policy in categorical terms); 'Britainne Gandhijini chetavni' (Gandhiji's warning to Britain). 'Ahimsano antim vijay nishchit the' (the ultimate triumph of non-violence is certain); 'Congresse kareli spashta vaato' (The Congress talks plainly). Thus the views of the Gujarati press on the Indian political situation tallied with those of the nationalist sections in the country. On 22nd October, 1939, the Congress called upon all Ministries run by that party in the provinces to resign their offices by the 31st of that month. It also called upon the legislatures in such provinces to adopt a resolution asking Britain to declare her 'War-Aims'. While all the Gujarati newspapers published this news with big headlines, some of the dailies and weeklies wrote editorials in which they expressed concern. Gandhiji commenting in the Harijanbandhu, "The resignation of the Congress ministries was a necessity, but the next step is by no means clear. Congressmen seem to be expecting some big move."[34] Soon after this, the Congress decided to launch Satyagraha by individuals who were to make propaganda against the war efforts of the Government and was to court arrest as a consequence. It started with the arrest of Vinoba Bhave on 31st October, 1939, following the arrest of almost all Congress leaders in the country. Vallabhbhai Patel was arrested in Ahmedabad on 17th November, 1940, followed by many congressmen in Gujarat who offered Satyagraha and courted arrest. The Gujarati newspapers had made arrangements to publish the names of the individual Satyagrahis, the details about their background, the notices that they had served on the Government and the manner in which they courted arrest. By December, 1941 about 20,000 Congressmen throughout the country were held in detention but they were released by the beginning of 1942.

Quit India Movement

As the tempo of the war in the Far East gained momentum, the Allies saw the defeat of the Colonial powers in their erstwhile colonies largely due to the lack of sympathy and local support. Statesmen in the USA and China, therefore, suggested that Britain should pay heed to the demands of the Indians voiced by the Congress party. Unwillingly, Britain sent Sir Cripps to India on a mission intended more to satisfy Britain's allies than to see any breakthrough in the Indian situation. Holding no promise of Independence, the mission exposed the hollowness of the British claim that they were fighting a war for the establishment of democracy in the world.

In India, things were in a bad shape. There was division in the Congress ranks over the nature of struggle against the British and the Jappanese,[35] communal atmosphere was full of recrimination as Gandhi's remarks were mutilated and given malicious construction[36], food shortages and famine crushed the people of Bengal, stories of refugees from Burma poured in with harrowing accounts of the British discriminated between the Whites and Indians. Under the circumstances, though it seemed that the conditions were far from favourable for launching a movement in order to overcome the conditions yet a movement became necessary.

A forceful movement asking the foreign powers to withdraw completely from India was the Quit India Movement. Thus, to the different mass-movements launched by the Indian National Congress under the leadership of Gandhiji against the Government, one more was added with the passing of a resolution by that organization (Congress) in August 1942, asking the British to withdraw from India.

Prior to the passage of the Quit India resolution, Gandhi wrote an appeal 'To every Briton", wherein he asked them to "retire from every Asiatic or African possession and at least from India." He believed that such a step was "essential for the safety of the World and for the destruction of Nazism and Fascism" He further went ahead with his request for a "bloodless end of an unnatural domination for a new era, even though there may be protest and wailing from some of us."[37] He also made appeals to the conscience of international leaders and common people in other countries to see the genuineness of his request for the end of foreign domination.[38] Hostilities were declared on 3rd September, 1939, between Britain and Germany, involving India once again. Those who were running the Gujarati press knew from the past experience the interest that the reading public showed in news about the war. They were aware of the fact that information about the war was in greater demand than before, because of the affect that the war had on Indian economic and, more particularly, political conditions. Now that the war news was supplied by the news agency (the Associated Press of India in collaboration with the Reuters news agency which was working on a global level) more rapidly than before and also because the bigger printing machines (mostly cylinder and in some cases rotary machines) could print their copies more speedily, with the latest information and in bigger type, some of the Gujarati news papers brought out special supplements. These supplements announced in big headlines the outbreak of the war. The newspaper headlines and comments pertaining to the war during September 1939 were: Poland has been a sufferer at the hands of the Nazis; German action is blind and brutal; Herr Hitalare chhadeehok kareli vachanbhangni parampara par prakash (A searchlight on the series of open breaches of promises by Herr Hitler); German jahajo par British vimani fojoe karelo hallo (The British Air Force attacks the German ships); Lokshahi Juthono Germanono Samno Karvano Nirdhar (Determination of the democratic forces to meet the challenge of the Germans), The Gujarati press thus evinced a support of Britain against the Nazis in the initial stages, as in the case of World War.

But the nationalist sections in the country viewed the situation in a rather different vein and wanted the people also to view it similarly. Hence the Working Committee of the Indian National Congress meeting at Wardha during September 1939 passed a resolution saying that the British Government should declare its war aims in regard to Democracy and imperialism in Songadh, Dhoraji and Anjar (Kuchh). Of these 18 fortnightlies, the Jyotirdhas, was the organ of some social reformists in Ahmedabad. Two were trade bulletins, one was a cinema magazine and the rest were meant for different castes or sects. The monthlies included the Navrachana and 13 others from Mumbai; the Yuvak, the Street Jeevan, the Kumar, the Rekha and six others from Ahmedabad; two from Surat; the Patidar from Anand, the Sharda, the Gunsundari, the Pustakalaya, the Gramjeevan and fourteen others from Baroda; the Samaj Sheekshak and two others from Navsari; the Jyoti, the Gharshala and fifteen others from Bhavnagar; three from Rajkot and one each from Mehsana, Visnagar, Patan, Jamnagar, Wadhwan Jetpur, Gondal, Limbd and Junagadh.

The dailies were of a uniform size—22 inches long and 17 inches broad with seven columns each, printed on bigger size cylinder or rotary machines. They contained mainly news procured through the news agencies and through accredited correspondents. In some cases, the dailies published weekly sections addressed to women or children or devoted to health and hygiene and to religious matters. The weeklies and the bi-weeklies such as the Gujarati, the Prajabandhu, the Gujarati Punch and the Sayaji-Vijaya used to give weekly round-ups of the news, comments and literary articles. The monthlies like the Rekha were devoted to political and literary comment while others were full of diverse matters. Generally, the weeklies were seventeen inches in length and eleven inches in breadth while the monthlies were nine by six inches length and breadth wise. All these Gujarati journals—dailies, bi-weeklies, weeklies, fortnightlies and monthlies—contained advertisements which occupied considerable space. These advertisements, both display and classified, had increased on account of the war-time fillip that the economy received. It is to be noted here that the industrialists who spent profusely on advertisements were indirectly strengthening the press which was supporting the nationalist movement against the Government.

By the beginning of 1942, the war situation was becoming unfavourable to Britain. The British possessions in South East Asia were going over to the Axis. The war-news at that time was reported by the Gujarati press in a way which indicated a change after the nationalist sections in the country had become more active. The reporting provided, besides, a contrast to that of World War I when the nationalist sections had not grown so influential. The headings were: 'Britainne boom padavvani German yojna' (German plans to gag Britain) 'Japani sainyoni aage kuch' (Advances made by the Japanese troops); 'Sathi sainyoni lagaataar pichhe hath' (successive retreats of the Allied forces). Under these circumstances, the war-cabinet in Britain announced their decision on 11th March, 1942, to send Sir Stafford Cripps to India for consultations with the Indian leaders and for finding out some solution to meet the emergencies created by the war situation. The announcement was made by the British Premier in the British Parliament and was reported in India by the Reuter's news agency. It was reported and commented upon by the Bombay Samachar by saying 'Cripps was coming to India to mislead the leaders' (undha pata bhanavava) and that 'the proposals must be devoid of any substance' (Damvagarni). Similar comments were made by the Gujarat Samachar and the Vande Matram.

The negotiations lasted from 22nd March to 11th April, 1942, when Sir Stafford Cripps left India after an announcement of the failure of the negotiations was made. But some of the Gujarati newspapers which had made special arrangements to procure intelligence about the negotiations between Sir Stafford Cripps and the Congress leaders had started writing since March 30, in the following words: 'Crippsji bhens laya ke bada paap' (Cripps had defined expectations); 'Cripps yojana sicikarashe nahin' (the Cripps proposals will not be acceptable). Gandhiji had been writing on all these issues in his weeklies. On 11th May, 1942, he wrote an article captioned. 'To Every Briton'. Gandhiji had requested (as had the Congress organization in a resolution adopted earlier) Britons to support him in his demand for a withdrawal of British rule from India. That article appeared in the Gujarati Weekly Harijanbandhu under the heading, Angrejo Jav (Britishness Quit).[39] The Gujarati press which had been quoting Gandhiji's articles took up this phrase in subsequent writings. It exhorted the people to 'respond to the call of the nation' and to 'be ready for a fight till the finish.'[40] In view of the situation, the Congress organization resolved, on 14th July, 1942, to request the withdrawal of the British rule from India and to launch a struggle under the leadership of Gandhiji, should negotiations between the Congress and the Government fail. This resolution was published by all the Gujarati dailies under big headlines and was commented upon from that day onwards. The Bombay Samachar said, "Delhi had been shaken due to this resolution" and the 'Janmabhoomi and the Vande Mataram' said, 'still there is time for Britain to enter into a compromise with India'.[41] Then these papers published the following words of Gandhiji, 'Bhale mari ane bijaoni dharpakad they' (what of that if I and others be arrested) and added that Gujarat would not 'lag behind in such an eventuality'. Then followed a series of addresses by Vallabhbhai Patel in Ahmedabad and Mumbai from 25th July to 3rd August. These addresses were given the front page treatment and were published under different headings which read as: 'Kolpan bhog apava taiyar raho;

agnipareekshano samaya aavipabonchyochhe. (The moment for an ordeal by fire has come: be prepared to give any sacrifice). Along with this the Janmahhoomi, the Vande Matram and the Bombay Samachar published the photographs of the different Congress leaders reaching Mumbai during the first week of August and this practice of the press made the news more lively and the situation more tense.

The All India Congress Committee met as scheduled on 7th and 8th August and adopted a resolution asking the British to quit and to declare India free. The message that Gandhi gave to the nation was as following:

> "Everyone is free to go to the fullest length under ahimsa. Complete deadlock by strikes and other non-violent means. Satyagrahi must go out to die not to live. They must seek and face death. It is only when individuals go out to die, the nation will survive. Karenge ya Marenge."[42]

The meeting concluded late at night on the 8th and soon afterwards the Government declared the Congress organization as an unlawful association and arrested Gandhiji and Congressmen throughout the country in the early hours of the 9th. This led to a series of disturbances involving lathi charges, tear-gas shelling and firing by the police throughout the country. The Gujarati newspapers gave that news on the afternoon of the 9th in special supplements, and from the 10th onwards, there were other reports of the disturbances from all parts of the country. The Government's attitude towards the press in this respect took the form of a series of restrictive orders affecting the nature of comment and reports. Ever since hostilities were declared early in September 1939, the Government had passed the Defence of India Act and the rules interalia which provided for a pre-censorship of material published in the press relating to certain matters. When the Congress organization launched the 'Individual Satyagraha' movement in 1940, the Government had issued a notification according to which, the publication of any matter calculated directly or indirectly to foment opposition to the prosecution of the war and publish accounts of speeches, meetings, etc. calculated to that effect were prohibited. When the Indian National Congress adopted its August resolution asking the British to withdraw from India, the Government of India issued a fresh notification on 8th August, 1942. In that it was said, 'the printing or publishing of any factual news (which expression shall be deemed to include reports of speeches or statements made by the members of the public) relating to the mass-movement sanctioned by the All India Congress Committee or relating to the measures taken by the Government against that movement, except news derived from official sources or from the Associated Press of India or the United Press of India or the Orient Press of India or from a correspondent regularly employed by the newspaper concerned and whose name stands registered with the District Magistrate of the district in which he carries on his work, shall be prohibited.

The declaration of various Congress committees as unlawful associations rendered them liable to prosecution under the Criminal Law Amendment Act anyone who assisted their operations. It follows, therefore, that the editor of any newspaper who supported or encouraged the mass movement sponsored by the bodies referred to above, or who opposed the measures taken by Government to avert or suppress that movement, would be guilty of an offence against the law. Moreover, the publication of factual news, both by the selection of events reported and by the manner in which they are displayed, can do even more to advertise and thus support the movement than editorial comment thereon. The responsibility of the press is, however, as great as its undoubted influence and in order to ensure that, responsibility may be exercised in a manner that will not bring the press into conflict with authority. Government consider it necessary: (a) to exercise a measure of control over the origins of factual news relating to the movement so as to ensure that what is published is derived only from recognized and responsible sources, and; (b) while imposing no direct control over the expression of editorial views, to leave editors themselves in no doubt as to the limits beyond which it will not be in their own interests to go (but)

Government wishes it to be clearly understood that they do not propose to allow any newspaper to continue to publish matter, whether it takes the form of news or views, which in their opinion, will encourage the movement or incite people to take part in it or which will excite popular feelings in favour of the movement or against the measures that Government will be compelled to take to combat it.

The notification and the press-note have been quoted here at length to indicate the nature of the news and comments the press could publish about the mass-movement that had begun after the arrest of Gandhiji and other Congressmen in the country. Many a Gujarati journal had to close down and many more were called to book by the Government. Subsequent events were the cessation of war in Europe and the release of the Congress leaders followed by a series of negotiations, culminating in the transfer of power to India on 15th August, 1947. We have brought out that phase of the Gujarati press when it was associated with the mass-movements launched by the nationalist organization under Gandhiji's leadership. It has been seen that the nature of content in the journals changed as a consequence and particularly because Gandhiji, during his stay in Gujarat, provided the Gujarati press with specific guidance and elaborate arguments through his weekly Navajivan. With increasing mass-awareness and popular participation in the movements, the nature of the news coverage and press comment became such that the Government issued prohibitory orders restricting not only editorial comment but also the publication of factual news. However, preoccupied with the news and views of the nationalists as the Gujarati press was, it secured a vast readership throughout Gujarat. It kept up the popular interest in the mass-movements and received in turn a further fillip, functioning thus as an initiator and sustainer of the nationalist agitation till the British withdrew from India in 1947.

GANDHI AS JOURNALIST

Romain Rolland, one of the best biographers of Gandhi, assumes: "Nations have short memories and I should have but slight faith in India's power to remain true to the Mahatma's teaching if his doctrines were not an expression of the deepest and the most ancient longings of the race. For if there is such a thing as genius, great by its own strength, whether or not it corresponds to the ideals of its surroundings, there can be no genius of action, no leader, who does not incarnate the instincts of his race to satisfy the need of the hour, and require the yearning of the world.[43] A year after Gandhi's death, the Harijan wrote: "All work in whatsoever sphere was a means mainly of service in Gandhiji's eyes. Newspapers and journals can build up a fitting memorial to him in this matter by conforming or trying to conform to the unimpeachable standards of journalism practiced by our revered and beloved."[44] As a journalist, Gandhi wanted to educate the people so that they could understand not only the significance of independence—political, economic and social—but also participate actively in freeing humanity from the bondage it was in. Gandhi's motto as a journalist was service. He once said, "One of the objects of a newspaper is to understand the popular feeling and give expression to it, another is to arouse among the people certain desirable sentiments, and the third is fearlessly to expose popular defects."[45] Such was the conviction of Gandhi in South Africa that he constantly kept a companion for his writings and gave him expression for publication through his journals and newspapers. Thus he used the press as a tool for political mobilization is confirmed by the fact that he brought out four major journals: Indian Opinion, Young India, Navajivan and Harijan, all with the purpose of arousing 'among the people certain desirable sentiments', besides a number of books producing a total of two million English wordage. "His instrument for creating social change was to create mass awareness. His tools were letters, articles and speeches."[46] Gandhi has been termed as the most influential writer and journalist that India has produced. He knew the power of the word, spoken and written, in inspiring people to action. He resembled a charismatic arbiter when airing grievances, be it in South Africa or India. His words were loaded with purpose, "No one who has used the words on a massive scale has been as passionately purposive as Gandhi.

No one has brought into use words with such intense longing to be down-to-earth on the one hand and paradoxically, to reach for the stars on the other."[47] Gandhi plainly wrote his objective, "I write as the spirit moves me at the time of writing." He further said, "I write to propagate my ideas."[48]

Gandhi's journey in journalism started quite early in his life, when he made contribution of nine articles on Indian diet, customs and festivals in a magazine Vegetarian in London. When on arrival in London in September 1888, to study law, Gandhiji, at the age of 19, for the first time realized how actively he would be associated with the newspaper for the rest of his life. Gandhi consistently wrote for the next six decades. The press, for him, became a tool for informing, educating and mobilizing the masses. He used newspapers to educate masses about public causes for which he led mass movements. The Indian Opinion was the first journalistic tool of Gandhi that was unveiled on June 4, 1903 in South Africa. It was a weekly newspaper and was published in English, Gujarati, Tamil and Hindi for the advantage of Indians inhabiting in South Africa. As Gandhi recalled later about the purpose for which the Indian Opinion was launched, "A struggle which chiefly relies upon internal strength cannot be wholly carried on without a newspaper. We could not have educated the local Indian opinion, nor kept Indians all over the world in touch with the course of events in South Africa in any other way, with the same ease and success as through Indian Opinion, which was a most useful and potent weapon in our struggle."[49] Next in Gandhi's armoury was Navajivan, a Gujarati monthly that was started as a weekly on October 7, 1919 with Gandhi as the editor. And the magic of Gandhi's pen soon showed up. Writing the editorial for the first issue of Young India, which was also relaunched under Gandhi's editorship a day after Navajivan, Gandhi exulted: "The editing of Navajivan has been a perfect revelation to me. Whilst Young India has little more than 1,200 subscribers, Navajivan has 12,000. The number would leap to 20,000 if it would get the printer to print that number. It exhibits that a vernacular newspaper is a felt want. I am proud to think that I have numerous readers among farmers and workers. They make India... the

English journals touch but the fringe of the ocean of India's population."[50]

Gandhi was aware of the readership while writing in various languages. He wrote trilingual, in English, Gujarati and Hindustani. Gandhi's tone and tenor changed while writing in different languages, because he had the ability to empathies with the audience and understand their expectations and requirement in a newspaper. Gandhi said that he was editing the English Journal, Young India, which along with Navajivan, priced at one anna each, mainly for the advantage of his friends in the Madras constituency. Still, however, Young India sold more copies than the combined total of several newspapers in India. There was not only a new thought but a new language in newspaper writing, and what he wrote was finest in journalistic writing. The last of Gandhi's journals, Harijan, also priced at one anna, began publication on February 11, 1933 from Poona. While the first Gandhi decade in India is often called the story of Young India, the decade of the thirties was dominated by Harijan, which was begun to help Gandhi in his crusade against untouchability. Introducing the weekly to his readers, Gandhi wrote in the inaugural issue: "The English edition of the Harijan is being published by and for the Servants of Untouchables Society at my request. Ten thousand copies are being printed. If you diligently study the Harijan, it will give you an epitome of the week's doings in the different parts of India in connection with the campaign against untouchability."[51] Besides the English version, Harijan was brought out in Hindi and Gujarati and it went by the names of Harijan Sevak and Harijanbandu, respectively. In subsequent years, the journal was also published in Urdu, Tamil, Oriya, Marathi and Kannada.

Initially, Gandhi wanted to keep politics out of Harijan but soon the journal became the voice of Indian reaction. The message of 'Do or Die' rang from the meek looking pages of the Harijan. When Gandhi and his followers were locked up after the Quit India Resolution, the government confiscated and destroyed it. Harijan was revived in February 1946, survived Mahatma's death, only to peter out in 1956. Today, the crafts of Gandhi's journalistic charisma are repositories of vivid memories and scholarship, adorning the thousands of libraries over the world, these journals reveal stories of India's emancipation from colonial rule, distend the richness of India's heritage and culture, and give innumerable leads to social scientists for pursuing research. The existing work, which looks into the role of these journals in political mobilization, is based on one such lead. The vastness of Gandhi makes it very difficult to keep the focus of the topic intact. However, every attempt has been made and precautions taken, to ensure that the focus remains.

GANDHIJI'S IMPORTANT WRITTINGS

Gandhi was a prolific writer who has left behind a vast body of articles and books. These are now complied in a hundred Volumes of "**The Collected Works of Mahatma Gandhi**" published by publication division, Government of India, New Delhi. His compilation also includes a mindboggling number of letters, drafts, petitions and circulars written by him.

Gandhi's journalistic career spanned nearly half a century. Beginning with his unpublished "**London Diary (written in 1889)**", his first publication was a series of articles published in "**The Vegetarian (1891-95)**", a journal of the Vegetarian Society of England. These attempts have been noticed only in retrospect. What established Gandhi as journalist was his editorship of the weekly "**Indian Opinion (1904)**" published from South Africa. Similarly, "**The Green Pamphlet**" on the conditions of Indians in South Africa followed by a note on the same topic, were the most widely distributed propaganda material on any public question at that time.

Green Pamphlet

Gandhi's first major essay in journalism was the 'Green Pamphlet' (so called because its cover was green) describing the condition of Indians in South Africa. Gandhi wrote the piece while he had come from home to Rajkot on a brief visit from South Africa (1901). Ten thousand copies of the Pamphlet were published. The success of the Pamphlet made

Gandhi more confident of the efficacy and publicity value of the print media. Open letters from Gandhi to public men in India followed. Gandhi came to be acknowledged as an authority on South African affairs. India's English Press solicited letters and articles from Gandhi.

Back in South Africa, the 'Green Pamphlet' was a subject of publicity, though of a different kind. In India, the Pamphlet had turned Gandhi into hero of the Indians in South Africa while in South Africa, the same Pamphlet had made him a villain in the eyes of the white settlers. When after a brief visit to India, Gandhi returned to South Africa with his wife and family and other Indians, the whole convoy was not allowed to land on the African soil. Gandhi was man-handled and beaten up by a hostile white crowd. But for the cunning of his friend in the police department, Gandhi would have lost his life. Later on, there was widespread denunciation of the violence in the white press and Gandhi managed to score a point over his detractors by refusing to book culprits.

It should be noted here that the misinterpretation of the subject was largely the doing of the British news agency, the Reuters,[52]which showed that the world came to know about the affairs of the South Africa through Gandhi's writings and was exercised over it. Thus even before taking up his own journal to publicise the cause of Indians' Gandhi had made extensive use of the print media via the local newspapers and by printing pamphlets. This was in spite of the fact that he wrote very few articles on the conditions of Indians in South Africa till he was requested by the The Times of India to do so. Except for the series of six articles that he wrote for The Times of India between June 1899 to April 1903, most of his articles dealt with non-political issues.

Indian Opinion

Indian Opinion, a fullscap-sized-three-column weekly journal, was started at Durban on June 4, 1903 by two of Gandhi's close aides, Madanjit Vyavaharik and Manshukhlal Hiralal Nazar. The former looked after the press. The latter was a journalist from Mumbai and held editorial charges till 1906.[53] The Indian Opinion was begun to vent the feelings of the Indians in South Africa and to improve their condition. It was a non-commercial venture. Initially, the journal was started in Hindi, Gujarati, Tamil and English languages. Later, the Hindi and Tamil versions were withdrawn. The journal was a mirror of an important part of Gandhi's life. "Week after week, I poured out my soul in its columns and expounded the principles and practice of satyagraha"[54], beginning from the first issue in which Gandhi wrote an editorial titled, 'Ourselves', Gandhi continuously wrote for Indian Opinion till 1914, the year of his departure from South Africa.

Gandhi's touched upon different aspects of exploitation of Indians in South Africa. Gandhi made the journal a potent weapon in his fight against the racial and discriminatory policies of the British Government. He declared at a later date that Satyagraha would probably have been impossible without Indian Opinion. Gandhi outlined three objectives of the journal: first, to make Indian grievances known to the governments in South Africa and in Britain and to the people of India; second, to make the Indians in South Africa aware of their own defects so that they could make effort to overcome them; and third, to eliminate the prevailing distinctions between Hindus and Muslims and among Gujaratis and Tamilians and others. Gandhi wrote in one of the initial issues of the Journal, "The British rulers in India follow a different policy. They do not desire that we should come together and become united. Here, in South Africa, these groups are small in number. We are all confronted with the same disabilities; we can easily essay an experiment in achieving unity." [55]

Many years later, acknowledging the importance of Indian Opinion in his struggle in South Africa, Gandhi wrote in his autobiography: "Satyagraha would probably have been impossible without Indian Opinion. The readers looked forward to it for a trustworthy account of the Satyagraha campaign as also for the real condition of Indians in South Africa. It was as though the community thought audibly through me. It made me thoroughly understand the responsibility of a journalist and the hold I secured in this way over the community made the future campaign workable, dignified and irresistible."[56] Gandhi describes himself as a General and Indian Opinion as his weapon in his book 'Satyagraha in South Africa' in the following statements: "I propose to acquaint the reader with all the weapons, internal as well as external, employed in the Satyagraha struggle and now therefore proceed to introduce to him Indian Opinion, a weekly journal which is published in South Africa for him every day."[57] At another place, he wrote:

> "I know of many, whose first occupation on receiving the paper would be to read the Gujarati section through, from beginning to end. One of the readers would read it, and the rest would surround him and listen. Not all who wanted to read the paper could afford to subscribe to it by themselves and some of them, therefore, would club together for the purpose."[58]

The journal was very interactive and readers were always invited to contribute their opinions and suggestions on crucial issues. In fact, the style of Gandhi's struggle—passive resistance—got an Indian name through a campaign in the Indian Opinion. Looking for an apt name for his technique of struggle, Gandhi invited suggestions from his readers. There was an overwhelming response and finally 'Sadagraha' was chosen which was changed as 'Satyagraha' by Gandhi. This instance reflects the wonderful ability of Gandhi in involving the masses constructively and instilling in them a sense of participation. The files of Indian Opinion incorporate a series of growing images of the Gandhian spirit. In the early editorials, only a mild protest against the racial segregation was seen. At the initial stage, Gandhi had firm faith in the British Constitution which was steadily shattered. Indian opinion continuously carried a vivid portrayal of the shattered Indian community in South Africa. It successfully made effort to educate public opinion and indicated the line of duty that every Indian was needed to follow in order to assert his or her basic human rights. There existed a close link between the readers and the editorial office of Indian Opinion. Gandhi himself was in close touch with the readers through the regular correspondence column. The editorials and columns of letters in Indian Opinion carried many features of popular interest. It had contributors writing from abroad too. Gandhi kept Indians in South Africa informed about the progress of the freedom movement in India. He wrote in strong protest against the Bengal partition and encouraged the boycott of foreign goods by Indians in South Africa. He stood for the adoption of the Vande Mataram as the Indian national anthem. Gandhi called it "A Passionate Prayer" and published it in Gujarati and Devanagari scripts in the Indian Opinion.

Young India

The success of Indian Opinion in educating and awakening the Indians in South Africa had been epoch-making effort on the part of Gandhi. He realized the requirement for a similar organ after he intensified his campaigns against the British rule in India, a couple of years after coming to his motherland in 1915. This need became more pronounced after Gandhi started his satyagraha against the Rowlatt Act and the Jallianwallah Bagh massacre in 1919. Gandhi assumed the editorship of Young India, which was published by the management of the Bombay Chronicle, in 1919. The objective of the Indian Opinion, as declared in the newspaper, was a "desire to promote harmony and goodwill between the different sections of one mighty empire."[59]

But by the time Gandhi became related to the Young India and Navajivan, his hopes in the British justice had been shattered. He was becoming more and more conscious of the true nature of colonialism and was preparing the country to fight injustice through satyagraha, as practised in South Africa. Gandhi thus spelt the policy of Young India. Apart from its duty of drawing attention to injustices to individuals, it also devoted its attention to constructive satyagraha as also sometimes cleansing satyagraha. Cleansing satyagraha is a civil resistance where resistance becomes a duty to remove a persistent and degrading injustice such as the Rowlatt Act. Gandhi poured out fire through his pen. He sincerely felt that the alien government had no right to govern. He wrote a number of fiery articles like 'Tampering with Loyalty' and

'The Puzzle and its Solution' in the pages of Young India to arouse the Indian masses. Apart from this the journal was also used to educate the masses on different socio-political and economic issues of national and international importance. Gandhi used articles written by renowned personalities of the freedom struggle on various issues. The Journal was also utilized as a forum for intellectual debates, for instance the debates between Gandhi and Tagore on 'Khadi' and 'Scope of Education'. The management of Young India entrusted its editorship to Gandhi. Writing about this development later, Gandhi noted in his Autobiography: "I was anxious to expound the inner meaning of Satyagraha to the public, and also hoped that through this effort, I should at least be able to do justice to the Punjab situation. For, behind all this writing, there was potential Satyagraha, and the Government knows as much."[60]

Navajivan

The first issue of the Navajivan came out on 9th September, 1919. Gandhiji, as the editor, said, "There is no dearth of journals in Gujarat at present. But, being a Gujarati by birth and a Gujarati indeed, I aspire to be absorbed into the life of Gujarat, for I can serve the country only by doing so. This will be the first occasion when I shall be known publicly in Gujarat as an editor. I wish that the Navajivan should reach the huts of the farmers and the weavers because I am going to write in their language; I am going to pray that the Navajivan be read by the women folk as well"[61]. Gandhiji had announced in the same issue that it was the solemn resolve of all associated with the Navajivan to say whatever they felt, no matter what restrictions Government had enacted for the press. He also declared that the Navajivan would not contain any advertisement.

In the inaugural issue of Navajivan, Gandhi wrote: "I think I have a service to render to India by delivering a message to her. I am convinced that I have no gift better than this for India. I have always been avid of placing before the people this priceless thing, and several others of which I have had ample experience. One powerful modern means for this purpose is the newspaper."[62]

The Navajivan, in its issues during December that year, took up the Khilafat and the Punjab issues in view of the 34th session of the Indian National Congress due to meet at Amritsar (Punjab) and after the session concluded gave details in its issues during January 1920 about the resolutions adopted with the text of the speeches made thereon. Gandhiji wrote in successive issues about the demands made by the Congress organization and explained their implications. The weekly frequently gave information about the tours undertaken by Gandhiji and published in detail the speeches made by him from place to place. In addition to that the weekly used to include articles on Swadeshi, Khadi, Spinning, Satyagraha, and Cow-protection, Gandhiji used to request those who were literate to read the Navajivan aloud before those who were not capable of reading; he also expressed his satisfaction that the Navajivan was read so extensively by the people of Gujarat. Navajivan was a regional journal in Gujarati, published along with Young India under the editorship of Gandhi. Outlining its purpose, Gandhi wrote in the March 12 issue of the Young India that it was published "for the sole purpose of educating the nation to win Purna Swaraj through truthful and non-violent means."[63]

Harijan

A couple of years after the Young India and Navajivan were silenced, Gandhi realised the requirement for another journal. But this time the need was different, the pitch was different and the motives or goals were different to help him in his crusade against untouchability. Born in 1933, the paper Harijan initially carried items only devoted to social issues. "It will be solely devoted to the Harijan cause," Gandhi wrote after being released from prison in May 1933, "and will scrupulously exclude all politics."[64] So much so that there was a complete blackout of important political news of the day, there was no mention of the Congress session and the Government of India Act of 1935. The Harijan became a mouthpiece for the Harijan movement and village industries. The paper published useful extracts from books on rural problems. However, the tide of surging nationalism in later years did not let Harijan maintain its focus. Increasingly, it started carrying the messages of the non-violent satyagraha of Gandhi and became a chief messenger of the Quit India Movement. The slogan of 'do or die' given by Gandhi during the movement was conveyed to the masses through the Harijan. It became a fiery propaganda vehicle, so much so that just after the arrest of Gandhi on 8 August 1942, the Harijan was closed down. However, even after that, Gandhi's message appeared to be echoing: "The Harijan may be suppressed, its message cannot be, so long as I live. Indeed, the spirit will survive the dissolution of the body and somehow speak through the millions."[65] The millions did speak, and Harijan lived up to its cause.

Hind Swaraj

One of Gandhi's seminal works is Hind Swaraj which was written in Gujarati and published in a book form in Gujarati in January 1910 by Gandhi's own International Printing Press. The English translation by Gandhi himself came out a few years later. Hind Swaraj is written in the literary genre of dialogue: a dialogue between a newspaper editor and a reader. It was addressed to a mixed audience: the expatriate Indians who were attracted to terrorism and political violence, the extremists and moderates of the Indian National Congress, the Indian nation and the English. As to why he wrote the book, he said there was first of all the consequent urge to communicate. Secondly, he wanted to clarify the meaning of Swaraj. Thirdly, he realised it was essential to respond specifically to the ideology of political terrorism adopted by the expatriates. Fourthly, Gandhi was anxious to teach the Indians that modern civilization posed a greater threat to them than did colonialism. Lastly, he wanted to contribute towards the reconciliation of Indians and Britons. Finally, Gandhi believed that through Hind Swaraj, he would be able to provide Indians a practical philosophy, an updated conception of Dharma that would fit them for life in the modern world. The urgency with which Gandhi wrote Hind Swaraj shows that it was written with a definite purpose in mind. He wrote: "During my stay in England, I had occasion to talk with many Indian anarchists. My booklet, Indian Home Rule, had its birth from the necessity of having to meet their arguments as well as to solve the difficulties of Indians in South Africa who held similar views.[66]

Hind Swaraj was the seed from which the tree of Gandhian thought has grown to its full stature. No wonder that it has been known as 'a very basic document for the study of Gandhi's thought', his 'confession of faith', a 'proclamation of ideological independence', and the nearest he came to producing a sustained work of political theory. Anthony J. Parel has very convincingly elaborated upon the reasons that impelled Gandhi to write this Hind

Swaraj. By the Indian nation, Gandhi means ordinary Indians, irrespective of their religious, linguistic, regional or caste differences as well as the new emerging middle class, referred to in the text as doctors, lawyers and the wealthy. And by the English, he means both the British ruling class living in India and Britons living in Great Britain.[67] Dennis Dalton, in his book, 'Gandhi's Power' writes: The aim of Hind Swaraj was to confront the anarchists and violence-prone Indian nationalists with an alternative to violence derived from Gandhi's earliest experiments with satyagraha. Equally important is the book's concern with the concept from which it takes its title: this is Gandhi's first extensive statement on swaraj, his idea of freedom[68].

AN AUTOBIOGRAPHY OR THE STORY OF MY EXPERIMENTS WITH TRUTH

The first edition of Gandhiji's Autobiography was published in two volumes. Volume I in 1927 and Vol. II in 1929. The original in Gujarati which was priced at Rs. 1/- has run through five editions, nearly 50,000 copies having been sold. Gandhi said, "If I had only to discuss academic principles, I should clearly not attempt an autobiography. But my purpose being to give an account of various practical applications of these principles, I have given the chapters, I propose to write a title of 'The Story of My Experiments with Truth'. These will of course include experiments with non-violence, celibacy and other principles of conduct believed to be distinct from truth. But for me, truth is the sovereign principle, which includes numerous other principles. This truth is not only truthfulness in word, but truthfulness in thought also and not only the relative truth of our conception but the Absolute Truth, the Eternal Principle, that is God."[69]

Gandhi further clarified in his writing that "If anything that I write in these pages should strike the readers as being touched with pride, then he must take it that there is something wrong with my quest and that my glimpses are no more then mirage. Let hundreds like me perish, but let truth prevail. Let us not reduce the standard of truth even by a hair's breadth for judging erring mortals like myself."[70]

The book 'An Autobiography or The Story of My Experiments with Truth' is divided into Five Parts. He started the book from the Chapter "Birth and Parentage" and concluded it by the Chapter of "at Nagpur's Farewell." The book proved to be a masterstroke of communication and it was soon translated into various foreign and Indian languages and still continues to change lives across the globe.

Satyagraha in South Africa

Other original work of Gandhi was Satyagraha in South Africa published in the form of book in 1928 written in Gujarati and translated into English by Valji Govindji Desai and had been revised by Gandhi himself and assured the reader that the spirit of the original in Gujarati has been very faithfully kept by the translator. He admitted that, "The original chapters were all written by me from my memory. They were written partly in Yervada Jail and partly outside from my pre-mature release. As a translator knew of this fact, he made a diligent study of the file of Indian Opinion and whenever he discovered slips of memory, he has not hesitated to make the necessary corrections. The reader will share my pleasure that in no relevant or material particular has there been any slip. I need hardly mention that those who are following the weekly chapters of my experiments with truth can not afford to miss these chapters on satyagraha, if they would follow in all its detail the working out of the search after truth."[71]

The Satyagraha struggle of the Indians in South Africa lasted eight years. The term Satyagraha was invented and employed in connection therewith. In the preface of the book 'Satyagraha in South Africa', Gandhi expressed his feelings regarding the launching of Satyagraha in South Africa by saying, "I had long entertained a desire to write a history of that Struggle myself. Something only I could write. Only the general who conducts a campaign can know the objective of each particular move and as this was the first attempt to apply the principle of Satyagraha to politics on a large scale, it is necessary any day that the public should have an idea of its development."[72]

Yervada Mandir

Gandhi in Yervada Central Prison wrote weekly letters to the Satyagarha Ashram, containing a cursory examination of the principle Ashram observance. As the Ashram influence had already travelled beyond its geographical limits, copies of the letters were multiplied for distribution. They were originally written in Gujarati. There was a demand for translation into Hindi and other Indian languages and also into English, translated by Valji Govindji Desai in English and his translation was revised by Gandhiji himself during his incarceration. He said, "I have gone through it carefully and touched up several passages to bring out my meaning more to my liking. I need hardly add that if I was writing a news for the English reader, perhaps I should write a wholly new thing. But that would be going beyond my commission and perhaps it is as well, that even the English reader has the trend of my thought as expressed to the inmates of the Ashrams, and in the year 1930. I have, therefore, taken the least liberty with the original argument."[73] The book contains Sixteen Chapters written in 38 pages while the last chapter on 'Swadeshi' was written when he was released from Jail in 1931.

Constructive Programme

The Constructive Progamme may otherwise, and more fittingly, be called construction of Purna Swarajya or complete Independence by truthful and non-violent means. Gandhi first wrote Constructive Programme in 1941 and revised it in 1945. The items included in it have not been arranged in any order, certainly not in the order of their importance. When the reader discovers that a particular subject, though important in itself, in terms of Independence, does not find place in the programme, he should know that omission is not intentional.

Gandhi, while drafting his Constructive Programme of rural development took care of social, economic, political and moral aspects of development. His approach to constructive programme can be classified into five segaments, viz., economic, educational, social, environmental and political. The Constructive Programme, as revised, has 19 items including Improvement of Livestock. These include (i) communal unity; (ii) removal of untouchabilities; (iii) prohibition; (iv) khadi; (v) other village industries; (vi) village sanitation; (vii) new or basic education; (viii) adult education; (ix) women; (x) education in Health and hygiene; (xi) provincial languages; (xii) national language; (xiii) economic equality; (xiv) kissans; (xv) labour; (xvi) adivasis; (xvii) lepers; (xviii) students; and one more to be included (xix) improvement of Livestocks.[74]

Key to Health

Key to Health, according to Gandhiji, this new name was given to his earlier articles written under the heading Guide to Health in or about the year 1906 for the benefit of the readers of the Indian Opinion in South Africa. These articles were later published in a book form but the copies were not available in India. Late Swami Akhandanand took permission from Gandhi to publish an Indian edition which proved fruitful. The book was translated into several Indian languages. An English translation also appeared. This reached the West, and was translated into several European languages. The result was that the book became the most popular of all his writings. For this, Gandhi said, "I have never been able to understand the reason for this popularity. I had written those articles casually and I did not attach much importance to them. But perhaps the reason for the popularity is to be sought in the fact that I have looked upon the problem of health from a novel point of view, somewhat different from the orthodox methods adopted by doctors and vaidyas. Whether my presumption is correct or not, many friends have been pressing me to publish a new edition putting forth my views to date."[75]

'Key to Health', according to Gandhi, is that anyone who observes the rules of health mentioned in this book will find that he has got in it a real key to unlock the gates leading him to health. He will not need to knock at the doors of doctors or vaidyas from day-to-day.

Gandhi was a born journalist and writing was in his blood. His writings were different in both style and content from the writings of the leader-journalists. Their style usually was grand and aimed at impressing the educated class of Indians. In contrast, Gandhiji's language was simple devoid of embellishments yet clear, straightforward and easily understandable. He wrote on a variety of topics not confined to politics and he was a diligent correspondent who replied to every letter written to him. His compassion, humility, nobility and his concern for the poorest of the poor breathed through his writings. His writings also focused on economic issues like poverty and unemployment with suggestions as to how to remove them. Health and hygiene also occupied an important place in his writings. Spiritual growth was another important area which he usually touched upon. Infact, one can find him writing on almost everything under the sun which had relevance for human beings. The vide range of topics also shows that Gandhi was aiming at not only freedom of the country but also the building of the nation which further differentiated him from the other leaders.

After going through the whole gamut of Gandhi's writings, it becomes clear that print media occupied an important place in Gandhi's communication. His insistence on putting the minutest detail in black and white and his belief in publicity of a cause he thought right further strengthens his view. In view of the style and content of his writings, Broomfield has described him as a great "scribbler."[76] Whatever came to his mind was put on the paper. That is why there was never much of a difference in the content of what he wrote or what he spoke. This is not to say that what he wrote was of inferior quality but to emphasise that for Gandhi who was continuously practicing self control like a yogi to get a right expression was never a problem. It is said that Gandhi liberated his writings from the tradition of written word. Infact, the written words constitute only half of Gandhi's repertoire of communication. One, however, draws solace in Gandhi's words, "After I am gone, people will remember my words." This indicates that Gandhi knew that the dialogue he had initiated will not end with his death. And even in the absence of his physical body, his words would carry weight.

Notes and References

1. Harold Koontz, and Heinz Weihrich, Essentials of Management (Singapore: McGraw Hill Book Co.), 1990, p. 365.
2. Gandhi, M.K., An Autobiography or The Story of My Experiments with Truth (Ahmedabad: Navajivan Publishing House), 1956, p. 47.
3. Parekh, Bhiku, Gandhi (Oxford: Oxford University Press), 1997, pp. 8-9.
4. Tendulkar, D.G., Mahatma Gandhi: Life of Mohandas Karamachand Gandhi, Eight Volumes (New Delhi: Publication Division, Ministry of Information and Broadcasting, Government of India) 1953, p. 247.
5. Mehta, D.S., Mass Communication and Journalism in India (Bombay: Allied Publishers Private Limited), 1979, p. 11.
6. The Times of India, Bombay, October 20, 1896.
7. Natarajan, S.A., History of the Press in India (Bombay: Asia Publishing House), 1962, p. 59.
8. Homer, A. Jack (ed.), The Wit and Wisdom of Gandhi (Boston: Beacon Press), 1951, p. 19.
9. Oriental and India Office Collections, London, Mss Eur F 238/3, Reading papers, Reading, the Viceroy to Montague, the Secretary of State, 19 May 192.
10. The Collected Works of Mahatma Gandhi (New Delhi: Publications Division, Ministry of Information and Broadcasting, Government of India), (hereinafter CWMG be used), Vol. 19, p. 277.
11. Sitaramayya, B. Pattabhi, The History of Indian National Congress (Bombay: Padma Publications), 1946, Vol. 1, p. 18.
12. Harijan, 28-10-1939, p. 283.
13. Parel, Anthony, Hind Swaraj and Other Writings (Cambridge: Cambridge University Press), 1997, p. 6.
14. Mukherjee, Hiren, Gandhi: A Study (Calcutta: National Book Agency Pvt. Ltd.), 1958, p. 45.
15. Parekh, Bhiku, Gandhi, *op. cit.*, p. 42.
16. Wadhwa, Priyanka, Development of Journalism (New Delhi: Murari Lal and Sons), 2007, p. 153.

17. *Ibid.*, p. 153.
18. Gandhi's letter published in Rand Daily Main on 6th August, 1910
19. CWMG, Vol. XV, p. 102.
20. Young India, 1-6-21, p. 172.
21. CWMG, Vol. XX, pp. 161-64.
22. Young India, 21.7.1920, p. 203.
23. CWMG, Vol. XVIII, pp. 68-70.
24. Young India, 21-07-1920, p. 89.
25. *Ibid.*, 19-01-1921, p. 19.
26. *Ibid.*
27. *Ibid.*, 20-01-1921, 91.
28. *Ibid.*, 22-01-1922, 94.
29. Navajivan, 12-01-1930.
30. CWMG, Vol. XLIII, pp. 352-53.
31. *Ibid.*, Vol. XLII, p. 455.
32. Deluca, Anthony R, Gandhi, Mao, Mandela, and Gorbachev, Studies in Personality, Power and Politics (London: Praeger Publications), 2000, p. 30.
33. Navajivan, 12-03-1930.
34. CWMG, Vol. LXXIII, pp. 125-26.
35. CWMG, Vol. LXXV, p. 13.
36. *Ibid.*, Vol. LXXVI, p. 29.
37. *Ibid.*, pp. 98-100.
38. *Ibid.*, pp. 311-12.
39. Harijanbandhu, 18-05-1942.
40. *Ibid.*
41. The Bombay Samachar, 14-07-1942.
42. CWMG, Vol. LXXVI, p. 403.
43. Rolland, Romain, Mahatma Gandhi (New Delhi: Publication Division, Ministry of Information and Broadcasting, Government of India), 1990, p 119.
44. Harijan, 2-02-49, p. 87.
45. Gandhi, M.K., An Autobiography or The Story of My Experiments with Truth, *op. cit.*, 1927, p. 260.
46. Harijan, 2-02-49, p. 98.
47. *Ibid.*
48. *Ibid.*, p. 100.
49. Gandhi, M.K., An Autobiography or The Story of My Experiments with Truth, *op. cit.*, pp. 262-63.
50. Navajivan, 08-10-1919.
51. Harijan, Vol. 1, Introduction
52. Doke, J. Joseph, Gandhi—A Patriot in South Africa (New Delhi: Publications Division, Ministry of Information and Broadcasting, Government of India), 1994, p. 52

53. Indian Opinion, 27-01-1906, pp. 56-60.
54. Gandhi, M.K., An Autobiography or The Story of My Experiments with Truth, *op. cit.*, p. 214.
55. Indian Opinion, 27-01-1906, pp. 61-62.
56. Gandhi, M.K., An Autobiography or The Story of My Experiments with Truth, *op. cit.*, p. 214.
57. Gandhi, M.K., Satyagraha in South Africa (Ahmedabad: Navajivan Publishing House), 1972, p. 131.
58. *Ibid.*, p. 133.
59. The Bombay Chronicle, 20-04-1919.
60. Gandhi, M.K., An Autobiography or The Story of My Experiments with Truth, *op. cit.*, Vol. 1, p. 518.
61. Navajivan, 09-09-1919.
62. CWMG, Vol. XV, pp. 419-21.
63. Young India, 12-03-1920, p. 45.
64. Harijan, 05-05-1933, p. 99.
65. CWMG, Vol. LXXVII, pp. 343-44.
66. Gandhi, M.K., Satyagraha in South Africa (Ahmedabad: Navajivan Publishing House), 1928, p. 211.
67. Parel, Anthony, Hind Swaraj and Other Writings (London: Cambridge University Press), 1997, Introduction.
68. Dalton, Dennis, Gandhi's Power: Non-violence in Action (Oxford: Oxford University Press), 1998, pp. 16-17.
69. Gandhi, M.K., An Autobiography or The Story of My Experiments with Truth, *op. cit.*, p. xiii.
70. *Ibid.*, p. xiv.
71. Gandhi, M.K., Satyagraha in South Africa, *op. cit.*, p. vii.
72. *Ibid.*, preface, p. xi.
73. Gandhi, M.K., From Yervada Mandir (Ahmedabad: Navajivan Publishing House), 1932, preface.
74. Gandhi, M.K., Constructive Programme: Its Meaning and Place (Ahmedabad: Navajivan Publishing House), 1941, pp. 3-32.
75. Gandhi, M.K., Key to Health (Ahmedabad: Navajivan Publishing House), 1948, p. v.
76. Broomfield, J.H., "Gandhi: A Twentieth Century Anomaly" in Richard L. Park (ed.), Change and Persistence Tradition in India: five Lectures (Michigan: Michigan Papers on South and South East Asia, No. 2), 1971, p. 55.

3

Media in Globalized World

The waves of privatization and pressures toward liberalized rather free trade that have marked the world economic order at the turn of the 21st century have also shaped the world media order. But the media industry is not only affected by these trends but also turned into a potential instrument to combat the poverty and inequity that continue to plague so many of the world's inhabitants. Mass media can not only be the ideological army in support of globalization, but can also become the grassroots weapons to fight its impact. As coalitions and activists around the world demand that sustainable development become a priority in the world's changing political and economic systems, many civil-society advocates are urging the use of mass media to help communities find local solutions to economic, political and social disempowerment from centralised or oligopolistic set-up. International news flow and cultural problems are significant in global journalism, perhaps too significant.

Global news almost always is centred in the West. As Stuart Hall says, "Western technology, the concentration of capital, the concentration of techniques, the concentration of advanced labour in the western societies, and the stories and the imagery of western societies: these remain the driving powerhouse of this global mass culture. In that sense, it is centred in the west and it always speaks English."[1] The reaction to globalization, of course, is localization of news and reporting. However, journalism needs to be global journalism; it needs journalists who practice journalism in the global context.

This globalization of journalism became practical with the advent of satellite distribution. It provoked global journalism that transcends borders and has no artificial boundaries. This globalization was further speeded up by the fairly uniform policy throughout the world of deregulation and privatization of existing broadcasting organizations. Globalization excited all western media organizations/and their owners. Technology let loose vast new markets for electronic media—viewers and readers all over the world who now use western news and programming to find out what's happening in the rest of the world. What is happening—and is it important for journalists in the global workplace to understand—is that local media companies and their newsrooms are beginning to hit back; to master western journalistic and production techniques for their own local ends and for their own markets. Global news sources are very uneven. Some cities have hundreds of reporters around the world covering stories of events that happen there; some countries and even continents are inevitably the poorer in the matter of coverage. More remote areas have hardly any journalists at all from outside for covering events. This, of course, affects the picture of the world as a whole because local individual trouble spots are left out. The other problem about global news coverage is the pressure to over-simplify. Time and space constraints inevitably cause to reduce coverage of what is happening-however important and whatever the global repercussions—simplifying and curtailing events to one basic story around which all other events are made to float. Practising global journalism also means allowing entry of fresh air like other attitudes, other cultures, and other approaches. It clearly means that there can often be many truths, not just the one western certainty that western journalists have grown up with. News implies views ... and that means subjectivity. But even with the subjectivity of reporting, there can be truth. International reporting too often is about mega-disasters. International reporting of the life of countries and people should be more about developmental issues emerging from disasters and wars. It should give outsiders an understanding of the people of a country with their social and cultural context. News must have a human angle.

Global journalism teaches us that there are many ways of working, of thinking and of understanding what is going on in the world. Different perceptions may indeed have equal value. However, traditional journalism finds place in global media. Its crucial role of being watchdog of democracy is being increasingly valued by the audience in all countries. The practice of global journalism also means not being too dependent on official sources; we should see for ourselves, be there, judge, and report for ourselves. News manipulation can be easy when reporters don't know the country, the people, and the politics there. Journalists live in a world where they have to take risks. This risk is more in the global context. The sovereign virtue in western-trained journalists is that they believe that risk taking is necessary in their profession. They are not only in the firing line when the situation is dangerous, but also they are in the firing line when the story is more mundane; but politicians, statesmen, business people, owners and rich influential people throughout the world try to change the true face of journalism and what it publishes. Journalism has never been more dangerous, both in the national and global context.

Each time the death of a journalist covering some global conflict or story is reported, it reminds of the unique risks and responsibilities of practicing global journalism and covering the world's disaster spots. A French correspondent once divided up journalists who cover international or serious conflicts into three types: the first type was the Tourists who popped in for a few days sniffed round. They got their passports stamped and then quietly left. The second type came with all the right equipment, but weren't really engaged with the story or the country or its people. These were the people, he said, who allowed the idea of themselves as 'war correspondents' to get in the way of telling the story. And finally there were those who cared and stayed when everyone else was leaving. They were the experts, the real global journalists, who always asked the extra intelligent question; worked that little bit harder to get the real story; who weren't afraid to dig that little bit deeper. And sadly, they are often the ones at greatest risk, the ones who get killed in the line of duty.[2] It is the journalists of this last type who show in an increasingly skeptical world, that journalism really does matter. They really can be the messengers of horror and suffering. Such global reporting and seeking after the real truth of what is going on in the world does have an effect. It can affect foreign policy, public opinion that something should be done. Bcheading of Daniel Pearl in one of the Islamic nations intensifies this view.

Global journalists, by practising their craft to the best of their ability, also remind the world of something else: that we live in a world where journalists and journalism are under constant attack. More foreign correspondents died in Croatia and Bosnia than in Vietnam. But most of the journalists who die doing their job are not the international journalists practising global journalism; they are the local reporters, often killed by their own people. In Serbia, President Milosevic closed down all the independent media. In Zimbabwe and Iran, the independent media is prohibited to flourish and are under serious attack. The enemies of freedom understand very well that independent journalists, whether local or those parachuted in for the story, are enemies who must be controlled, destroyed or suppressed.

Journalists practising global journalism must understand this better than anyone else. They must also understand that in today's world, there are times when journalists have to stop working. Objectivity does not mean ignoring the plight of those whose story is being told. The best stories are those that the people in power do not want to be told. If journalists stop practising global journalism, the bad people will get away with it and win. Practising global journalism means being there, bearing independent witness, reporting what is happening and then communicating this to the outside world. Practising global journalism is about taking risks. News organization is about risk. And risk is becoming so much worse now that there is an increasing danger that reporters will stop going into the real trouble spots for fear of their lives. News organizations are now assessing the risk and often deciding on working if it is too great. There is also risk to be avoided in terms of the various new technological issues that affect the lives and work of global journalists in the digital age. These too have to be confronted. As more and more news becomes available instantly or semi instantly throughout the world across borders, via all the new digital forms and satellite transmissions, not to mention the Internet via which the world of the global journalism is entering into a democracy.[3]

The new technology and speed of transmission is forcing journalists throughout the world to ask themselves the basic question, "what is it all about?" Journalism is deeply embedded in the traditions of the last 300 years of western history. Journalism culture has meant that all journalists brought up in the western tradition since the rise of the printing press have instinctively scrutinized society and its institutions starting, of course, with the democratic government institutions on behalf of the people, the readers. After that scrutiny always comes publication of the information so that the voters, readers, can judge for themselves. Hence the term watchdogs of democracy, in the western tradition/journalism, and democracy, are sisters. The global journalism of today, helped and hindered as it is by the digital revolution, by convergence of media onto one communicating platform, by instantaneous distribution of facts and information throughout the world, in a way never dreamt of 50 years ago, is changing its focus. Rather than reporting facts and events the global journalist is now more and more reporting about each and every aspect of human behaviour and nature while someone else reporting events and facts, what people thinks their sources, authorities of different types saying about a factual event. More and more journalist is trying to find out what will happen rather than what is happening thus it is becoming a medium of conjecture rather than fact.[4]

As global journalism increases in importance and envelops the world, there is a new role for global journalists, i.e. that the sheer size of the businesses and political institutions they are covering, forcing them not to divulge the actual happening at ground level; there, the journalists be increasingly kept at a bay. And, of course, global journalism is becoming explanatory as well as factual and opinion-based. The digital age global journalist, as never before, has to find ways of putting fast-moving stories into a simple, immediately understood context, analyzing what's going on, looking at the historical perspective of a story and how it might affect other events globally or is not necessarily linked to countries. Global journalism has to find stories that go beyond politics and government; it has to find new leads, new ways of presenting stories to a global audience. And that means "global localness."[5] It has to make the global local and the local global. Then, there is the all pervasive influence of the global media moguls. Global journalism is the product of the digital technology provided by the big international companies, the multinationals. Some of these huge companies are news corporations; but an increasing number aren't. They are more to have electrical pods or washing powder, or Hollywood, as their foundation but incidentally also own an international media corporation.

These new media moguls are forming an increasingly global network which provides journalistic and broadcast pre-production, production, post-production and distribution. Take the empire of News International: Rupert Murdoch's media empire stretches from the South Pacific across Britain and Europe to North America. He owns a Hollywood film studio, a satellite TV network and the largest TV magazine in the United States. In addition, of course, he owns newspapers, magazines and broadcast stations throughout the world. In Britain and Europe, he owns the most advanced direct broadcast satellite system and the largest-selling tabloid paper in the world. He is extremely powerful in China. Murdoch is not alone, there are others, perhaps not as well known or as powerful but such power makes the job and integrity of global journalism practice more and more difficult.[6] Another aspect of digital age global journalism is the all-pervasive nature of the telecommunications principles that allow journalism to be truly global. It is also inextricably entwined with news flow. The news gets from the journalist to the radio/television, newspaper/magazine or increasingly, the Internet via a complex web of telecommunications that includes satellites/cable, phone lines/mobile phones, laptops connected direct to the newsroom, thousands of miles away and the Journalist needs to know how to work such technology, which is constantly changing, being upgraded all the time. It is impossible to talk about the practice of global journalism at the same time talking about the growth in digital communications. As messages are sent on the uplink from the reporter via the earth station to the satellite and then down again to another earth station on the other side of the world instantaneously, it is becoming more and more difficult to separate one reporter's voice report or news copy from any other. Globalization is having the effect of homogenization on news flow, news content, news style, news presentation. No reporter/broadcaster can be seen to be beaten by another reporter/broadcaster. No broadcaster. And they all have to show the same pictures; have the same idea; speak with same analysis but trying every time to be different in the eyes of readers/viewers.

The controls being faced by journalists in the digital global age are increasingly technological; they also have to face the laws of each country with or from which they file stories, whether text, voice or pictures by whatever means at their disposal in the rapidly converging media operation that is global journalism practice. These laws, particularly in democratic countries, can be specially engineered to help journalists in their work. In some countries, for example, journalists cannot be forced to reveal their sources in court proceedings. Countries have their own restrictions and regulations that in one way or other affect the job that broadcasters and print journalists have to do. These legal and ethical restrictions as well as restrictions placed on journalistic work by technology or lack of it affect the degree of freedom to report that journalists have in their global practices.[7] Most countries in East and West, in democratic and non-democratic societies, have some kind of expression of press freedom. The devil, as always, is in the detail. Freedom to report is often described as the right to speak/print or broadcast what we want without prior restraint. Press freedom allows publication without prior restraint on the specific understanding that, after publication or broadcast, action can be taken by aggrieved parties against the reporter or news organization either by simple criticism or court action. That's the way the game is played. Action takes place afterwards, not before publication. This is the ultimate test of news freedom to report, the laws to guarantee access to information, such as increasingly across the world various kinds of freedom of information, laws, recognize the importance of access to information and for freedom to publish. Unfortunately, it becomes increasingly obvious that as global journalism increases, so do the efforts by governments of all persuasions to influence the way the media reports events in the country and about that country. There are other global pressures increasingly affecting global journalism practices. One problem is the rapid expansion of media, particularly broadcasting which is controlled by private industry, which, of course, is there to make a profit for shareholders and owners. This pulls journalism towards tabloidisation of news and reporting which is at the same time entertaining—infotainment.

World's 100 Largest Newspapers

Rank	Title	Country	Circulation (000)
1	Yomiuri Shimbun	Japan	14,067
2	The Asahi Shimbun	Japan	12,121
3	Mainichi Shimbun	Japan	5,587
4	Nihon Keizai Shimbun	Japan	4,635
5	Chunichi Shimbun	Japan	4,512
6	Bild	Germany	3,867
7	Sankei Shimbun	Japan	2,757
8	Canako Xiaoxi (Beijing)	China	2,627
9	People's Daily	China	2,509
10	Tokyo Sports	Japan	2,425
11	The Sun	United Kingdom	2,419
12	The Chosun Ilbo	South Korea	2,378
13	USA Today	USA	2,310

14	The Wall Street Journal	USA	2,107
15	Daily Mail	UK	2,093
16	The Joongang Ilbo	South Korea	2,084
17	The Dong-A Ilbo	South Korea	2,052
18	Nikkan Sports	Japan	1,965
19	Hokkaido Shimbun	Japan	1,922
20	Dainik]agran	India	1,911
21	Yangtse Evening Post	China	1,715
22	Sports Nippon	Japan	1,711
23	The Nikkan Gendai	Japan	1,686
24	Times of India	India	1,680
25	Guangzhou Daily	China	1,650
26	The Mirror	UK	1,597
27	Yukan Fuji	Japan	1,559
28	Shizuoka Shimbun	Japan	1,479
29	Nanfang City News (Guangzhou)	China	1,410
30	Dainik Bhaskar	India	1,405
31	Sankei Sports	Japan	1,368
32	Hochi Shimbun	Japan	1354
33	Yangcheng Evening New (Guangzhou)	China	1,320
34	Malay Manorama	India	1,309
35	Liberty Times	Taiwan	1,300
36	Thai Rath	Thailand	1,200
37	New York Times	USA	1,121
38	Hindustan Times	India	1,108
39	Chutian Metro Daily (Wuhan)	China	1,084
40	Gujarat Samachar	India	1,051
41	Ananda Bazar Patrika	India	1,046
42	Xinmin Evening News (Shanghai)	China	1,045
43	Eenadu	India	1,039
44	Nishi-Nippon Shimbun	Japan	1,025
45	Kronen Zeifcung	Austria	1,009
46	WAZ Mediengruppe	Germany	1,001
47	United Daily News	Taiwan	1,000
48	China Times	Taiwan	1,000
49	Daily Sports	Japan	999
50	The Hindu	India	989
51	Hindustan	India	957
52	Beijing Evening News	China	950
53	Mathrubhumi	India	904
54	Los Angeles Times	USA	902
55	Information Times	China	900
56	Daily News	Thailand	900
57	Al-Ahram	Egypt	900

58	Peninsula City News	China	860
59	Kom Chad Luek	Thailand	850
60	Kyoto Shimbun	Japan	825
61	Kobe Shimbun	Japan	821
62	Punjab Kesari	India	817
63	Komsomolskaya Pravda	Russia	817
64	Rajasthan Patrika	India	804
65	Dahe Newspaper	China	796
66	Chugoku Shimbun	Japan	789
67	Quest France	France	783
68	Daily Sakai	India	783
69	Jang	Pakistan	775
70	AJ	India	759
71	De Telegraaf	The Netherlands	753
72	Qianjiang Evening News	China	750
73	Qilu Evening News	China	750
74	Nanfang Daily	China	750
75	Daily Thanthi	India	750
76	Moskovskiy Komsomolets	Russia	750
77	Sandesh	India	750
78	Daily Express	UK	720
79	New York Daily News	USA	715
80	The Washington Post	USA	708
81	Daily Star	UK	720
82	Today Evening News	China	699
83	New York Post	USA	686
84	Corriere della Sera	Italy	677
85	Wuhan Evening News	China	660
86	Modern Express	China	651
87	Yanzhao Metro Daily	China	650
88	Metro Express	China	650
89	Zeitungsgruppe Koln	Germany	628
90	Kahoku Shimpo	Japan	622
91	La Repubblica	Italy	622
92	Trud	Russia	613
93	Beijing Youth Daily	China	606
94	Chicago Tribune	USA	601
95	New Express	China	600
96	Daily Sunshine	China	600
97	Matichon	Thailand	600
98	Khao Sod	Thailand	600
99	Apple Daily	Taiwan	600
100	Min Sheng Pao	Taiwan	600

GLOBAL NEWS FLOW

Global news flow is all about journalists and their ability to find out what is happening in countries that are not their own. Like all journalism, it has a fondness for anniversaries, for summaries, for analysis, for looking for the simple, single story amidst the confusion of the war or disaster or political insurrection. Before there can be proper global news flow, there must be an idea of what is news, what is happening. All proper journalists are supposed to have it: only a few can identify or define it. Journalists speak of 'the news' as if events select themselves. Further, they speak as if which is the 'most significant' news story and which 'news angles' are most salient are divinely inspired. Yet of the millions of events which occur daily in the world, only tiny proportion ever becomes news. One approach is to try to define the news values that come into operation when journalists select stories. In this context, Norwegian Johan Galtung and Mart Ruge's paper, has long been regarded as a landmark study of news values and news selection.[8] The factors making up their news values continue to be cited as 'prerequisites' of news selection in the twenty-first century. Their approach is particularly interesting for journalists practising global journalism because their research was specifically into the way foreign news operated. The central question at the heart of their paper was how events become news.[9]

Galtung and Ruge's study began as a paper presented at the First Nordic Conference on Peace Research, which took place in Oslo in January 1963. They presented a series of factors that seem to be particularly important in the selection of news, followed by the deduction of some hypotheses from their list of 12 factors as follows:

1. *Frequency*: An event that unfolds at the same or similar frequency as the news medium is more likely to be selected as news than is a social trend that takes place over a long period of time.
2. *Threshold*: Events have to pass a threshold before being recorded at all.

After that, the greater the intensity, the more gruesome the murder, the more casualties in an accident—all these put greater impact on the perception of those responsible for news selection.

3. *Unambiguity*: The less ambiguity, the more likely the event is to become news. The more clearl an event can be understood, and interpreted without multiple meanings, the greater the chance of its being selected.
4. *Meaningfulness*: The culturally similar is likely to be selected because it fits into the news selector's frame of reference. Thus, the involvement of the UK citizens will make an event in a remote country more meaningful to the UK media. Similarly, news from the USA is seen as more relevant to the UK than is news from countries which are less culturally familiar.
5. *Consonance*: The news selector may predict or indeed want something to happen thus forming a mental image of an event which in turn increases its chances of becoming news.
6. *Unexpectedness*: The most unexpected or rare events within those that are culturally familiar, will have the greater chance of being selected as news.
7. *Continuity*: Once an event has news, it remains in the media spotlight for some time, even if its amplitude has been greatly reduced because it has become familiar and easier to interpret. Continuing coverage also acts to justify the attention an event received in the first place.
8. *Composition*: An event may be included as news, less because of its intrinsic news value than because it fits into the overall composition or balance of a newspaper or news broadcast. This might not just mean 'light' stories to balance heavy news; it could also mean that, in the context of newspaper reports on alleged institutional racism within the police, for example, positive initiatives to combat racism which would normally

go unreported might make it on to the news pages.

9. *Reference to elite nations*: The actions of elite nations are seen as more consequential than the actions of other nations. Definitions of elite nations will be culturally, politically and economically determined and will vary from country to country, although there may be universal agreement about the inclusion of some nations (e.g. the USA) among the elite.
10. *Reference to elite people*: The actions of elite people, who will usually be famous, may be seen by news selectors as having more consequence than the actions of others. Also, readers may identify with them.
11. *Reference to persons*: News has a tendency to present events as the actions of named people rather than a result of social forces. This personification goes beyond human interest stories and could relate to cultural idealism, according to which man is the master of his own destiny, and events can be seen as the outcome of an act of free will.
12. *Reference to something negative*: Negative news could be seen as unambiguous and consensual, generally more likely to be unexpected and to occur over a shorter period of time than positive news.[10]

Bell adds some more factors concerned with news-gathering and news- processing rather than with the events and actors featured in the news. He argues for the importance of:

- Competition (the desire for a scoop);
- Co-option (a story that is only tangentially related is presented in terms of a high-profile continuing story);
- Predictability (diary stories which can be pre-scheduled are more likely to be covered than events which turn up unheralded);

- Prefabrication (readymade texts such as press releases, cuttings, agency copy which journalists can process rapidly will greatly increase the likelihood of something appearing in the news).[11]

A vital part of news selection and decision-making for journalists, particularly those working in foreign countries, from their base newsroom, is a firm focus on what is the type of the government, an idea of what type of the story reporters are looking for considering which newspapers decide the angle, the headline and tone and the facts that are gathered. The global reporter's job often is to see that the facts fit the headline. Or come up with a better native from their own local knowledge. The practice of journalism needs a local map, with appropriate map references; along with that, it also needs a spirit of adventure so that these can be thrown away as the reporter finds out the facts. Reuters Media serve both traditional and new media. Together with other parts of the Group, it provides news and information to over 900 internet websites reaching an estimated 40 million viewers and generating approximately 140 million page-views per month in addition to serving the traditional print and TV media. Some 330 subscribers plus their networks and affiliates in over 90 countries use Reuters television news coverage. Reuters is the world's largest international news and television agency with 2,100 Journalists, photographers and camera operators in 254 bureaus serving over 100 countries. News is gathered and edited for both business and media clients in 23 languages. Approximately 30,000 headlines, including third party contributions, and over three million words are published daily. Reuters Television goes to 900 television broadcasters in 81 countries.[12]

Associated Press (AP) serves more than 1,500 newspapers and 5,000 broadcast outlets in the United States. Abroad, AP services are printed and broadcast in 112 countries. Worldwide, AP serves more than 15,000 news organizations. Associated Press is the oldest and largest news organization in the world, serving as a source of news, photos, graphics, audio and video for more than one billion people a day. It has 8,500 newspaper, radio and television subscribers in 112 countries. AP's mission is to provide factual coverage to all parts of the globe for use by the media around the world. News bearing the AP logotype can be counted on to be accurate, balanced and informed. With 3500 employees working in 240 bureaus around the world, AP operates as a not-for-profit cooperative with its subscribing member organizations. AP supplies a steady stream of news (20 million words a day) to its domestic members and foreign subscribers. It also has the industry's most sophisticated digital photo network, a 24-hour continuously updated online news service, a state-of-art television news service and one of the largest radio networks.

AP has received 45 Pulitzer Awards, more than any other news organization in the categories for which it can compete. It has 27 photo Pulitzers, the most of any news organization. Its mission statement says: The Associated Press is in the information business. Its fundamental mission is to provide state, national and international news, photos, graphics, broadcast and online services of the highest quality, reliability and objectivity to its readers, and to domestic owners as economically as it can. The AP seeks no special privilege beyond free access. It believes that the more journalistic voices the world hears, the better informed it will be.[13] The major obstacles the AP encounters in collecting a factual global news report are restricted access, explicit or implicit censorship and pressure against correspondents, extending as far as expulsion and kidnapping. The most serious and widespread of these constraints is the inability to gain entry for professionally qualified AP representatives. In cases where the AP lacks regular access, information must be obtained from radio broadcasts and visitors. Explicit and implicit censorship is another news barrier. Explicit censorship results in deletions or refusal to transmit correspondents' copy. An example would be the inaccessibility in some countries of key government officials. Often, the most difficult specific sources for the foreign correspondent to reach are those who can best explain the story of their countries to the world. Then the local press is restricted to publication of only environment approved news, foreign correspondent's access to balanced local information suffers. This makes it more difficult for the foreign correspondents to understand and explain the country to readers in distant places. Direct action against foreign correspondents is the most extreme and dangerous step to free news coverage. The Associated Press often hires correspondents expelled by various countries, and in many cases kidnapped, as in the case of Middle East co-respondent Terry Anderson, who was held hostage for more than six years in Lebanon.[14]

Agence France Presse (AFP) has about three thousand employees including 900 correspondents and 2,000 freelancers in 165 countries. United Press International (UPI) is one of the world's most famous news agencies, although it is also one of the most troubled. It has its headquarters in Washington although it was owned by the London-based ARA group, which, in turn belonged to a Saudi Arabian corporation. UPI had very Eve radio interests which it sold to raise money for repaying its mounting debts. UPI originally went bankrupt in this which was its second bout of bankruptcy under its fourth owners since being sold originally by the family of its newspaper magnate E.W. Scripps. He launched one Press in 1907 because he needed a news agency to service morning and evening news papers. The other American news agency, Associated Press, at the time only serviced morning news papers. In 1958, UP merged with William Randolph International News Service and thus UPI was born. It never made a profit and grew smaller as the years went by. However, it has had considerable journalistic prestige, particularly in its coverage of the American White House, where Helen Thomas has been the chief of its White House Bureau for many years. In the last few years, the agency has moved towards its restructuring which created an Internet based service.[15]

Global news flow, whether from agencies or individuals, by practising global journalists, has, of course, been at the forefront of new technological advance to gather and distribute news and information. Journalism has always gone hand in hand with new technology. Journalists have always used basic forms of communication of whatever type they could manufacture or find. After the telegraph was invented, came cable for overseas and international dissemination of news by journalists. In fact, newspapers and particularly news agencies such as Reuters, were largely responsible for the early cable distribution which allowed stories to be sent electronically from one country to another. Then came radio, then the telephonic cable, then satellite communication and now the computer aided by the Internet. Photo services developed in the early part of the twentieth century, television began in the 1950s; now global journalism is a vast multimedia complex principally using satellite for delivery of print, audio and television news and online news services in 21st Century. One of the big challenges about the practice of global journalism is that global and local are becoming mixed. This is particularly the case in relation to television news, which is now instantaneous from anywhere to anywhere. As with print, television receives most of its pictures not from its own correspondents around the world but from the television news agencies which are totally global in their coverage and distribution.[16]

Broadcast newsrooms throughout the world receive the latest news in sound and pictures from basically three news agencies and a variety of co-operative news exchanges (the largest of them being the Geneva-based Eurovision). In two of the three cases, Reuters and Associated Press, are the same organizations which distribute print as well as pictures. The third, Worldwide Television News (WTN) is, like the others based in London, a convenient centre of world communication. They gather videotaped sound and pictures and story information from around the world and from individual television stations throughout the world with which they have an exchange agreement. These global television agencies take the stories that pour into their London offices, edit them into news story packages, but without any narration in most cases, and transmit them via satellite to their clients throughout the world. They also provide on demand complete stories ready for broadcast with voice-over material recorded on the package. As Boyd Barren says, "Many new commercial stations around the world have been designed from the outset to rely heavily on the agencies in this way."[17]

The international agencies are the major agenda-setters.

They make the first decisions on how and whether international stories will be covered. They choose where to allocate their resources, and hence which stories will be covered and where. They decide on which stories to send to their clients; how much visual element they will provide; what kind of audio and accompanying background text they will send. Broadcasters then write their stories around the video clips these organizations offe, and without video, there is usually no story to send. International events without pictures are non-stories as far as the global agencies are concerned. Of course, the press, and sometimes, the global news magazines set an initial agenda for which the global broadcast news agencies then pick up and produce pictures and sound. An agency's decision to cover a story may be influenced by the interest shown amongst global journalists and news media but they will then make their own individual choices about what to photograph, whom to interview, how many seconds to give each part of the story, how to package it and whom to send the story to? On the other hand, agencies usually only provide the raw material for local journalists to expand, edit, change as they see fit for their local audience. So, the global again becomes local. That's if there are journalists and newsrooms available to spend the time doing this. Too often, the footage that comes into a newsroom from a global news agency is the footage that viewers eventually see. So, the news agenda is often set not in the domestic news market, but thousands of miles away in London. Often, too, the first decisions about how an international story is to be covered, if at all, is made not in the domestic market but in London within the studios of these major news agencies.

The growth of news agencies throughout the world also has an effect on news globalization. British Broadcasting Corporation World Service Television and CNN International broadcast across the globe round the clock and others such as News Corporation, General Electric and Microsoft's MSNBC are doing likewise. Non-English language news programmes are available throughout most of the world via the German language Deutsche-Well, Spanish language Tele-Notices and Japanese NHK services, STAR TV, South Africa's M-Net.

Other satellite services provide a wide range of news channels where before there were no news channels at all. The major news channels still deliver the news globally in English and even vernacular services such as Deutsche-Welle and NHK provide considerable international news in English. The emergence of global satellite television has led to a rearrangement of the global news industry. Satellite television has brought into existence regional and global news channels and that too on a single platform, the most prominent is CNN International, which reaches over 200 countries, and thus coveres a vast majority of the world population. However, the big four western news agencies AP, UPI, Reuters, and AFP still dominate the global print market. The rapid spread of cable and satellite technologies has meant many news operations have arisen with a multinational feel. CNNI has done it quite successfully with outputs in several parts of the world, such as London and Hong Kong. Euronews tries to do this in Europe, but, of course, as Boyd Barrett and Rantanen state: The problem is defining European flavour. Its principal source is Eurovision which, in turn, takes international stories from WTN, Reuters and APTV. Sky TV has a European news service reaching 33 countries.[18] They describe them as:

- *Reuters*: Reuters TV, Reuters wire services, ITN, Tele-Noticias, global programme production, Polish and Russian commercial broadcasting;
- *Murdoch/News Corp*: STAR TV/Sky, BSkyB, Fox network, global broadcasting and production;
- *BBC: BBC, BBC*: World, IBBC News 24;
- Carlton: UK programme producer and broadcaster, majority owner of ITN;
- *Disney/Capital Cities-ABC*: besides ABC in the US majority shareholder in WTN, Scandinavian Broadcasting;
- *General Electric*: NBC, CNBC, NBS Super channel/ Asian Business Channel, MSNBC;
- *Time-Warner*: US production, broadcasting and third largest US cable operator, German-Language regional news in Europe, owner of Turner broadcasting which includes CNN, CNNI.[19]

In the annals of International Communication research, the 1970s may very well be referred to as the decade of the New World Information Order (NWIO). It is a UNESCO sponsored effort to achieve more equalization in the production and distribution of information between the First World and the Third World. Massive cries from developing countries about the imbalance in information flow from the North to the South and from the West to the East have prompted several countries to press for a realignment of information producers and consumers which resulted in NWIO.

GLOBAL JOURNALISM FREEDOM

The globalization of journalism over recent years has had repercussions for the way journalism is practised in individual countries as well as by the global journalists. The effects of globalisation are seen in all areas, both in the way stories are reported domestically and internationally, as well as in other areas such as those concerning legal and ethical matters.

ASIA

Hongkong, The Phillipines, Singapore, Malaysia

Asia is a region that has been undergoing massive changes, not just economically but also in the taste of its news. Like all countries faced with the problems of globalization, this region, which borders the Pacific, and, therefore, with American influence, is struggling to hold on to its strong cultural traditions. The media of the region, as in all developing regions throughout the world, have become all pervasive. No longer are newspapers a luxury reserved for the highly educated and rich: today, they are for everyone as are radio and television. And this includes international satellite broadcasts of news and other programmes from a wide variety of sources, but mostly from the UK and the US. These are rich media markets. As Asia's people have sought a wider voice in government, so has the media, press and broadcasting expanded its role to take on more of the western ideals of political watchdog and voice of the people. The size of the Pacific-rim countries' media is striking. Japan's five top dailies have circulations more than 40 million.

Korea's four leading dailies have circulations between 1 and 2 million—larger than most American daily and many UK national dailies. Hong Kong's STAR TV, an international satellite broadcaster, has a potential viewing audience of 2.5 billion. Technological advance has also been rapid in these Pacific-rim countries. This exposure to western styles of journalism has brought tensions. The adversarial, critical, cynical style which western journalists use and audiences expect, are new to these countries. This style and the approach of western journalists can also be offensive to Eastern different moral codes and ethical considerations. This, in turn, has also led to criticism by individual countries, used to a certain local approach of bias in the reporting by international journalists of their own domestic affairs.[20]

Hong Kong, the Philippines, Singapore and Malaysia, all have strong multilingual media systems, utilising English, Chinese, Malay, Tamil and Tagalog. In Malaysia, press law originally drafted by the English colonials is still in use. In Thailand, there is strong and well read English-language newspapers. However, the vernacular language press is growing in status and influence. In Malaysia, the Malay-language press is expanding rapidly. In Vietnam and Cambodia, the English and French language press has dropped in importance while local newspapers are on the increase. Many countries in the Pacific-rim, as elsewhere throughout the world, are strong on developmental journalism. The media is expected to work cooperatively with the government in helping educate people, while at the same time promoting the government policies, preaching harmony and in Chinese terms, Confucian values. In China, Singapore and Malaysia, the most important papers are owned by the government.[21]

In some countries, particularly those with a Confucian tradition, which emphasis consensus, loyalty to family and discipline, there is obviously a reluctance to criticise those in authority. Journalists from other cultural traditions find this difficult to live with and work in. Journalists and politicians often cooperate; the politician provides information and in return the journalist does not publish embarrassing information. The same applies in financial stories as well. Links between big business and the media often inhibit the press and broadcast media from reporting dodgy business practices. In many countries, the press is not encouraged to expose the relationships between business and government; or to investigate allegations of graft, nepotism and corruption. Journalists are often discouraged from in-depth reporting and they hesitate in many cases to criticise government actions. In some countries, ownership makes additional problems for reporters. Often, the most influential media are controlled by large companies with interests in many businesses outside the media itself. This, of course, causes problems for reporting not about businesses that might belong to the same owner.[22]

Japan

Other countries are managing to come to reconcile their own cultural traditions and the modern approach to journalistic practice as seen from the West. Take Japan for example. Japan shares a Confucian ethos with other Eastern countries such as South Korea, Taiwan, China and Singapore, but this doesn't stop Japanese media reporting frankly and freely. The media system in Japan is huge: five national dailies, five commercial networks and a fast developing satellite TV system. Japan has also had a legal framework that ensures freedom of expression for much longer than other countries in the region.

Japanese media is very strong and saturates the country. I't is also extremely well. advanced. Freedom of expression has been enshrined in Japanese life since the American occupation after the Second World War. The country's television stations fit no particular political profile and Japan's newspapers are committed to independence. Censorship is forbidden and government censorship is virtually unknown. Japan has no statutory laws covering freedom of information of privacy. The Supreme Court has, on many occasions, upheld the right of the media to receive information and gather news in the public interest. Other court decisions have recognized the right of journalists not to divulge confidential sources. In Japan, there is a strong code of ethics and with it a strong sense of self-regulation. The newspapers' publishers' association subscribes to a code committing the press to independence, a non-partisan stance and fair writing for the public interest. Election laws guarantee the media's right to report and comment on elections but they prohibit any attempt to influence the election, such as through the publication of data that might affect election outcomes. Papers, however, often ignore this restriction and print poll results without getting into trouble. Libel and privacy codes are the only formal boundaries on the Japanese press. Newspapers do not like to be involved in libel suits and so take great care and try to avoid attributing any statements or actions to particular individuals. Juvenile law in Japan demands anonymity for criminal suspects under the age of 20. Tabloids and magazines, however, are much freer in publishing stories and are occasionally sued. Usually, the plaintiff wins. The broadcast media are regulated more closely than the press. The Ministry of Post and Telecommunications is responsible for the broadcast laws. NHK, the Japan Broadcasting Corporation, is one of the world's largest public broadcasters. Broadcasters must be politically impartial.

Japan is media saturated, and both a difficult and an easy place for global journalism, to flourish. Freedom of expression is enshrined in the Japanese constitution and any form of censorship is practically unheard of. The media is not muckraking as in many western countries but has Confucian values in the practices of the media. There are, of course, some taboo subjects such as criticism of the Royal Family.

In Japan, the pattern of news coverage influences public perceptions of what the important issues of the day are. Many Japanese scholars have accepted the idea that the mass media have powerful effects, because the media overwhelm Japan's information environment. Compared to the United States, Germany and Hong Kong, for example, the Japanese are more dependent on the mass media and less dependent on interpersonal communication and personal observation for information. The Japanese media, particularly the five national newspapers, have great influence on what readers think about, if not how to think. The media in Japan have a concentration of ownership, integration with other elite power groups and an ability to exercise direct influence over government policy. This implies strong potential power in exerting control on the flow of information. News executives and managing editors have the power to cover up or reveal political scandals or to campaign for or against any interest.The Japanese are among the greatest readers per head of newspapers in the world. Every day about 70 million newspapers are printed in Japan, more than one newspaper for every two people. Surveys suggest that an enormous 90 per cent of adults read at least one newspaper a day, the average reader devoting about 40 minutes each day to it. There are about 160 daily newspapers in Japan that are, on the whole, aimed at the general rather than the specific reader. The two biggest dailies Yomiuri Shimbun and Asahi Shimbun are the flagship papers of large, wealthy companies. These two papers have existed since 1874 (Yomiuri) and 1879 Asahi). The production networks are impressive. Asahi is printed in 18 plants throughout Japan, Yomiuri at slightly fewer. Yomiuri has about 100 offices throughout Japan and 360 regional reporters' offices. Asahi has about 830 reporters throughout the country. Both have over 30 overseas offices each. Amidst this, they have a daily circulation of 26 million and are the largest in the world.

Apart from the big national dailies, there are important, high quality regional newspapers such as Hokkaido Shimbun in Sapporo, ChunichiShimbun in central Japan and the Nishi-Hjhon Shimbun on Kyushu. There are also many high quality city newspapers such as Kyoto Shimbun, Kobe Shimbun and Shizuoka Shimbun. The biggest regional newspapers have overseas correspondents while the smaller ones rely on the Kyodo News service. The English-language press does not play an important role since there is little market for it. The most important Japanese language newspaper is the Japan Times with a circulation of almost 70,000. Japans newspaper consumers also devour magazines hungrily. There are more than 2,000 monthlies and hundreds of weeklies. All the major dailies publish news weeklies. The Japanese media are dominated by five national newspapers, in order: the Yomiuri

Shimbun, the Asahi Shimbun the MainichiShimbun the SankeiShimbun and the Nihon KeizaiShimbun. In recent years, the Youmiuri has had a daily morning circulation of more than 14 million, the Asahi Shimbun more than 12 million, and the Mainichi more than 5 million copies a day. In addition to having the highest per capita circulation in the world, Japan's top five newspapers either own or are affiliated with Tokyo's commercial television networks. Asahis affiliated with TV Asahi Yomiurs with NTV, Sankei Shimbun with Fuji Television, Mainichi Shimbunw TBS and Nihon Keizai Shimbun with TV Tokyo. Of perhaps even greater importance is the fact that there is no significant difference in content among the top national papers, with the exception of the Nihon Keizai Shimbun, which is a business newspaper. The five large daily newspapers speak in one voice. Their commentary on the issues of the day is almost indistinguishable and their selection of what to report and what to ignore is virtually identical. The systematic and heavy self-censorship the newspapers engage in is without parallel in the industrialized world. The Japanese newspapers' tremendous circulations do not guarantee that political stories, for example, are well-read by most of the population. The media cannot influence the public if the public is not paying attention; what if the public is paying attention? The question is that and the newspapers offer unbalanced coverage of an important international issues, or they never raise certain issues?

Several scholars and journalists have reported on the array of sources routinely used by Japanese journalists. Their articles tend to focus on the Japanese press club or kisha kurabu system. Every major government department and agency and all significant business groups have their own press club. Since the 1880s, the press clubs have graduated from waiting rooms for reporters to almost exclusive channels of information regarding the pertinent institutions and is within the confines of the club walls that much of the reporter official interaction takes place. Generally, only journalists affiliated with the major media companies can belong to press clubs. Upto 1993, Magazine writers, freelance writers and, foreign correspondents were not allowed to join, which meant they could not attend most news conferences, background briefings or receive news releases. The off-the-record briefings are particularly important to journalists because that's when politicians and bureaucrats explain the real meaning of their often ambiguous official comments. Scholars and journalists have pointed to several adverse consequence of press club system. The kisha kurabu tend to encourage uniformity in reporting and discourage critical reporting. The news tends to be uniform partly because it originates from same sources: everyone attends the same news briefings and receives the same news releases. Japanese reporters, especially political writers, must cultivate the friendship of their news sources. Complicating the situation, Akhavan Majid notes that political reporters are often assigned to a politician for the bulk of their careers, "tying the fortunes of the journalist to those of the official assigned to him." The closer the reporter is to his or her source, the greater the constraint in reporting information, disadvantageous to their patron. Under such circumstances, the reporter can either remain reticent or can go on to write only favourable stories promoting the political interest of his patron. Reinforcing a reluctance to write stories detrimental to one's subject politician is a cultural norm of obligation. A reporter's expose about a politician would be in violation of the unwritten code of conduct and might jeopardize future access to other politicians. The kisha kurabu system ensures that much of the news that is reported is initiated by the government and reported primarily from the government's perspective. As a result, the government appears to have a strong role in influencing the media's agenda. For the most part, government officials and not journalists decide which issues are salient and worthy of discussion.

As mentioned earlier, Japan's national papers have been characterised as essentially uniform. They appear to influence each others' news judgements to the extent that no one wants to risk being different. Intermediate agenda setting also may help explain another aspect of Japanese politics and media. Despite significant influence politicians and bureaucrats appear to yield over journalists and despite the Japanese tendency to be non-aggressive and conformist, the country's political system has not lacked for scandal. In politics, of course, scandals often are publicized by an officeholder or candidate's political opponents. But when does a scandal become news if main-stream Japanese journalists are reluctant to print that which might embarrass or anger their sources? In several instances, experts say, the mainstream Japanese newspapers picked up a controversial story only after it had first been reported by a foreign news organization or a freelancer. For example, it was a magazine reporter who disclosed the financial scandal that led to the resignation of Prime Minister, Kakuei Tanaka in 1974. Press club reporters apparently knew about the scandal but chose not to print anything until after the magazine did.

Freelance and western journalists influence mainstream Japanese journalists because they remind those journalists of professional norms such as being a watchdog of government and thus being objective. No matter how deferential a Japanese journalist may appear to someone with a western perspective, Japanese journalists themselves say they believe in many of the same journalistic values. Indeed, nearly all the journalists, asked questions in one survey, said they should act as watchdogs over government and most characterized government-press relations as basically conflicting. Japanese journalists generally believe that they should shape public opinion, attempt to influence government policy, and act as watchdog.

Also shaping the attitudes of Japanese journalists is the socialization process that occurs at every newspaper. To get a job with a Japanese newspaper, applicants must first pass a highly competitive and rigorous exam. As a result, those who succeed usually have similar, elitist educational backgrounds. Reporters at the major newspapers spend a year or two on a particular local beat and move up to a more prestigious beat every few years until they join the ranks of management. Like employees of most Japanese companies, they have lifetime employment which means plenty of time to be fully indoctrinated into the customs of their organisation and plenty of motivation to do so. In addition to the press clubs and socialisation within newsrooms, cultural ideas about what it means to be Japanese, not necessarily what it means to be a journalist, also come into play when the media's agenda is being set. Japanese journalists have for centuries lived in a Confucian culture that places great value on the group over the individual and on harmony over conflict. As a result, the Japanese media tries to preserve harmony by refraining from disturbing the status quo. Senior Japanese newspaper editors view themselves as public guardians, entrusted to help maintain a disciplined society with a maximum of order and a minimum of conflict. The Japanese media are huge business conglomerates. Money influences coverage. The Japanese national papers earn a larger percentage of their income from circulation than from advertising. Japan's national newspapers are characterized by ownership in which key employees have a financial stake in the company. Thus the papers must be extremely careful to avoid alienating any segment of their diverse readership by their content, style, or political slant lest their circulation and hence financial stability should suffer.

Japan has been a television culture for a long time. In Japan, everyone lives by television. Japan's television system is extensive. There are five large commercial television networks, a huge public television organization, satellite and pay-TV services and a growing cable system to which about 16 per cent of the population were connected in 2000. Japan leads the way in satellite television. Cross-border satellite broadcasters have also made their presence felt in Japan. And as satellite TV has expanded, Japanese broadcasters have bought the rights to international satellite transmissions such as CNN, ESPN and MTV. Japanese news journalism on TV is brash and somewhat flashy to western eyes and ears. News journalism can be opinionated rather than straight laced. The public service broadcaster, NHK, however, remains more-mainstream in its journalism. However, the TV networks have links with the major press organizations. For instance, all the five of the Tokyo commercial television networks are owned by the big five national dailies. The Foreign Press in Japan (FPIJ) was officially organised in 1964. Its objective is to provide opportunities for the best possible news coverage in Japan for its members. All foreign news organizations in Japan accredited or otherwise recognized by the Ministry of

Foreign Affairs for coverage in Japan, are eligible to join. The FPIJ regularly allocates pool positions for coverage of special events in Japan for which Japanese government or other organizations have approved limited coverage by reporters, both Japanese and foreign. The FPIJ pool members then provide pool coverage (video and audio tape and pen coverage) to all registered members. The FPIJ also lobbies for greater access to Japanese government ministries and agencies, as well as with other 'kisha clubs' for more transparency and fairness in regards to allowing coverage by the international media.

One of the biggest problems for global journalists is how to crack the code of the Japanese press clubs. These can inhibit freedom of information for those not part of the network. The press club is an essential part of journalistic life in Japan. It is criticized by foreign journalists who are often excluded from the personal clubs and from Japanese journalists themselves who object to the bland pro-establishment style of journalism that the culture tends to foster. Most government agencies, political parties, important industrial and economic organizations, local government, the courts and police all have their own press clubs. One of their important functions is to hold news conferences for top policy-makers often at the request of journalists; unlike in many other countries, where an official with information calls a press conference. One guess puts the number of stories filtered through these press clubs as high as 75 per cent. Foreign correspondents who are often excluded from membership, criticise the practice of exclusion because they feel that it puts them at a severe disadvantage. Some clubs now allow foreign journalists to become members.

The more developed media landscapes of Japan, Taiwan and South Korea face other key concerns. Particularly contentious is the perceived decline in the standards of journalism as media outlets battle for market share. In Japan, some even took the view that a leading newspaper's coverage led to Princess Masako's miscarriage. South Korean politicians denounce journalists as chaebol (family-owned conglomerates) representatives and the Taiwanese media is often accused of going down a sensationalist path.

Japan's parliament passed a controversial law allowing police to use wiretaps to investigate certain serious crimes. A key concern for journalists is that the law fails to protect journalists' right to protect their confidential sources of information.

South Korea

In South Korea, censorship laws have been considerably softened over the last few years. Newspapers are now freer than in the past to criticise the government and to write investigative stories that would have been unthinkable a few years ago. Censors no longer sit in newsrooms and there are no more government directives telling newspapers how to handle sensitive stories. The number of dailies published in South Korea has doubled in 2007. There are still some old practices remaining such as journalists taking money from officials or businesses for favourable coverage.

Seoul has about 16 dailies of various types and the major papers have foreign offices in the major world capitals. The industry has some of the most advanced technology and the bigger papers can produce multiple editions of sharp coloured newspapers. There are two English language dailies in Seoul—the Korea and Korea Times, but they are mainly read by westerners. The government has no restrictions on private ownership of satellite dishes. Satellite channels, including international ones, are available to viewers and cable television is also developing fast. Radio is very influential throughout the country and there are more than 50 stations, some government owned, some a mixture of public-private ownership and some owned by religious organizations. Most newspapers are owned by wealthy families or large industrial companies. South Korea has a high quality of journalism. Journalists are well paid and have high status.[23]

China

In China, the media has very little freedom. It is a branch of government and news is filtered by authorities. China's newspapers are all state owned. Virtually all printed material is first scrutinized by Communist Party officials.

Newspapers do not tend to espouse different opinions. The People's Daily, which is well known outside China, is the official newspaper of the Communist Party. Perhaps the major influence for news and journalism in China rests in the hands of the Xinhua news agency (www.xinhua.com). It employs over 10000 people and has more than 100 offices throughout the world. Within China, Xinhua has over 30 offices, one for each province plus one for the army. In Hong Kong, Xinhua acted as the virtual embassy employing hundreds of people who performed news-gathering and intelligence communications. Xinhua oversees three main areas: domestic news, international news, and a translation department which takes foreign stories and translates them for circulation to government officials. There are more than 2,000 newspapers in China and the majority of them cannot post correspondents, so they use Xinhua, People's Daily for daily stories. It prints about 25 per cent Xinhua stories, has only about 50 overseas correspondents compared with Xinhua's 400. Xinhua is not involved in anti government stories; still it, does provide news stories to China Central Television. China has a couple of other, but much smaller, news services: the China News service which covers news about Chinese people living overseas and China Features news service which produces feature stories about China, written in English, for newspapers around the world. In China, broadcasting is massively important, possibly more important than print. About 150 million Chinese now own television sets. Radios are even more widespread. Television is controlled by China Central Television (CCTV), which falls under the Ministry of Radio, Film and television. CCTV has over 2,000 employees, and much of it is beamed throughout China via satellite. CCTV broadcasts not only which it produces itself, three times a day, often drags on some foreign news such as NHK or CNNI as sources. The audience for its news is probably in excess of 500 million. China also has about 100 regional, provincial and municipal networks throughout the country. [24]

Hong Kong's media remained ostensibly free but two reinterpretations of the Basic Law by Beijing effectively overturned the judgements by the Hong Kong court. This greatly blurred the boundary between the legal systems of Hong Kong and the mainland, weakening the human rights safeguards. Legal restraint is a hanging sword over the head of the media and all the indications are that the Hong Kong Special Administrative Region authorities plan to enact legislation to implement more stringent provisions in the Basic Law, signals that the enjoyment of rights is being gradually eroded.

Taiwan

Taiwan's media law formally guarantees freedom of speech, but it is, of course, not always as simple as that. Journalists find that while there might be freedom of speech, it is often extremely difficult to find out information from government departments that have a deep seated notion of secrecy. There is, however, a new freedom of information bill, which is based on the US Freedom of Information Act. In Taiwan, as elsewhere, globalization is bringing western influences to bear on the local media. Taiwan has about 160 newspapers of various kinds. The main newspapers print multiple editions of high quality colour and distribute them throughout the country. They have the latest computerized newsrooms, printing plants and high-speed presses. Taiwan is fast becoming a television culture for news and information, despite the large number of newspapers available throughout the country. There is more than one TV per household. TV stations are mainly in Mandarin with some Taiwanese, English and Hakka programmes. Radio is also booming with more frequencies than ever before. The networks broadcast newscasts throughout the day, particularly at the morning, lunch and evening peak times. For foreign coverage the networks have their own correspondents stationed overseas and also have arrangements with American networks to rebroadcast their news programmes.

In Taiwan, the four main media representative organizations publicly condemned the government-initiated wiretapping of reporters and searches of news media premises, describing the moves as an infringement of press freedom. The application of criminal law however, continues to be the major blot on Taiwan's press freedom copybook. On the 1st January 1988, the government ended its ban on new newspapers and a page limitation was also lifted.[25] According to an IPI Report, in 1991, "the Taiwanese press witnessed an almost entire absence of restriction on press freedom."[26] In 1992, the legislature revised the sedition law, formally allowing open discussions about the Taiwan independence movement. Since the lifting of martial law, the number of newspapers in Taiwan skyrocketed, from 31 in 1987 to 300 by the end of 1994. Among these new newspapers, the first opposition daily newspaper started in June 1989, the Capital Morning Post. However, this paper went out of business 14 months later, due to inability to attract advertisers.[27] The number of daily newspapers has declined to 25.[28] The print media have tended to become more liberal in their views and reporting than the electronic media. The main television stations are still influenced by political ideas.

The Taiwanese media are characterised by considerable partisanship, something which a KMT spokesman described is "a natural part of the democratization process." Opinions that were not allowed to surface during martial law are now spoken and written about openly. Editorial writing tends to be fiercely opinionated. The Taiwanese are very interested in financial laws. As Taiwan has developed economically, it has grown in television culture. Television has overtaken newspapers as the primary source of information. Taiwan receives several channels operated by government-owned networks where broadcasting is mainly in Mandarin, with some Taiwanese, English and Hakka programmes. Radio is booming. For foreign overage, the networks have their own correspondents stationed overseas and they rebroadcast a number of overseas law channels. The most dynamic aspect of Taiwan's media scene is the rapid development of cable. For years, owning a satellite dish, was prohibited; but as dishes became smaller, this law became possible to police. The government first lifted the ban on u-band equipment which allowed Japanese signals. In 1992, the ban was further lifted so that STAR TV could be made available. For many years, cable operations were not covered by any laws and programmes, which could be received in well over a third of Taiwan households, tended to be full of pirated programmes downloaded from international satellites without permission. But now the government has awarded a number of franchises for cable systems, each offering about 30 channels.

While print media have enjoyed freedom since 1988, electronic media remained under stringent government control through licensing, ownership and the appointment of top managerial staff who serve as news gatekeepers.[29] The three broadcast television stations, Taiwan Television Enterprise (TTV), China Television Company (CTV) and Chinese Television System (CTS) have been owned and controlled by the provincial government, the ruling kuomintang and the Ministry of Defence, respectively.[30] The situation started to change in the early 1990s. By 1993, the Cable Act had been passed, allowing private ownership of cable channels. Since then, the cable television industry has boomed; more and more private cable ventures have become involved in news, offering alternatives to government-owned broadcast networks' news programmes.[31] Taiwan now has 11 national cable news operations, with eight offering 24-hour news services, while four other over-the-air broadcasters offer newscasts. The proliferation of television news has turned this small island of 13,900 square miles with a population of 21 million into a society where news happens anytime, everywhere.

Cable news in Taiwan has not clearly shed its partisanship. The partisan nature of cable news operations is proven further by journalist perceptions of cable news founder motivations in starting news ventures. Most journalists, however, agree that cable news was an attempt to offer different news perspectives. Before the late 1980s when the Kuomintang (KMT) imposed authoritarian rule in Taiwan, television news was dominated by the three state-owned broadcasters: TTV, CTS and CTV. For the last 30 years, television news from these three broadcasters has been strongly criticised as biased towards KMT.[32] With the transition from authoritarian rule to democracy, the electronic media scene has been changing because of private ownership of cable T.V. Even though cable might be offering different news angles, journalists in Taiwan also say how hard it is for the old idea of using news operations as tools of power to die. Even though cable news stations are privately owned and free from direct government control, they still fail to function independently of political interference. Well over half the journalists working in Taiwan think they have autonomy in their daily reporting and editing. For Taiwanese journalists, the organisation's editorial policy influences the degree of autonomy they experience. Journalists' experience of autonomy also affects their job satisfaction. The more autonomous journalists feel, the more satisfied they are with their job. Cable journalists in Taiwan on the whole are a dissatisfied group. More than half of them feel dissatisfied with their work and only a third of them say they are satisfied in their work. Like American journalists, age and income also affect Taiwan Journalists' job satisfaction.

Journalists in Taiwan reject the authoritarian, and Confucian concept that media should support government policies in order to promote stability. They believe in the watchdog philosophy so dear to western journalists and believe it is the job of a journalist to report what happens critically. However, there is then a difference in interpretation of what being a watchdog of society means. Many Taiwan journalists say that being critical does not translate into being adversarial toward government; they emphasize more the media's responsibility of being neutral, giving equal weight to different opinions. A study by Lee[33] described journalists under the KMTs authoritarian rule as holding libertarian views. A later study found that journalists working under the present system in Taiwan continue their beliefs in the libertarian role of the press. Their perceptions resemble those of the American journalists, who emphasise more the media's interpretative and information dissemination functions and less the media's adversarial role.[34] Taiwan's political reform towards democracy has brought changes in its media system. The television news arena is no longer dominated by government-controlled broadcasters. Private ownership of cable has boosted local entrepreneurs to venture into the news business and this freedom has resulted in a proliferation of cable news channels. This phenomenon, as perceived by journalists, can be explained by cable's desire to offer audiences new perspectives different from the government-controlled broadcasters. This change, however, has not brought independence to private cable news channels.

Thailand

While Thailand continues to be a beacon of hope for media freedom in the region, recent worrying developments showed that freedoms are far from guaranteed. The media were not allowed to carry senate candidates' views, policies or perceived role in the Senate in the run-up to the country's first Senate election. Official intimidation also showed its ugly face. Several government officials tried to intimidate journalists for criticising the deputy prime minister.

Thailand has about 150 newspapers, about 40 of them dailies based in Bangkok. Almost all of the country's 73 provinces have local newspapers. Tabloid journalism of the most lucid and scandalous type is very popular. But broadsheet, more serious journalism, is also popular. The Thai media has its own taboo subjects, first among them the Royal Family. No paper, not even the most scurrilous and racy tabloid, would ever consider criticising the monarchy. Buddhism is also a taboo subject for media criticism. There is an English-language press, which is well read and highly regarded. Bangkok has two important English-language dailies, the Bangkok Post and the Nation. There are several Chinese language dailies which produce high quality journalism.

The Philippines

The Philippines and Thailand have a sharp news system that allows for aggressive, critical reporting. One of the major problems of reporting in countries of the Pacific-rim is to do with perceived and accepted taboo subjects. These might include criticism of the imperial family in Japan or the royal family in Thailand, and in countries such as Singapore and Malaysia, any writing that might inflame ethnic hostility, especially between the Malay and Chinese communities.

Freedom of the press is highly prized in the Philippines. And press freedom is enshrined in the law which states; "no law shall be passed abridging the freedom of speech, of expression or of the press. It also guarantees the right of the people to information on matters of public concern."[35] Libel law is particularly troublesome in this country.

Journalists have easy access to government information and can write critically about the people in power and serve as a watchdog on government functioning. Manila has over 20 daily newspapers. Television is of high quality, featuring both public and privately owned networks. Almost all the country's broadcast's belong to a self-regulating association known as the KBP (Kapisanan ng mga Brodkaster sa Pilipinas). Radio is the country's most important medium for communication, reaching 85 per cent of the country, compared with about 50 per cent for television and 25 per cent for newspapers. There are about 300 radio stations—commercial and non-commercial. Many radio stations do not have newsrooms and simply read stories from the newspapers. Radio also has the ability to reach listeners in their native dialects. Radio Veritas, for example, is a Catholic radio group based in Manila but which runs 45 radio and several TV stations throughout the archipelago. It broadcasts a number of news bulletins every day in about 35 different dialects. Ownership of the press in the Philippines is in the hands of powerful families. Large businesses are also buying up the industry.

Since President Joseph Estrada took office in the Philippines, several developments have brought the administration's commitment to freedom of the press into question. Critics have accused Estrada of curtailing media freedom in a country that has embraced the principles of free expression in recent years. In particular, an advertising boycott of the Philippine Daily Inquirer, the most widely circulated newspaper in the country, was generally considered to be official retaliation for critical reporting. Estrada also filed a huge libel suit against the Manila Times newspaper, seeking US$2.6 million in damages over a story that allegedly linked him to a government contract scandal. The paper apologized and the president withdrew the suit. A few months later, however, the Manila Times was shut down, having been bought by investors who reportedly have close political connections with the government. Relations between the media and the Office of the President have been fraught with tension but, promisingly, Estrada recently held a news conference in which he announced he had a millennium 'wish' for a "cease-fire" with the media.

Even in countries such as the Philippines or Macao, where the media remains among the freest in Asia, journalists often come under attack from local organized crime groups and drug syndicates, intimidating reporters who investigate their activities. Almost 40 journalists have been killed in the Philippines since democracy was restored in 1986, two of them in 1998. Most of the journalists killed were investigating official corruption and drug trafficking. In September 1998, a bomb blast injured ten journalists in Macau. This was just the latest in a series of attacks against journalists who openly reported criminal activities. Macau has been rocked in recent years by rising crime and frequent bombing, made worse by rival gangs or triads, fighting violent turf wars to gain control of illicit businesses.

Malaysia

As in other countries in the region, critical journalism is difficult in Malaysia. Much of this is to do with the culture of the country, and culture is not something that can be dismissed lightly. Development journalism is widely practised in Malaysia and there is a general expectation that the press will communicate government-supporting values and ideas. As in Singapore, government campaigns are regularly implemented for specific ends, and the media usually takes full part in these. However, government attitudes to the media and freedom of reporting are being liberalised, not least because of satellite television. New technologies continue to make it difficult here, as elsewhere, for Malaysia to be insulated from international journalism. Direct censorship is relatively rare but foreign newspapers and magazines sometimes have trouble with the authorities. Many Malaysian and international journalists familiar with Malaysia think that Malaysian newspapers generally perform their basic functions well and some feel better than in neighbouring Singapore.[36]

Malaysia's constitution does not explicitly provide for

freedom of the press but there is a Fundamental Liberties section, which guarantees free speech and expression. The government relies on several pieces of legislation to keep the press under control. These pieces of legislation give the Home Affairs minister, the power to ban publications deemed contrary to the country's interests, national security or public morality. Publishers also have to apply every year for a licence. The Official Secrets Act, of course, hinders investigative Journalism, as it does in many countries both West and East, but in this case, journalists writing a story have to prove that the information they are using is not classified before the story can be published. The Broadcasting Act gives the minister of information many powers to intervene and remove journalistic material that is going to be broadcast, if it is damaging to Malaysian values. The most important restraint is the Internal Security Act, which was originally implemented by the British colonial authorities. It was originally intended to combat communist insurgents but it is broad enough for subsequent governments to use it to stop opposition and criticism. Malaysia has also kept tight control over new media technologies. As in Singapore, satellite dishes are banned. The Malaysian Press publishes in four languages: English, Malay, Chinese and Tamil. The English-language press is the oldest and probably the most influential. These newspapers go back to 1845 (when the paper was called the Straits Times and published in Singapore which was then part of Malaya). When Singapore separated from the rest of the Malay Peninsula in 1965, the Straits Times continued to be published in Singapore and a new newspaper, the New Straits Times, was published in Kuala Lumpur. The Malay-language newspapers now are the most read in the country. Chinese-Language newspapers are also widely read. There is also a small Tamil-language press. Editorial decisions often reflect pro-government bias.

Newspapers are also widespread throughout the regions. In the states of Sabah and Sarawak, there are a number of small local Chinese papers. Some of these are multilingual, published in Chinese, Malay, English or local languages in varying combinations. Apart from the papers in states such as Sabah and Sarawak, the majority of Malaysian newspapers are based in Kuala Lumpur. There is not a strong provincial press and the larger cities like Penang and Malacca are served by the Kuala Lumpur papers.

Malaysia has a mixture of government run and private television. Satellite news services are provided through a government Pay-TV system. Ownership of Malaysian media often puts extra stresses and strains on press freedom. All the major newspapers are either owned by one of the ruling coalition parties or by financial interests closely associated with government in one way or another. Broadcasting is in a similar position. This gives politicians a strong means to influence editorial decision-making. As elsewhere, foreign publications and journalists sometimes run into trouble over reporting matters about Malaysia. Coverage of foreign affairs is largely dependent on the international news agencies, although there are sometimes complaints that these international news agencies are often too western in their reporting approach. The newspapers rely very heavily on the official Malaysian news agency, Bernama, as well as AP and Reuters. Bernarnei acts as the sole distributor of foreign news and it distributes it to client newspapers and takes a commission.

Singapore

Singapore, like Malaysia, uses the concept of 'Asian Allies' as justification for silencing critics. Self-censorship is for the news media which are largely state-controlled, permits are required for public speaking and publications, censorship is strict and libel laws are rigorously enforced. The former Soviet Asian republics are making only nominal progress in adopting a democratic system and journalists, broadcasters, and individual citizens enjoy little freedom to report facts or to express their opinion.

Additionally, Singapore's theories of a so-called Asian model of journalism are spreading fast through Asia, adopted by more and more governments to justify censorship and prohibit the import of specific publications, which apparently could undermine the stability of the state or contravene moral norms. Asian leaders often criticise what they call the western model of journalism, in which the media are free to report the news as they see it. They argue that the role of domestic media is to act responsibly, which is generally understood to mean supporting the goals of the elected leadership and the preservation of social harmony. Malaysian Prime Minister Mahathir has described westerners' notion of a free press as the freedom to tell lies and said that western media coverage is interested only in attracting readers without considering the damaging implications for society.[37]

In Singapore, a government-linked company operates all four 'independent' television channels and 10 of 15 radio stations. The Internet must be accessed through a government censor's server. All major newspapers and 20 per cent of cable television are owned by a commercial company with strong ties to the government. The English language paper, Straits Times, is well known internationally. Singaporeans are very comfortable with English, and so, the circulation of this paper is growing. While its domestic coverage remains close to the government line, its foreign news is drawn from a variety of sources and offers a comprehensive coverage. There are several Chinese-language and Malay-language newspapers and one Tamil language newspaper. All of them generally mirror the government line.

Singapore is a puzzle. It has a rather controversial media reputation. It is restrictive and the government makes no efforts to disguise the fact that its media are not free in the western sense to write and report everything it chooses. It is all a question of western versus eastern thought and ideas of freedom of the press. The original Singaporean leaders, notably Lee Kuan Yew, believed that western ideas of freedom were a mixed blessing and were not necessarily the right thing for a Confucian society such as Singapore. For western journalists working in Singapore, as well as for Singaporean journalists themselves trying to report Singapore affairs, this argument poses certain problems. Singapore has long held the view that foreign journalists should not criticise the domestic affairs of Singapore. Singaporean law allows much latitude in dealing with difficult journalists, and for overseas correspondents. One way of doing this is by refusing accreditation. But there is a thaw in government control, which has been noticed in the last 10 years, when the journalists worked there and during their subsequent visits. There is more questioning of government decisions but still reporters are inherently afraid to cross the line of discretion; so self-censorship is still rife. Singapore does have strict censorship laws. Any story that would fan the flames of ethnic tension is not allowed. Therefore, race, religion, language, relations with Malaysia and Indonesia—anything that might damage Singapore's reputation in the wider world—are subjects that the media in Singapore treat with extreme care and allow themselves to self-censorship. In their words, they take a cautious approach. The Singaporean constitution explicitly limits freedom of expression. There are laws which range from those concerned with internal security and sedition, which limit freedom of reporting and there are also powers which allow the government to close down what they deem to be undesirable publications if they are thought to be against the public interest. Then, there is the Newspaper and Printing Presses Act, which gives the government powers to restrict, but not ban, the circulation of any publication sold in the country that is deemed guilty of biased reporting. This is a power often used against foreign newspapers and magazines. Whether these powers are used or not is largely irrelevant. Journalists know the powers exist and so tend to be careful in what they report and how they report. Radio and TV news output is also closely controlled. Satellite TV is available but only through the government controlled cable system. Private ownership of satellite dishes is banned although some institutions such as newspapers have permits to operate them. The government's second strategy has been to develop its own satellite television system based on cable. It feeds some international networks direct to homes.

With few exceptions, Asia has still a long way to go before freedom of expression becomes a real part of life. Suppressing news is still very much an accepted practice. According to Barbara Trionfi, writing for the International Press Institute, "freedom of the press in many parts of Asia remains bleak."[38] All too often, she says, Journalists in the region have a choice when it comes to dealing with sensitive issues: avoid confrontation with officialdom or face imprisonment and brutal repression. Subtler methods of stifling unwanted voices such as harsh defamation legislation, advertising boycots and legal provisions designed to protect national security are also being widely and effectively deployed. Consequently, the practice of self-censorship is nudging towards epidemic proportions.[39]

Vietnam

The press in Vietnam remains shackled by the Communist government. Virtually all media outlets are operated by government-controlled or party-affiliated organisations. Most editors, publishers and reporters are Communist Party members and independent thinking is often violently repressed. The government controls all administrative aspects of the press, including approval and appointment of publishers and staff members. The party's Central Committee on Thought and Cultural Affairs controls press content by issuing guidelines and directives to editors.

Laos

Similarly, in Laos, the media is tightly restrained; domestic newspapers and radio and television broadcasting are under the government's watchful eye. Under Communist rule since the 1970s, Laos is one of the most tightly controlled societies in Asia. Recently, the Laotian government has initiated a tentative process of economic liberalisation, but there have been no moves to reform the political structure. The ruling Laos People's Revolutionary Party (LPRP) holds 98 out of the 99 National Assembly seats. Cambodia, on the other hand, is showing some signs of positive development in terms of media freedom. Prime Minister Hun Sen has recently become a proponent of press freedom, publicly praising the benefits to society of an unfettered media. While the motives may be linked more to foreign investment and donor aid than democratic principle, the policy has left some breathing room for the Cambodian media. The official rhetoric does not, however, guarantee the right to freedom of expression in Cambodia. For example, an anti-royalist newspaper was shut down in 1999, after it printed articles critical of King Sihanouk. The paper was banned from appearing for 30 days.

Besides, criminal charges were filed against it, and its printer was warned to stop printing the paper for the month. Legislation in Cambodia has a chilling effect on the press, containing provisions of jail terms for journalists found guilty of defamation and restrictive elements which are susceptible to official abuse. Furthermore, the independence of the judiciary is seriously questioned by many journalists. The elections in 1998 could not be deemed free and fair, largely because access to the media for the opposition parties was severely restricted.

Indonesia

Indonesia's media continues its battles to hold on to its new-found freedom. The fall of President Suharto gave a new lease of life to Indonesian journalists. To the surprise of man, his successor B.J. Habibie, started his tenure promisingly from the media's perspective, presenting grounds for cautious optimism. His short-term in office was significant in media terms as he systematically dismantled the oppressive legislative infrastructure that shackled the press during the 32-year Suharto era. Civil unrest simmers in many parts of Indonesia and many still consider the media a major agitator and claim that journalists don't behave responsibly. The chaos and unrest that regularly besets parts of the country makes reporting an immensely dangerous profession. Journalists have been killed and attacked, often by the security forces. Havoc and violence played a prominent role in East Timor in 1999 as the people voted on the issue of self-determination. The violence took a heavy toll of the media. Two journalists were murdered and about 300 were attacked and threatened. All the evidence suggests that Indonesian soldiers were responsible for the killings, and paramilitary groups backed by the Jakarta government identified the media as prime targets in the run-up to the referendum.

Turkmenistan

IPI describes the five Central Asian Republics as a virtual media freedom, desert. Probably the most repressive of the former Soviet states is Turkmenistan, where freedom of speech violations against local and foreign reporters have not diminished since 1992 and the government-controlled television and press provide few details on the country's political and social troubles. In Turkmenistan there is no need for censorship as self-censorship is so prevalent that newspapers silence themselves. There is no government harassment or repression of the independent media because there is no independent media. In recent years, independent media outlets have been shut down one by one.

Uzbekistan

Uzbek president, Karimov, professed a commitment to democratic media and reform, which he attempted to prove with the passage of a Law on the Mass Media. Several articles of this law, however, are worded in such a way that they could be used to punish government critics; one provision, for example, makes journalists responsible for the truth of the information contained in their news stories, potentially subjecting journalists to prosecution if a government official disagrees with a news report. Uzbek newspapers continue to be funded, and therefore, controlled by government organs like ministries and city governments, and meet direct censorship. In practice, the electronic mass media is stifled by an effective state-imposed self-censorship on journalists via highly bureaucratic re-registration requirements that each TV station must pass annually.

Tajikistan

Even though the political situation seems to be slowly normalizing in Tajikistan after the end of the civil war, the country remains a dangerous place for journalists, as the killing of a noted Tajik editor in 1998 shows. In Tajikistan, most private newspapers only survive with the help of government subsidies. Challenging the performance of the authorities would jeopardize their financial lifeline. The fact that there are no private printing presses or distribution networks also gives the government many opportunities to wield influence over private papers. On the private broadcasting front, however, there are local stations operating and, while under-resourced, they do have a reasonable presence in pockets of the country.

Kazakhstan

Censorship of the media and harassment of journalists have been common tactics used by the government in Kazakhstan to successfully curtail freedom of expression, association and assembly and the right to political participation. These tactics were glaringly evident in the run up to the recent elections. Kazakhstan president, in anticipation of the presidential elections, consolidated his control over the media, strictly banning any criticism of the president and the government.

The official attitude toward the media in countries such as Burma (Myanmar) or Afghanistan is now much more clearly defined, though not for the better. Even minimal attempts to report the facts are ruthlessly crushed. Burma's military junta keeps a strict control on the media, leaving no freedom either to local or foreign journalists. The Burmese press operates under strict censorship and citizens risk jail if they are found guilty of giving false information domestically or internationally. Since the junta took over, at least 14 Burmese journalists have been sent to jail, some have died there and the situation has not shown signs of much improvement. In 2000, Burma (Myanmar) was holding at least 13 journalists as prisoners. In 1999 censual assessment, Burma continues to be governed by draconian decrees and continues to brutally disregard human rights, including freedom of expression. Well over 1,000 political prisoners remain behind bars enduring the most appalling, inhumane conditions.[40]

Afghanistan

In Afghanistan, the fundamentalist Taliban regime has closed down local media and prevented, sometimes through physical means, the foreign press from covering the war and other sensitive issues. Any source of information or contact with the outside is considered a possible threat. An Iranian journalist was killed in 1998 by the Taliban forces and journalists working for foreign radio stations broadcasting from outside the border of the Taliban territory, are often harassed and even physically attacked.

Sri Lanka and Nepal

Civil wars and internal conflicts in Sri Lanka and Nepal are the major causes of harassment of journalists. In the course of 1998, in Nepal, at least eight journalists ended up in prison and newspapers were seized by police for denouncing police violence, corruption and the misconduct of security forces, who were presumed to have killed civilians in clashes with a Maoist rebel group in the west of the country. The Sri Lankan government, in its fight against the Tamil separatist movement, imposed direct censorship of military news under emergency regulations. This is obviously more as part of a political strategy than a military requirement for national security, which the government pretends.

Turkey

Twenty-five journalists are in prison in Turkey, more than any other country in the world. Journalists who are interpreted as advocating secession for the Kurdish people are the primary targets of the Turkish government's clampdown, and criticising the military has also resulted in the imprison-ment of journalists.

Africa

More than two-thirds of the world's least developed countries are in Africa. But despite the poverty, not everything is gloom. The movement towards democracy accelerated in the 1990s and this, in turn, meant that a number of independent newspapers and magazines became more influential. The press always had an important place in African political life, as have journalists. Africa is also one of the most dangerous places on earth for journalists practising global (and local) journalism. Many African leaders over the years started life as journalists but curiously, when they got power and became leaders of their country, they tended to exercise excessive control over the media. Africa has an image of having a problem over censorship and press freedom. The continent has fewer newspapers, radio and television sets than any other continent.[41] But there is hope that things are improving. Their two main problems, however, continue to be autocratic governments and poverty. Many African countries still control the media, and

harassment of journalists by governments and other groups is still prevalent. Press freedom is not as advanced as elsewhere in the world. Almost half of the 53 African countries that have signed human rights charters routinely violate the press freedom, and it is clear violation of those agreements, according to Reporters Sans Frontiers (RSF). The organization (RSF) says that a survey carried out in 2,000 shows that at least 22 African nations do not respect press freedom. They are Algeria, Angola, Burkina Faso, Cameroon, the Democratic Republic of Congo, Djibouti, Egypt, traditional Guinea, Ethiopia, Gabon, Kenya, Libya, Mauritania, Nigeria, Rwanda, Sierra Leone, Sudan, Swaziland, Togo, Tunisia, Zambia and Zimbabwe.

The watch group stated: Although the violations are not very serious, what their governments have in common is the fact that they do not respect the African Charter for Human and Peoples' Rights and the International Covenant on Civil and Political Rights. However, all 22 countries have signed and ratified at least one of those agreements.[42] In September 1999, Sudan's President Omar Bashir, launched numerous verbal attacks on the independent media, accusing them of serving the party of Satan, atheists and agent's of the opposition. In Tunisia, press freedom does not exist. Both state-run and private newspapers are subject to censorship, even when dealing with subjects seemingly unrelated to government; such is the environment or cultural heritage.

In Algeria, state monopolies on printing and advertising are ways of putting pressure on the private media. It is not unusual for the country's four state-owned printing works to demand immediate payment of a newspaper's debts if it has published articles regarded as critical. In Mauritania, a publication may be banned if it attacks the principles of Islam or the credibility of ·the state. The group (RSF) also asked the governments of the 15 European Union countries to take into account the press freedom records of African nations when entering into cooperation agreements with them.[43]

Australasia: Australia

Australia's first newspaper, The Sidney Gazette, 1803-42 was published by authority and was censored by Governors or their secretaries. John Dunmore Lang wrote that it was conducted.... as if its editor's situation had been that of a mastiff to His Excellency. Samuel Bennett claimed it was a mixture of fulsome flattery of government officials and inane twaddle on the matters.[44] In 1833, "The Currency Lad" was going in for Yellow Journalism in Australia. It discovered the popular appeal value of the police courts; its columns departed entirely from the legalistic reportage of the major cases in favour of the technique later popularized by John Nortan on a grander scale in truth. It humanized in short paragraphs the cases before the court, without any regard to their significance, but with a jaunty eye to their entertainment value."[45]

The media in this part of the world is among the freest in the world. It also has some of the best newspapers, particularly in Australia. Australia's newspapers looked originally to Britain as their model. The oldest mass circulation newspaper is the Sydney Morning Herald, which is one of the country's great dailies and has an average circulation of more than 400,000. It is owned by a Sydney family. The Melbourne Age is also one of the most prestigious papers and is owned by the Canadian, Conrad Black. There are newspapers in every capital city in Australia as well as in many regional centres. There are also some very small, but important and prosperous newspapers that have circulations of about 6,000, such as the Nasacort Herald in South Australia, They are all very modern in their technology. Most of them including the very small ones, have an online presence. Australia broadcasting is a mixture of public and private, and is broadly modeled on the United Kingdom's broadcasting. Commercial broadcasting started in 1924 and is highly popular around the country. Every small and medium sized city and town in Australia has at least one radio and television station; most of the towns have more. Public Service broadcasting is run by the Australian Broadcasting Corporation (ABC), a fiercely independent organization that takes its government watchdog role extremely seriously. In a country of such vast size, but small spread-out population, satellites were a great innovation for radio and television transmissions across the country. In Australia, negotiations between media and government tried to resolve the many unsettled issues affecting ownership and media policies, despite heavy lobbying by media groups, especially over the rules to be applied to the introduction of digital television. Cross-media rules restrict the ability of TV operators and media publishers to invest across each other's traditional borders. Australian radio was thrown into chaos over the Australian Broadcasting Authority's so called 'cash for comment' inquiry into the activities of two well-known radio broadcasters who have been accused of giving favourable on-air comments to companies and industries in return for undisclosed financial payments. The ownership of Australia's untrammeled media is already among the most concentrated in the world.

The newspaper press constitutes nearly the only literature published in the Australian colonies. It monopolises the greater part of the thought. The newspapers occupy the space of all literature and stop the channels of all information from all other sources, by far the largest class derives no information from any other quarter.[46]

New Zealand

New Zealand also has an excellent press and broadcasting system. The largest daily, the New Zealand Herald is published in Auckland. There are also newspapers in Wellington and in the south island. New Zealand broadcasting also adopted the BBC model in 1932. Television started there in 1960 run by the government-funded New Zealand Broadcasting Corporation (NZBC). In 1984, independent non-governmental TV began. News and current affairs form a large and important part of the output. New Zealand continues to enjoy an essentially free and unfettered press but issues such as privacy and court gagging orders continue to impede legitimate reporting and stifle debate. Although the media was explicitly excluded from the 1993 Privacy Act, many journalists feel the law still significantly impedes news-gathering and disseminating and acts as a deterrent to sources of information who are covered under the privacy law. Reflecting a global media concern, New Zealand's journalists are struggling with the privacy issue. Current legislation struggles to find an acceptable balance between rights relating to privacy and other rights relating to freedom of expression. The reporting of suicide also continues to be a thorny issue in New Zealand, which has one of the highest rates of youth suicide in the world. The current laws restrict the media from reporting on specific cases for fear that the reports will encourage other people to follow suit.

Papua-New Guinea (PNG) is located north of Australia in the Pacific and has a larger population than New Zealand's (which itself has a population of about the size of Sydney). The media in PNG is dependent in many ways on Australia. PNG has radio and television inherited from Australia. It broadcasts in more than 30 languages. While the principles of press freedom and freedom of expression are generally respected in Australasia and Oceania, the situation has deteriorated badly in some Pacific Island states. Papua New Guinea has a robust and essentially free news media. Peace agreements in the secessionist war on the island of Bougainville have eased tensions considerably. There were, however, reports of intimidation of the media by government supporters. Elsewhere in the Pacific, weeklies are the main staple diet with English as the dominant language for publication. Tahiti and New Caledonia, however, have French language newspapers. Radio came to the Pacific islands in 1935, with Fiji being the first country to have its own radio service. However, more than half of the current services in the Pacific started as late as 1960. They are, of course, strongly influenced by British and Australian broadcasting. Until the 1970s, most of them were staffed by expatriates from Australia and Britain; that is no longer the case. Television came generally to the Pacific islands in the 1950s and 1960s. They can all link into INTELSAT.

News agencies in the Australasian region are not well developed in number but in quality they are world class. The non-government New Zealand Press Association (NZPA) and the Australian Associated Press (AAP) serve their own countries and also the Pacific communities. AAP is based in

Sydney and serves both Fiji and Papua-New Guinea with output that it puts together from major world agencies and the output of its own members.

Media freedom came under heavy attack in the Solomon Islands when the government introduced emergency legislation that provided for imprisonment of up to two years, or a fine, for journalists who violated state-imposed reporting regulations. The legislation followed the declaration of a state of emergency following ethnic tension on the main island, Guadalcanal. The restrictions forbade printing, broadcasting or communicating information that incited violence or was likely to cause racial or communal disharmony. They also forbade printing, broadcasting or communicating information prejudicial to the safety or interests of the state or likely to cause disaffection with the government or hatred or contempt for the administration of justice or national security. The powers also restricted the printing, broadcasting or communicating of information from official documents. In order to avoid the risk of harsh penalties, the Solomon Islands Broadcasting Corporation stopped all live broadcasts of news produced by the British Broadcasting Corporation, Radio Australia and Radio New Zealand International. Foreign journalists covering the ethnic conflict in the Solomon Islands were also warned that they could be jailed, fined or banned under the state of emergency regulations.

World's Oldest Newspapers still in circulation

Post och Inrikes Tidningar (Sweden)	1645
Haarlems Dagblad (Netherlands)	1656
La Gazzetta di Mantova (Italy)	1664
The London Gazette (UK)	1665
Wiener Zeitung (Austria)	1703
Hildesheimer Allgemeiner Zeitung (Germany)	1705
Worcester Journal (UK)	1709
The Newcastle Journal (UK	1711
The Stamford Mercury (UK	1712
The Northampton Mercury (UK)	1720
Hanauer Anzeiger (Germany)	1725

The Belfast News-Letter (N. Ireland)	1737
Feuille d'Avis de Neuchatel (Switzerland)	1738
Darmstaedter Tageblatt (Germany)	1740
Press & Journal (UK)	1747
Berlingske Tidende (Denmark)	1749
Giessener Anzeiger (Germany)	1750
Leeuwarder Courant (Netherlands)	1752
The Yorkshire Post (UK)	1754
La Gazzetta di Parma (Italy)	1755
Provinciale Zeeuwse Courant (Netherlands)	1758
Norrkopings Tidningar (Sweden)	1758
Saarbriicker Zeitung (Germany)	1761
Schaumburger Zeitung (Germany)	1761
24 heures/Feuille d'Avis de Lausanne (Switzerland)	1762
Hersfelder Zeitung (Germany)	1763
Quebec Chronicle Telegraph (Canada)	1764
The Hartford Courant (USA)	1764
Lippische Landeszeitung (Germany)	1766
Aalborg Stiftstidende (Denmark)	1767
Adresseavisen (Norway)	1767
Feuile d'Yverdon (Switzerland)	1773
The Gazette (Canada)	1778
Neue Zurcher Zeitung (Switzerland)	1780
Golarsche Zeitung (Germany)	1783
Northampton Daily Hampshire Gazette (USA)	1786
The Times of London (UK)	1788
The Berkshire Eagle (USA)	1789
Zwolse Courant (Netherlands)	1790
The Observer (UK)	1791
Tauber-Zeitung (Germany)	1791
Jeversche Wochenblatt (Germany)	1791
Norwich Bulletin (USA)	1791
Greenfield Recorder (USA)	1792
Rutland Herald (USA)	1794
Thurgauer Zeitung (Switzerland)	1798
Gazette de Lausanne (Switzerland)	1798
Keene Sentinel (USA)	1799
Nijmeegs Dagblad (Netherlands)	1800
Bote vom Unter-Main (Germany)	1803
The Bedford Gazette (USA)	1805

Schleswig-Holst. Landeszeitung (Germany)	1807
Concord Monitor (USA)	1808
Soclinger Tageblatt (Germany)	1809
New Haven Register (USA)	1812
Mobile Register (USA)	1813
Arnhemse Courant (Netherlands)	1814
Le Journal de la Corse (France)	1815
Cellesche Zeitung (Germany)	1817
Ludwigsburger Kreiszeitung (Germany)	1818
Westfalischer Anzeiger (Germany)	1822
The Bombay Samachar (India)	1822
Abo Underrattelser (Finland)	1824
Cannstatter Zeitung (Germany)	1824
Union-News & Sunday Republican (USA)	1824
Kennebec Journal (USA)	1825
El Peruano (Peru)	1825
Le Figaro (France)	1826
El Mercurio de Valparaiso (Chile)	1827
Stamford Advocate (USA)	1829
Providence Journal (USA)	1829
Aftonbladet (Sweden)	1830
Sydney Morning Herald (Australia)	1831
The Gleaner (Jamaica)	1834
Kalamazoo Gazette (USA)	1837
The Tuam Herald (Ireland)	1837
The Times-Picayune (USA)	1839
Sidney Morning Herald (Australia)	1840
The Geelong Advertiser (Australia)	1840
The (Tasmania) Examiner (Australia)	1842
The Plain Dealer (USA)	1845
Straits Times (Singapore)	1845
The Herald (South Africa)	1845
The Witness (South Africa)	1846
The Age (Australia)	1854
The Daily Telegraph (UK)	1855
The Sacremento Bee (USA)	1857
Atuagagdliutit (Greenland)	1861
The Northern Scot (Scotland)	1870
The Daily Californian (USA)	1871
The Salt Lake Tribune (USA)	1871

The Mainichi Shimbun (Japan)	1872
The Bay City Times (USA)	1873
Diario de Noticias-Madeira (Portugal)	1876
Cape Times (South Africa)	1876
Dagens Nghter (Sweden)	1878
Asahi Shimbun (Japan)	1879
The Ohio State Lantern (USA)	1881
The Financial Times (UK)	1888

EUROPE

Britain has a free press. There is no censor and no licensing and any one can publish a newspaper provided he does not break the law in doing so. The press is in private hands. There is no government control over newspapers, no government shareholding in a newspaper and a press gets no form of government help other than exemption from value added tax. The sessions of parliament are open to the press. The working of the government is reported and commented on, as is the working of all other public institutions. The freedom of the press is not inscribed on tablets as it is in the American constitution; it exists by consensus and the freedom British newspaper enjoy and for which Journalists fought over the centuries has to be guarded by editors, by political parties and by the people who care about these matters.[1]

Regular newspaper publication in United Kingdom dates from the mid 17th century. Prior to that, it was believed that the "reckless" reporting of news might endanger the Crown and the country. A limit was placed on the printing of news other than of events abroad, natural disasters, royal declarations and crimes. There were weekly Corantos published from the 1620s containing these kinds of news. Publication grew following the general relaxation after the ending of the Star Chamber in 1641. During the Civil War, there were regular news-sheets and then news books carrying general information along with propaganda. Following the Restoration, there arose a number of publications including the London Gazette (first published on November 16, 1665 as the Oxford Gazette), the first official journal of record and the newspaper of the Crown.

Publication was controlled under the Licensing Act of 1662, but the Acts lapsed from 1679-1685 and then in 1695, that encouraged number of new titles. There were twelve London newspapers (the Daily Currant was the first London newspaper) and provincial papers by the 1720s and by the early 19th century, there were 52 London papers and over 100 other titles.

As stamp paper and other duties were progressively reduced from the 1830's onwards (and all duties on newspapers were gone by 1855), there was a massive growth in overall circulation as major events occurred and improved communications developed the public's need for information. The Daily Universal Register began life in 1785 and was later to become 'The Times' from 1788. This was the most significant newspaper of the first half of the l9th century, but from around 1860 there were a number of more strongly competitive titles, each differentiated by its political biases and interests. The Manchester Guardian was founded in Manchester in 1821, by a group of non-conformist businessmen. Its most famous editor, Charles Prestwich Scott, made the Manchester Guardian into a world-famous newspaper in the 1890s. It is now called The Guardian. The Chartist Northern Star first published on May 26, 1838, was a pioneer of popular Journalism, but was very closely linked to the fortunes of the movement and was out of business by 1852. At the same time, there was the establishment of more specialized periodicals and the first cheap/economical newspaper was the Daily Telegraph and Courier (1855), later to be known simply as the Daily Telegraph. From 1860 until around 1910 is the period considered a 'golden age' of newspaper publication, with technical advances in printing and communication combined with a professionalization of journalism and the prominence of new owners—Newspapers became more partisan and there was the rise of new or yellow journalism (see William Thomas Stead). Socialist and labour newspapers also proliferated, and in 1912, the Daily Herald was launched as the first daily newspaper of the trade union and labour movement.

First World War saw the rise of the 'press barons' initially, the Harmsworth Brothers (later Viscounts Northcliffe and Rothermere) and the Berry Brothers. A trend continued between the wars when in the WW-I, the barons were joined by Max Aitken (later Lord Beaverbrook) and the newspaper industry took on an appearance similar to today's. The post-war period was marked by the emergence of tabloid newspapers (or red tops) notably with Cecil Harmsworth King and his International Publishing Corporation. In the 1980s, the powerful print of trade unions were challenged and production moved away from Fleet Street, marked by the successes of Rupert Murdoch and the Sun in the 1980s and 1990s. Currently, their circulation is in a slow but steady decline but still comparatively high.

More recently, the National Union of Journalists (NUJ) has complained of declining wages in the local press, which some claim are a result of increasing consolidation of the local newspaper industry. In March 2006, Labour MP, Austin Mitchell, called for a debate on the matter and encouraged the UK parliament to enact legislation to regulate the sector. In the perceived gap left by local newspapers, many of which have closed 'district' offices in smaller towns, local news websites are emerging. Examples of this include a website for the town of Bourne, in Lincolnshire, which is run by former Fleet Street journalist, Rex Needle, and RuberyVillage.co.uk which is run by teenagers and provides news for the West Midlands village of Rubery.

British Newspapers according to Chronological Order

- 1900—April 24: Daily Express launched by Pearson and become first national daily to put news on the front page.
- 1902—Jan 17: Times Literary Supplement launched.
- 1903—Nov. 2: Daily Mirror launched by Harmsworth. First daily illustrated exclusively with photographs.
- 1907: National Union of Journalists (NUJ) founded.
- 1908—Nov. 14: Illustrated Weekly Budget launched and became the only newspaper in the world printed in colour. Only seven issues published.

- 1909—March 2: Daily Sketch launched and later merged with the Daily Mail in 1971.
- 1911: Copyright Act.
- 1911—Jan 25: Daily Herald launched and became first newspaper to sell two million copies.
- 1913—April 12: New Statesman founded by Sidney Webb.
- 1915: 'Teddy Tail'—first British comic strip—in the Daily Mail.
- 1915—March 14: Sunday Pictorial launched by Rothermere and became Sunday Mirror in 1963.
- 1916: Daily Express bought by Max Aitkin.
- 1918—Dec. 29: Sunday Express launched.
- 1922—Aug. 14: Death of Lord Northcliffe.
- 1924—Nov. 2: First crossword in a British newspaper, in the Sunday Express.
- 1926—May: Most newspapers suspended during the General Strike. Government publishes British Gazette;
- 1930—Jan. 1: Daily Worker launched and became Morning Star in1966.
- 1930—Feb. 1: First Times crossword.
- 1930—June 2: News Chronicle formed by the merger of the Daily News and the Daily Chronicle and later merged with Daily Mail in 1960.
- 1931: Audit Bureau of Circulations formed.
- 1932—Aug. 23: British Museum Newspaper Library opened at Condole in North London.
- 1934—Oct. 18 : Daily Mail publishes the first photograph be transmitted by beam radio (from Melbourne to London).
- 1938—Oct. 1: Picture Post launched by Edward Hulton and ceased its publication in 1957.
- 1940: Newsprint rationing introduced.
- 1940—Nov. 26: Death of Lord Rothermere.
- 1940— Daily Worker and Week suppressed.
- 1947: First Royal Commission on the Press.
- 1953: General Council of the Press formed.
- 1954—Oct. 3: The Manchester Sunday paper's Empire was set-up; its first Cardiff edition as

Wales's Own day Paper: Printed in Wales for Wales'.

- 1959—Aug. 24: Manchester Guardian changes title to Guardian based in London.
- 1961: Second Royal Commission on the Press.
- 1961—Feb. 5: Sunday Telegraph launched.
- 1962—Feb. 4: Launch of Sunday Times magazine as Sunday Times Colour Section.
- 1964: Press Council replaces General Council of the press.
- 1964—June 9: Death of Lord Beaverbrook.
- 1964—Sept. 6: Observer colour supplement launched.
- 1964—Sept. 15: Daily Herald becomes the Sun.
- 1964—Sept. 25: Daily Telegraph magazine launched.
- 1966: Times bought by Roy Thomson owner of the daily Times.
- 1966—May 3: Times begins printing news on the front page.
- 1969: News of the World bought by Rupert Murdoch.
- 1969: Sun re-launched as a tabloid by Rupert Murdoch.
- 1974 : Third Royal Commission on the Press.
- 1976 : Evening Post (Nottingham) becomes the first British newspaper to introduce direct input by journalists.
- 1978—Nov. 2: Daily Star launched.
- 1978—Dec. 1 : Publication of the Times and Sunday
- 1978—Times suspended for eleven months.
- 1979: Financial Times launches international editor, Frankfurt am Main, Germany.
- 1980: Daily Star printed simultaneously by facsimile in London and Manchester.
- 1980: British Library Newspaper, Library Newsletter, launched Became Newspaper Library News in 1997.
- 1980—Oct. 31: Closure of Evening News leaves London with just one evening newspaper.

- 1981: Rupert Murdoch buys the Times and Sunday Times.
- 1981—May 3: Sunday Express magazine launched.
- 1981—Sept. 6: News of the World magazine Sunday, launched.
- 1982—May 2: Mail on Sunday launched: the first photocomposed national newspaper in Britain.
- 1984: Robert Maxwell buys the Mirror Group.
- 1984—Oct. 2: Daily News (Birmingham) launched by Bullivant. The UK's first free daily title.
- 1985: Telegraph bought by Conrad Black.
- 1986: News International moves all national titles to it at Wapping.
- 1986—March 4: Today launched by Eddy Shah, first national coloured newspaper.
- 1986—Sept. 14: Sunday Sport launched.
- 1986—Oct. 7: Independent launched.
- 1987: Today bought by Rupert Murdoch.
- 1987: First women editors of national newspapers in modern times: Wendy Henry News of the World and (Sunday Mirror).
- 1987—Feb. 24: London Daily News launched by Robert Maxwell: the first attempt at a 24-hour newspaper in Britain. Ceased publication on 23 July.
- 1987—April· 26: News on Sunday launched. Ceased publication in November.
- 1988—Aug. 7: Scotland on Sunday launched.
- 1988—Aug 17: Sport launched, initially appearing every Wednesday.
- 1989—March 5: Wales on Sunday launched in Cardiff.
- 1989—Sept. 17: Sunday Correspondent launched. Ceased pu.blication on 25 November 1990.
- 1990—Jan. 28: Independent on Sunday launched.
- 1990—May 11: European launched by Robert Maxwell. Ceased publication on 14 December 1998.
- 1991: Press Complaints Commission replaces the Press Council.

- 1991—Oct. 7: Sport becomes daily.
- 1991—Nov. 5: Death of Robert Maxwell.
- 1992: Dundee Courier becomes the last daily in Britain to put news not advertisements on its front page.
- 1993: Observer bought by Guardian Media Group.
- 1994: Electronic Telegraph launched: first British national paper on the Internet.
- 1995—Nov. 17: Today ceases publication: first national paper to close since the Daily Sketch.
- 1996—April 21: Sunday Business launched.
- 1997—Nov. 11: Shetland Times versus Shetland News.
- 1998—March 15: Sport First launched: Britain's first national Sunday newspaper dedicated to sport.
- 1998—June 10: Death of Sir David English, the editor who transformed the fortunes of the Daily Mail.
- 1998—Sept.: Death of Vere Harmsworth, Third Viscount Rothermere.
- 1999—Feb. 7: Sunday Herald (Glasgow) launched.
- 1999—March 16: Metro launched: a daily newspaper distributed free to travellers on the London Underground.
- 2000—Sept. 20: Business a.m. launched: the first news, daily newspaper in Scotland for 100 years.

Press freedom is, of course, basic to countries of Western Europe and also now to the emerging countries from the old Eastern Europe. Having said that, there are in all European countries some forms of restriction on the media and its journalists.

Scandinavian countries rank at the top of the tree for press freedom, but even there, the government has set some rules. Swedish law, for example, not only forbids government officials from asking journalists to reveal their sources but also won't allow reporters to reveal a source without that person's permission. Scandinavia started the now widespread system of press councils and ombudsmen, but apart from

Sweden, Finland, Norway, Denmark and the United Kingdom no other European country has them. The ombudsman idea started in Sweden in the 1960s and then moved to the United States and elsewhere.

Europe has a wide range of libel and privacy laws. In France, such laws are very complex and restrictive. Nordic countries have strong protections against libel but cases are more often handled by press councils or those involved rather than by the courts. In this, they are very similar to Thailand, where the same principles broadly apply. The most radical changes in government-media relations in Europe have been the way broadcasting has evolved from being a highly controlled medium to being more independent and run by commercial organizations in a similar way to newspapers. There is also a great disregard for the idea that comes to the surface so often that there should be a Europe-wide set of press laws and guidelines for journalistic conduct for anyone reporting in Europe. That has not been popular with journalists. In Europe, as indeed around the world, the practice of global journalism has at its forefront the ideals of press freedom. Freedom of the press is a balance between protection from government interference and the right of an individual to personal reputation.

United States

In America the first Newspaper appeared in Boston in 1690, entitled as Public Occurrences. Published without authority, it was immediately suppressed, its publisher arrested and all copies were destroyed. Indeed, it remained forgotten until 1845 when the only known surviving example was discovered in the British Library. Boston, the largest town in the colonies with about 10,000 population in 1704 had John Campbell, A Canny, cautious Scotchmen, founded the Boston Newsletter, the first continuously published American Newspaper. Campbell was 51 when be began his paper, he had built up a small business as a bookseller and had been incharge of the post for two years. The newspaper which was the result of Campbell's substitution of the printing press for the pen was on what the printers called a half sheet. The early newsletter seems very unexciting to a modern reader but its news value should not be underestimated. Campbell had correspondents at several important points, though they were neither regular nor efficient.[2] The first successful newspaper was the Boston News-Letter, started by Postmaster, John Campbell, in 1704. Although it was heavily subsidized by the colonial government, the experiment was a near-failure, with very limited circulation. In the early years of its publication the News-Letter, was filled mostly with news from London. Journals detailing the intrigues of English politics and a variety of events concerning the European wars. The rest of the newspaper was filled with items listing ship arrivals, deaths, sermons, political appointments, fires, accidents and the like. One of the most sensational stories published when the News-Letter was the only newspaper in the colonies was the account of how Blackboard, the pirate, was killed in hand-to-hand combat on the deck of a sloop, that had engaged his ship in battle.

Campbell relinquished his stewardship of the paper in 1722 to Bartholomew Green, its printer. Editor Green devoted less space to overseas events and more to domestic news. When Green died after a decade as its editor, the News-Letter was inherited by his son, John Draper, also a printer. Draper proved to be a better editor and publisher than his predecessors. He enlarged the paper to four sized pages, filling it with news from Boston, other towns throughout the colonies and from abroad. Two more papers made their appearance in the 1720's, in Philadelphia and New York, and the Fourth Estate slowly became established in the new continent. By the eve of the Revolutionary War, some two dozen papers were issued in all the colonies, although Massachusetts, New York and Pennsylvania remained the centres of American printing for many years. Articles in colonial papers, brilliantly conceived by revolutionary propagandists, were a major force that influenced public opinion in America from reconciliation with England to full political independence. Many individuals and groups have claimed that the media in America care more about ratings and selling newspapers than they do about maintaining or developing the social and ethical fabric of their nation.

The "Mighty Pulitzer" of U.S. Journalism

The two main arms of U.S. journalism today, print media and electronic media, are divided as well into three main approaches:

1. the "new news" of daily journalism as exemplified by the daily newspaper, evening television news, or radio "news-on-the-hour" with the latest from AP, plus cable and Internet sources;
2. weekly or periodical journalism as typified by *Time* as well as the better television discussion shows like *Meet the Press* and *Washington Week in Review;*
3. commentary or opinion journalism in various periodicals; *The New Republic, Nation, Foreign Affairs, Atlantic,* and Sunday editions of some dailies, as well as books, are examples.

The expectations for objectivity, balance, and fairness are much higher, naturally, for daily journalism, which reports the first version of events, than for the more leisurely weekly and opinion publications or the talk shows of weekend television. Daily journalism also has room for editorial comment and interpretation, but the expectation is that comment and predictions should be clearly identified and separated from hard or just appearing news.

THE PRINT MEDIA

Daily Newspapers

Although viewed by some as a twilight industry, the daily newspaper is still the most effective means of supplying large amounts of serious late breaking news to the American public. A total of about 1,500 dailies are published, roughly 40 per cent in the morning and 60 per cent in the afternoon, with a total circulation of about 63 million. Almost all metropolitan papers come out in the morning to better compete with television.

Circulations vary widely. Fifteen dailies have a circulation of more than 500,000, whereas more than 1,129 dailies have circulations under 25,000 and are primarily concerned with serving small cities and communities.

The backbone and intellectual leadership of daily journalism comes from the 40-45 dailies, each with circulations of more than 250,000 and includes all those considered the best plus a number of mediocre or fading dailies.

A recent survey by the *Columbia Journalism Review* of 150 daily newspaper editors produced the following rankings for what they considered to be America's 21 best daily newspapers:

> 1. New York Times; 2. Washington Post; 3. Wall Street journal; 4. Los Angeles Times; 5. Dallas Morning News; 6. Chicago Tribune; 7. Boston Globe; 8. San lose Mercury News; 9. St. Petersburg Times; 10. The Sun (of Baltimore); 11. Philadelphia Inquirer; 12. The Oregonian; 13. USA Today; 14. Seattle Times;15. Newsday, 16. Raleigh News & Observer; 17. Miami Herald; 18. Star Tribune (of Minneapolis); 19. Atlanta Journal-Constitution; 20. Orange County Register (of Santa Anna); 21. Sacramento Bee.[3]

From this elite group, the largest and presumably the most influential dailies include: The *Wall Street Journal* (daily circulation about 1.7 million) is primarily a business publication but is noted for its excellent news coverage and fine writing on non-business topics. Owner is the Dow Jones Co., which has 14 other papers.

USA Today (circulation about 2 million) is also distributed nationally and is owned by the Gannett Co., which has 74 dailies and a total daily circulation of more than 6.6 million. The paper has received mixed reviews but is considered to be improving and is carrying more hard news.

The New York Times has a Sunday circulation about 1.7 million, of which about 200,000 comes from its national edition. Although undergoing marked changes in recent years, the *Times is* still considered by many as the nation's most influential newspaper and targets an elite readership.

As mentioned, the large circulations of *The Wall Street*

journal, USA Today, and *The New York Times* are due in part to their national distribution; facsimile newspaper pages are sent via satellite to regional printing plants around the nation.

The Los Angleles Times (about 1.3 million Sunday) is one of the notable success stories in U.S. journalism, changing in the past 40 years from a parochial, partisan paper into the finest newspaper west of the eastern seaboard. (In March 2000, the paper and the Times Mirror Company were purchased by the Tribune Company of Chicago.)

The Washington Post (Sunday circulation about one million) is highly regarded and wields great influence in the political vortex of the nation's capital. The Washington Post Co. also owns *Newsweek* as well as broadcast and cable properties. The paper competes head-to-head with *The New York Times* on major stories in Washington but targets the greater Washington area for readers.

The *New* York Times, *Washington Post,* Los Angeles Times and Wall Street journal—all maintain significant numbers of their own reporters in key capitals overseas. In truth, concern about the global economy and political instability of the world beyond American shores and the willingness to report foreign news is one of the hallmarks of a great news medium. Much of this outstanding reporting finds its way to other dailies through syndication.

Another major newspaper group is Knight-Ridder Inc. with 29 papers enjoying a circulation of 4,136,770. Highly regarded among its properties are The Miami *Herald, The* Charlotte Observer, San Jose Mercury News, and *The Phladelphia Inquirer, each* an outstanding daily, with great influence in its city and suburbs. For $1.65 billion, Knight-Ridder acquired two big additions, The Kansas City Star, circulation 291,000, and *The Fort Worth* Star-Telegram, circulation 240,000, from the Disney Co. in April 1997.

Finally, Newhouse Newspapers has 26 dailies with a circulation of 2,960,360 including The *Oregonian. Newhouse* also owns The New Yorker and the Conde Nast magazines.

Weekly Newspapers

At the other end of the circulation scales are the 7,400 to 7,500 weekly newspapers that average about 7,500

subscribers each. Total circulation of these publications, so important in so many small communities, is about 55 million, more than double the mid-1960s total. Although often small and unimposing, these papers are close to their readers and usually serve their communities well. Local news dominates these papers.[4]

Magazines

Certainly, the most diverse and perhaps the most changeable, yet resilient of the media, have been magazines, of which about 4,000 are published, up from 2,500 in the mid-1980s. Carmody reported that 832 new magazines started in 1994; 67 of these were about sports and 44 were related to sex. Each year, about 80 per cent of newly launched magazines fail.

Comparatively, few magazines are mainly concerned with journalism and news but, overall, magazines contribute tremendous amounts of diverse information and entertainment available to the public. As seen later, U.S. magazines are increasingly popular overseas.

Leading news magazines and their approximate circulations are: Time (4.1 million); *Newsweek* (3.2 million); and U.S. *News and World* Report (2.3 million). Business magazines such as *Money* (2.2 million), *Business Week* (900,000), and Fortune and *Forbes* (each about 770,000) contribute to the public affairs news as do *Atlantic*, Harper's, and *The New Yorker.*

Though modest in circulations, opinion journals such as the *New Republic, Nation,* and *National Review* have a disproportionate influence on politicians, opinion makers and intellectuals, particularly in Washington, DC and New York City.

Books

Over 50,000 new book titles are published annually in the United States and a significant number contribute directly to the swirling cauldron of journalism. Ever since Theodore H. White wrote The *Making of* the President, 1960, after John Kennedy defeated Richard Nixon, journalists have been writing numerous books on national politics and public affairs. However, the two political best sellers of 1996—Primary Colors by Anonymous (Joe Klein) and *Rush Limbaugh is a Big Fat Idiot* by Al Franken—were essentially satire and entertainment, not political journalism.

Nowadays, almost all candidates for the presidency kick off their campaign by publishing a book to publicize themselves and their political ideas; such efforts qualify as political journalism. Of interest here is that journalists have been writing books critical of media performance. Important recent efforts include *Breaking the News* by James Fallows, Hot Air: *All Talk. All the Time* and Spin Cycle both by Howard Kurtz, *Feeding the* Beast by Kenneth T. Walsh, *Don't Shoot* the Messenger by Bruce Sanford, Warp Speed by Bill Kovach and Tom Rosenstiel, Life: *The Movie* by Neal Cabler, and What the People *Know* by Richard Reeves.

Electronic Media

Radio is ubiquitous and has been for most of the 20th century. Receiving sets are everywhere, in almost every car, scattered around the house, and carried by young people and joggers. There are 500 million sets in America. The nation is served by more than 8,454 radio stations of which 3,764 are AM stations and 4,690 are FM stations. About 70 per cent of the audience listens to FM. Many big city radio stations today are quite profitable.

Hard hit by the advent of television, radio was slow in finding a new niche. It no longer seeks its previous mass audience and offers instead narrow formats in various kinds of music and news, plus a smattering of network programming, especially in news. Radio's survival has offered additional proof that older media are supplemented by new media, not replaced by them.

Radio's journalistic contributions appear to consist mainly of brief newscasts stressing local and regional news, as well as headlines and brief reports on national and foreign events. As mentioned, two shining exceptions are National Public Radio's *Morning Report* and All *Things Considered* heard all over the nation on public stations. These programmes make important contributions to the reporting and analysis of public affairs. Public radio has disproved the conventional wisdom that government support of broadcasting compromises journalistic quality and independence.

A good deal is written about television news and its ups and downs. To set the scene briefly, here are a few basic facts: More than 1,290 commercial licenses have been granted by the Federal Communications Commission (FCC). Of these, about half are VHF, with a far-reaching signal, and half are UHF stations, more numerous and limited in reach.

Viewers have access to about 350 noncommercial or public television stations. More than 400 commercial stations are independent, not affiliated with the four major networks—CBS, ABC, NBC, and Fox. (Two fledgling networks, UPN and WB, are trying to break into prime time.) Television markets vary widely from New York City with about 7 million television households, all the way to Alpena, Michigan, with just 15,600 households with television sets.[5]

Ninety-eight per cent of homes have television sets and research suggests that sets are on seven hours a day in a typical home. About 80 per cent of homes have a video cassette recorder (VCR) and 60 per cent receive cable. Both VCR and cable percentages are steadily increasing as are satellite receivers. There were 1,594 total cable systems across the nation. Cable channels such as CNN and MSNBC have become major outlets for both news and public affairs programming.

Most Americans are aware of television's importance as a news medium. If at any time, there are rumours of a disaster or other ominous event, people will first turn on their television sets or, if away from home, their radios. But they are more likely today to find the breaking news on a cable station than a broadcast outlet.

Public television stations have made their own significant contributions to broadcast journalism primarily in recent years through the *News Hour with Jim Lehrer* and various documentary news programmes such as *Frontline, Nova, The American Experience,* and so on. With the exception of CBS' 60 *Minutes,* news documentaries or news magazines on commercial networks rarely reach the journalistic quality of those on PBS.

Another important contributor to broadcast news is C-

SPAN, the non-profit cable channel created to report on the legislative process in the U.S. Congress. In addition, it provides television coverage, without comment or interpretation, of a wide variety of meetings, conferences, or seminars, all of which have some connection to public affairs. C-SPAN has a small but devoted group of listeners who care about public affairs.

These national media have overlapping audiences and, to a great extent, reach the movers and shakers of the American establishment leaders in government, politics, social affairs, business, and academia, especially along the eastern seaboard from Boston to Atlanta and throughout the Midwest and the West Coast.

Legal Restraints

All countries have legal issues that affect the way reporting occurs both internally and externally. Some of these concern the law; others are about more general principles of freedom to report and freedom to find out and gather the news. In countries such as the US, Sweden, Canada, Norway, Greece, Holland, Australia, New Zealand, Ireland and France, there is some kind of freedom of information legislation. In these countries, there is a presumption that the public has a right to know what is happening. Government files are by and large open for inspection. Freedom of information legislation has yet to be fully enacted in some other countries, most notably in the United Kingdom. In countries such as Australia, internal discussions can be disclosed if it is in the public interest. In the United States, the American Freedom of Information Act is a major tool for journalists wanting to find out what government or big corporations are doing. It is a federal act which requires federal agencies to provide certain information. It is also a federal act in Australia.

The degree of press freedom in the world has been declining over the recent years. Governments tend to use legal means rather than outright oppression or violence. A survey, "News of the Century: Press Freedom 1999," by Freedom House, monitored political and civil rights worldwide. Freedom House ranks press freedom on a scale of 1 to 100, with a lower score indicating a country with a freer press. In 1998, the average press-freedom level of 186 countries was 49.04, a decline from 1997 of nearly 3 per cent. The trend reverses the movement towards greater press freedom, declared Leonard R. Sussman, coordinator of the survey. "While physical attacks, even murder and arrest of journalists, have ended, regimes increasingly use subtle legislation such as 'insult laws' to restrict criticism,"[6] Sussman added and noted that some reductions in press freedom were found in 53 countries, while slight improvement was noted in only 20. The survey suggested that there was a growing form of censorship by stealth whereby innocuous-sounding laws were used to restrict reporting and inspire self-censorship. These laws generally emphasise the 'duties' of journalists to protect national security, public health and morals and the reputations of citizens, especially rulers and their parties. The survey listed 68 countries (36% of the world's total) as having a free press, 52 (28%) partly free and 66 (36%) with news media that are not free. Major declines in press freedom were noted in Ghana, Peru, and Jordan, whose media declined from partly free to not free, while Namibia and Samoa declined from free to partly free.

Most reductions in news media freedom were marginal. Yet only 1.2 billion people live in nations with a free press, 2.4 billion where the press is partly free, and another 2.4 billion in not-free nations. Improvement was noted in Bosnia-Herzegovina, Indonesia, and Nigeria, which moved from not free to partly free. Mongolia, Slovakia, and Thailand entered the free category from the partly free. The most notable improvement was registered in Nigeria. With the death of the country's dictator, many press restrictions were removed. In Asia, the press was rated not free in Malaysia and Singapore. The financial crisis that provoked riots in Malaysia caused the government to criticise and censor foreign journalists and to exert additional pressures on the domestic news media. With the fall of the Suharto government, Indonesian journalists enjoyed a marked improvement in press freedom. Peru's newspapers and magazines felt increasing pressure from President Fujimori, who, many believe, is planning to run for a constitutionally prohibited third term. Since 1992, many print and broadcast journalists have been intimidated by libel suits, detention, house arrest, and in one famous case the revocation of a television station owner's citizenship. As the Internet asserts itself as an increasingly dominant force for the dissemination of news and information, questions of professional ethics become even more serious. One of the big issues for journalists in their relationship with online journalism and the web is the vexed problem of intellectual property rights. The issue has been festering globally since at least 1996 when journalists began to discover that their work was being distributed without their knowledge on the Internet or in other electronic media. Internet-based publishers are eager to foster good relationships with dependable freelancers. One way to achieve this is to ensure that in the new digital journalism age, revenue is going to the journalists creating the original material. There can be no free press where those who are working within it are abused. For journalists and other freelancers, copyright is the foundation of their livelihood.

The subject matter of copyright is usually described as literary and artistic works, that is, original creations in the fields of literature and arts. The form in which such works are expressed may be words, symbols, music, pictures, three-dimensional objects, or combinations thereof. Practically all national copyright laws provide for the protection of the following types of works:

- literary works irrespective of their content (fiction or non-fiction), length, purpose, form (handwritten, typed, printed, book, pamphlet, single sheets, news-paper, magazine); whether published or unpublished;
- in most countries, computer programmes and oral works, that is, works not reduced to writing.

In certain countries, mainly in countries with common law legal traditions, the notion of copyright has a wider meaning than authors' rights. Copyright protection generally means that certain uses of the work are lawful only if they are done with the authorization of the owner of the copyright. Some strictly determined uses (for example, quotations, the use of works by way of illustration for teaching, or the use of articles on political or economic matters in other newspapers) are completely free, that is, they require neither the authorization of, nor remuneration for the owner of the copyright. In addition to economic rights, authors enjoy moral rights on the basis of which they have the right to claim their authorship and require that their names be indicated on the copies of the work and they have the right to oppose the mutilation or deformation of their works. Copyright generally vests in the author of the work. Certain laws provide for exceptions; for example, regard the employer as the original owner of copyright, if the author was, when the work was created, an employee and was employed for the very purpose of creating the work.

The laws of almost all countries provide that copyright protection starts as soon as the work is created. Copyright protection is limited in time. Many countries have adopted, as a general rule, a term of protection that starts at the time of the creation of the work and ends 50 years (in some countries, 70 years) after the death of the author. However, in some countries, there are exceptions either for certain kinds of works (e.g. photographs, audiovisual works) or for certain uses (e.g. translations). It was in order to guarantee protection in foreign countries for their own citizens that, in 1886, ten countries established the International Union for the Protection of Literary and Artistic Works by signing the Berne Convention for the Protection of Literary and Artistic Works. Today, over a hundred countries worldwide are signatories to this Convention.

Although freedom of expression is fundamental, the freedom of journalists to report what they see or hear is not as universal as it should be. Throughout the world, the struggle continues to maintain a free press in print, radio, broadcasting and increasingly online. Press reporting is, of course, always hampered by individual laws in individual countries which provide some fundamental legal constraints. There are universal restraints of one kind or another concerned with defamation and court reporting. But each country then puts its own individual spin and restrictions on these and other areas of information. Journalists in each country have their own specific requirements and these will be contained in relevant media law books and individual codes of conduct formulated by journalists' associations and trade union organizations of various types. It is essential, therefore, for any journalist working in a foreign country to be aware of these individual laws and ethical constraints. Some of them will, of course, border on copyright and intellectual property rights considerations.[7]

Libel is about protecting a person's reputation. If someone believes a story has been damaging to his reputation by a false statement, then he can sue. If the damaging statement published is true, then the journalist usually has a complete defence but the newspaper or journalist has to prove the truth of the statement; the libeled person does not have to prove it is untrue. Practising global journalism often means being involved in investigations of one kind or another and these can often lead journalists into great danger. It is important for all investigative journalists to be clear about any legal or censorship problems they might encounter in the country in which they are working.

Dangers of Global Reporting

During 2008, more than 157 journalists and media staff were killed or murdered making it one of the worst years on record, says the International Federation of Journalists (IFJ) and the International Press Institute (IPI). "In a century of unremitting slaughter, 1999 has been an infamous year," said Aidan White, General Secretary of the IFJ. "Once again, it is journalists and those who work with them who are among the victims of murder, crime and conflict."[8]

Journalists and media have been targeted everywhere. In India, media came under fire in the violent exchanges on the disputed border with Kashmir and in Chechnya, Russian forces bombed and struck at Chechen media facilities in Grozny. "Journalists are being slaughtered at a time when the public need impartial information most: during times of war and conflict," said Johann P. Fritz, Director of the International Press Institute.[9] Also that year were the horrifying deaths of Dutch journalist Sander Themes and Indonesian journalist Agus Muliawan in East Timor, who died, according to a later investigation, at the hands of Indonesian Security Forces.

In Africa, the civil war in Sierra Leone claimed some 10 victims among the local community of journalists and an undeclared civil war in Colombia claimed 6 victims, said the Report. According to IPI, 1999 was the second worst year on record. And it continued: "We end the century on a note of dismay. Despite much talk of ethical principles and human rights, the struggle for press freedom remains a lofty ambition in many parts of the world. Journalists are often murdered because someone, somewhere wants to keep story quiet. Latin American journalists remain vulnerable to pressure from criminal gangs and political terrorists and there is a fear in that region that the killing of journalists might again become routine.

"Governments and media employers must put the safety of journalists and media staff to the top of the agenda. Too often, however, we see that working conditions are getting worse, not better, creating an atmosphere of uncertainty and insecurity within journalism," said Aidan White, who reaffirmed the IFJ's call for an international Code of Practice for media workers. "Journalists, employers and media unions must lead the way in setting standards for security,"[10] he said.

PROBLEMS OF GLOBAL JOURNALISM

One of the most pressing problems for the global journalist is the question of ethics and the way reporting has to be shaped because of them. Ethics and regulatory issues transcend borders; global journalists have to have a global feel for these issues. Wherever journalists work, there are a number of basic moral problems associated with individual decision-making about story coverage and approach.

Working across national boundaries emphasises the differences between cultures. The Internet adds many more problems that have to be faced daily. No longer is it only the journalist who provides the slant of international news to the local reader. The Internet has changed all with its increased interactivity. Now, the reader can call the tune. Now, the

Internet reader can be active and track down more or less information about a story and supply an individual angle or respond instantaneously by email or via chatrooms. The filtering process at the reporting end and the selection end becomes more difficult. As the Internet becomes more widespread, journalism will become more global and transmission working will become more usual. Technology now means that reporters can research what is happening in a foreign country from their desk or indeed from their home. It also makes it more likely they will be working for a huge global company or publication. No longer do they have to work in London if they work for the London Times. The job can just as easily be done from anywhere, any country. And putting news on to the web means automatic globalization and a multinational audience. That is why data base and online journalism are catching pace.

Ethics and laws become more difficult to understand and follow uninformally. Something illegal in one country may be legal elsewhere; something ethical in one country may be unethical in another, perhaps in a neighboring country. The Internet also throws up ethical problems of its own. Concerns over copyright and intellectual property rights loom very large among these concerns and they will have to be sorted out internationally. Then, there is the spin problem; much of the material now being placed on the net is being done so precisely in the hope that journalists will access and use it, together with the particular spin. Many governments put out all their press releases on the web. Most companies do the same. There is a great temptation simply to cut and paste this material and use it without checking. And because Internet material is so easy to access, it is becoming a major research tool for global journalists. The danger is the assumption that what you see is what is true. The proof of the source is much more difficult on the Internet. Even if the press release or the site with the relevant facts carries a credible name, there's no guarantee that the name is as it should be. All but the most important thing here is that internet information needs to be treated with caution and checked. This information usually gives one side of the story—that of the government, the company/or the individual. It must thus be treated with the same skepticism that any source would be treated. Web sites and Internet information will probably also have to have an ethical code of conduct in some way.[11]

Journalists work on the assumption that their reporting is free of censorship and control. This definition of freedom, however, extends only so far as freedom is concerned with government. This definition does not consider the institutional requirements and restraints placed on journalists by the media corporations for which they work. There is strong evidence that newspaper journalists are not as satisfied in their jobs as they used to be and much of their dissatisfaction is with management and shrinking professional freedom. Meanwhile, newspaper management strategy has been changing, as digital technology takes hold on collection and dissemination of news throughout the world.

News has become a commodity and newspapers and broadcasting organizations are tending to adopt a more market-driven approach. This is rapidly changing the role of journalists and journalism. Some global journalists have rebelled against market-driven management principles, criticizing what they call the big business that newspapers have become. This big business approach on the part of owners also creates an impression that newspapers are giving up their historical roles of being government's watchdog and purveyors of truth but adapting their content to attract new advertisers. On the other hand, management, and increasingly editors, are embracing the market-driven approach as a necessary means of keeping newspapers competitive and profitable in a changing media marketplace. Journalists practising global journalism hold tightly to the belief in freedom to report and autonomy of decision-making in what makes news and how news is reported. And because journalists are creative beings, who need freedom and autonomy to operate properly, freedom and autonomy are important indicators of job satisfaction.

Journalists are happier when they are free from institutional restraints on their professionalism. They feel they have a meaningful say in decisions and they get feedback and support, but not too much supervision, from their superiors. Then they work better, self-censorship does not occur and the world is a better place for the journalism that is practiced. Journalism has historically been an occupation or profession that allowed its practitioners a great deal of freedom. Reporters are not supervised in news-gathering and are allowed discretion in choosing the news angles and contents of their stories, while editors often create their own standards for quality and ethical conduct. There is evidence that market-driven approach has cut into journalism autonomy, as corporations have standardized codes of conduct and job performance is increasingly evaluated by employees' abilities to attract new readers and advertisers. Newspapers serve an important function of providing news of government. Journalists, not surprisingly, think that the newspaper industry has a moral or ethical responsibility above and beyond making profits. Only about 25 per cent of journalists say they are very satisfied with their jobs. In a global study published in 1999, it was found that the proportions of journalists considering themselves very satisfied with their jobs varied greatly in the 14 countries studies. Those countries with the smallest percentages of very satisfied journalists were Hong Kong, Taiwan and Algeria, with China and Brazil not far behind. Those with the largest job satisfaction were Chile and Mexico.

This ability of journalists to feel free to pursue stories aggressively is one of several factors that have consistently ranked high in job satisfaction studies. Reporters enjoy their work best when they can choose which stories they wish to cover, and which aspects of the story should be covered. In a random national sample of all media workers in Canada,. George Pollard found workers were most satisfied due to a combination of intrinsic factors, such as autonomy, authority, and control of work, and extrinsic factors, such as job security and income. Pollard noted that news work is not a profession in the same sense as medicine or law, but news workers do embrace professionalism, and in some professions, perceived autonomy is the key determinant of job satisfaction. News organizations can increase job satisfaction by clear job definitions, meaningful employee participation in decision-making, and limited reliance on hierarchical authority and rule enforcement.[12]

Journalists worldwide tend to be motivated by achievement, power and public service. Newsroom managers work best with journalists (who mostly resist management control whenever possible) by motivating them to work for personal satisfaction and out of their commitment to journalistic ideals. Most management theories do not work in modern newsrooms or broadcasting stations. The best approach to newsroom management is to be aware of what is going on in the newsroom; get feedback from the journalists being managed; know the limitations of management style that is not founded on charisma and respect, and be flexible.[13] On the other hand, everyone wants to report in the global news fields. It is glamorous, prestigious and exciting. Most feel that global reporting and working internationally is the top of the journalism profession. It can also be dangerous. Global reporters often get caught up in the riot-earthquake-political coup equation, the main reasons why international reporting exists. So, global news often equates with conflict. That means being a war correspondent or a famine correspondent, or a disaster correspondent. They tend to cover the world's hot spots. But, of course, this too often means global reporters become filters, sorting streams of daily propaganda, assessing and judging both sides of a story and working out who are the goodies and the baddies. All practising global journalists have to hit the ground running when they arrive. There is not 'reading-in' time. They are expected to file reports as soon as they arrive with the surefootedness of those who have beenr there for years. Deadlines are sacrosanct. Correspondents who cost a lot of money (and they all do) must start paying their way as soon as possible. That is the law of the market. Another problem with global journalism is the lack of training for those who practice it. They are expected to use their transferable skills learnt doing domestic stories, even though they very often cannot speak the language. That means they often have to depend on local translators and researchers. They have to trust them or sink. It also means there is an immediate relationship struck up between the journalist and the diplomats, usually of their own country. These are often the journalist's most important sources. There are also problems of adapting to the technological and political changes that are occurring globally

Notes and References

1. Hall, Stuart, The Rediscovery of Ideology: Return of the Repressed in Media Studies (London: Methven Publications), 1982, pp. 56-86.
2. De Burg, H. (ed.), Investigated Journalism: Context and Practice (London: Routledge), 2000, pp. 15-17.
3. Bell, A., The Language of News Media (Oxford: Blackwell Publishers), 1991, pp. 186-88.
4. Harcop, T. Journalism: Principle and Practice (London: Sage Publications), 2004, pp. 11-21.
5. Randall, D., The Universal Journalist (London: Pluto Press), 2000, pp. 21-46.
6. Pavlik, J.V., Journalism and News Media (New York: University Press), 2001, pp. 47-56.
7. Weaver, D. (ed.), The Global Journalist (New Jersey: Hampton Press), 1998, pp. 47-64.
8. Watson, J. Media Communication: An Introduction to Theory and Process (Basingstroke: MacMillan Publishers), 1998, p. 117.
9. Herbert, J. Practicing Global Journalism (Oxford: Focal Press), 2001, pp. 72-73.
10. Galtung, J. and M. Ruge, "The Structure of Foreign News", Journal of International Peace Research, Vol. I, 1965, pp. 65-71.
11. Bell, A., The Language of News Media (Oxford: Blackwell Publications), 1991, pp. 158-60.
12. Wilson, J., Understanding Journalism: A Guide to Issues (London: Routledge), 1996, pp. 114-131.
13. http://www.ap.org
14. Frost, C., Media Ethics and Self -Regulations (London: Longman Press), 2000, p. 11.
15. Dyke, G., Inside Story (London: Harper Collins), 2004, pp. 63-65.
16. Harbert, J., Practicing Global Journalism, *op. cit.*, pp. 148-149.
17. Boyd, Barrett, The Globalization News (London: Sage Publications), 1998, p. 79.
18. Boyd Barrett and T. Rantanen, (ed.), News Agencies as Agent of Globalisation (London: Sage Publication), 1998, p. 89.
19. Compbell, C.P., Race, Myth and News (Chicago: Sage Publications), 1995, pp. 41-43.
20. Harcop, T., Journalism: Principles and Practice, *op. cit.*, pp. 11-21.
21. Curram, J. and M. Gurevitch (ed.), Mass Media and Society (London: Arnold Press), 2000, pp. 39-40.
22. De Burg, H. (ed.), Investigated Journalism: Context and Practice, *op. cit.*, pp. 110-112.
23. Pavlik, J. V., Journalism and News Media (New York: University Press), 2001, pp. 41-76.
24. Whale, John, Journalism and Government (London: Fontona Books), 1977, pp. 111-131.

25. www.jour.sc.edu/news
26. *Ibid.*
27. www.mediacentre.org/content
28. Bayod-Barrell, O., The Globalization of News (New York: New York Press), 1998, pp. 45-56.
29. www.mediacentre.org/content
30. Herbert, J. Practicing Global Journals, *op. cit.*, pp. 56-67.
31. Hall, Jim, Online Journalism (Sterling: Pluto Press), 2001, pp. 39-46
32. Herbert, J. Practicing Global Journals, *op. cit.*, pp. 56-67.
33. Bayod-Barrell, O., The Globalization of News, *op. cit.*, pp. 55-58.
34. Weaver, D. (ed.), The Global Journalist (New Jersey: Hampton Press), 1998, pp. 47-49.
35. Bahuguna, Akhil, World Journalism Today (Jaipur: ABD Publishers), 2004, p 112.
36. Bell, A., The Language of News Media (Oxford: Blackwell Publishers), 2001.
37. www.journalism.co.uk/news
38. International Press Institute, Vol. II, No. 4, 1999.
39. *Ibid.*
40. www.ojr.org/ojr/workplace
41. Bangal, Nicholas, Newspaper Language (London: Focal Press), 1993, pp. 93-100.
42. www.africanews.org
43. *Ibid.*
44. Meyer, Henry, The Press in Australia (Melbourne: Lanswdowne Press Pvt. Ltd.), 1968, p. 10.
45. *Ibid.*, p. 21.
46. Thomas, Mac Combe, The History of Colony of Victor (Melbourne: Dilldown Press), 1858, p. 323.
47. Walter, W. G., An Outline of Modern Newspaper (New Delhi: Arise Publishers), 2008, p. 178.
48. Mott, Frank Luther, American Journalism (New York: The Macmillan Company), 1962, pp. 11-12.
49. Gaur, Sanjay, Media Journalism in 21st Century, *op. cit.*, p. 9.
50. Smith, K., The Mass Media: Reporting, Writing (New York: Harper Row Publishers), 2000, p. 551.
51. *Ibid.*
52. Gaur, Sanjay, Media Journalism in 21st Century (Jaipur: Book Enclave), 2006, p. 98.
53. Butterworth and Hememann, Journalism in the Digital Age (London: Pluto Press), 2000, p. 89.
54. *Ibid.*, p. 90.
55. http://www prescouncils.org.
56. Keeble, Richard (ed.), Print Journalism: A Critical Introduction (London: Routledge Group), 2005, pp. 99-111.
57. http://www.actionsites.com
58. Bertrandt, C., Media Ethics and Accountability System (New Jersey: Transaction Publishes), 2000, pp. 112-118.
59. Herbert, J., Practising Global Journalism, *op. cit.*, pp. 120-122.

Investigative Journalism/Media Trial

Trial by Media is a phrase which was coined in the late 20th century and early 21st century to describe the impact of television and newspaper coverage on a person's reputation, by creating a widespread perception of guilt regardless of any verdict in a court of law. In the United Kingdom, there is a heated debate between those who support a free press which is largely uncensored and those who place a higher priority on an individual's right to privacy and right to a fair trial. During high publicity court cases, the media are often accused of provoking an atmosphere of public hysteria akin to a lynch mob which not only makes a fair trial nearly impossible but ensures that regardless of the result of the trial, the accused will not be able to live the rest of their life without intense public scrutiny. The counter argument is that the mob mentality exists independent of the media which merely voices the opinions which the public already has. There are different reasons why the media attention is particularly intense surrounding a legal case. The first is that the crime itself is in some way sensational, by being horrific or involving women and children; the second is that it involves a celebrity either as victim or accused.

Although a recently used phrase, the idea that popular media can have a strong influence on the legal process goes back certainly to the advent of the printing press and probably much further. This does not include the use of a state controlled press to criminalize political opponents, but in its commonly understood meaning, covers all occasions where the reputation of a person has been drastically affected by ostensibly non-political publications.

One of the first celebrities in the 20th century to be arguably tried by media was Roscoe 'Fatty' Arbuckle who was acquitted by the courts but nevertheless lost his career and reputation due to the media coverage. Parallels can be drawn between these cases and the trial of O.J Simpson. The connection is less about guilt or innocence but about the promotion of the media coverage in the public mind above the status of the court. Another interesting case in the US was the Rodney King incident and subsequent trial of the police officers involved. Once again, an acquittal is challenged by the media reporting with violent consequences. What makes this case particularly important historically is the fact that it was amateur video footage which provided the key evidence of perceived guilt. As video cameras and their digital successors and CCTV become widerspread, this type of 'caught on camera' incidents become more and more common. This can pose real problems for the legal system as the evidence they provide may be inadmissible for technical reasons but they give very strong images for the media to seize upon and the potential to manipulate by editing. Even where a criminal court finds somebody guilty, the media can still appear to sit in judgement over their sentence. Often, the coverage in the press can be said to reflect the views of the person in the street. However, more credibility is generally given to printed material than 'water cooler gossip'. The responsibility of the press to confirm reports and leaks about individuals being tried has come under increasing scrutiny and journalists are calling for higher standards. There was much debate over U.S President Bill Clinton's impeachment trial and prosecutor Kenneth Starr's investigation and how the media handled the trial by reporting commentary from lawyers which influenced public opinion.[1] Another example was the investigation into biologist Steven Hatfill allegedly sending anthrax through the U.S. mail as a terrorist attack, which resulted in no conviction, but Hatfill went on to sue as his reputation was severely tarnished and career destroyed. Families and friends of persons convicted of crimes have apparently successfully used the power of the media to reopen cases, such as the Stephen Downing case in Derbyshire where a campaign by a local newspaper editor resulted in a successful appeal and his release after twenty seven years in prison.[2]

In India, trial by media has assumed significant proportions. It has had both positive and negative results. However, many would think that the overall impact is for the betterment of the society. Some famous criminal cases that would have gone unpunished but for the intervention of media are Priyadarshani Mattoo case, Jesica Lal case, Nitish Katara murder case, Naina Sahni Tandoor murder case and Bijal Joshi rape case. The media, however, drew flak in the reporting of murder of Arushi Talwar when it preempted the court and reported that her own father Dr. Rajesh Talwar and possibly her mother, Nupur Talwar, were involved in her murder. The CBI later declared that Rajesh was not the killer. In another case, the media—print, audio and visual all wrote about Sri Jayendra Saraswathi Swamigal, a Hindu religious leader, suggesting his guilt in a murder case, but the High Courts of Madras and Andhra Pradesh and the Supreme Court of India repeatedly found that there was no material evidence to find him guilty and came down heavily on the media and the Government of Tamilnadu for misuse of government machinery. Another case was of Uma Khurana's fake sting operation which later proved to be gimmick to grab increasing TRPs (Television Rating Points).

STING: THE NEW FACE OF JOURNALISM

Sting Operations are generally implemented by undercover agents to apprehend criminals. It is a very complicated game, planned and executed with great care and confidence. In these types of operations, the police poses as criminals to trap law violators. Now a days, electronics and print media are very sensitive to sting operations.

However, the word sting derives its origin from 1930's American slang, meaning an act of theft or fraud, especially one that was carefully planned in advance and swiftly executed. The term then evolved in 1970's American usage to mean a police undercover operation designed to ensnare criminals. In this latter sense, "sting" is, therefore, a synonym for the expression "set a trap to catch a crook." Sting, as the dictionary defines, is a small sharp organ of an insect or a plant, capable of injecting a painful dose of poison.

In more refined terms, it can be called Investigative Journalism or Undercover Journalism. Sting Operation is an information-gathering exercise; it looks for facts that are not easy to obtain by simple requests and searches, or those that are actively being concealed, suppressed or distorted. An informed citizenry, the bedrock of a democracy, holding the government accountable through voting and participation, requires investigative journalism which cannot sustain itself on asymmetric dissemination of information.

In law enforcement, a sting operation is an operation designed to catch a person committing a crime by means of deception. A typical sting will have a law enforcement officer or cooperative member of the public play a role as criminal partner or potential victim and go along with a suspect's actions to gather evidence of the suspect' s wrongdoing. Sting operations may be a component of a conspiracy; law enforcement may have to be careful not to provoke the commission of a crime by someone who would not normally be inclined to do so. In common law jurisdictions, the defendant may invoke the defence of entrapment.

THE USE OF NEW TECHNOLOGY

The advent of miniaturised audio and video technology, specially the pin-hole camera technology, enables one to clandestinely make a video/audio recording of a conversation and actions of individuals. Such equipment, costing between Rs 60,000 to Rs. 1,20,000 depending on quality, generally has four components—the miniaturised camera, often of a size of a 25 naye paise coin or even smaller (pin top size), a miniature video recording device, a cord to transmit the signals and a battery cell. The use of the cord can be avoided through wireless transmissions.

There are various ways of hiding the camera—inside a briefcase, or a pager or a cigarette lighter or a cellular telephone or a fountain pen or a smoke detector or in the nose frame of sunglasses or other spectacles, etc.

Where a briefcase is used, the recording equipment, the transmitting cord and the battery can also be concealed in it. In other cases, the remaining components are generally attached to the body of the user. In the sunglass/spectacles version, the connecting cord looks like the safety cord which some people use with their glasses. In other cases, an observant person can notice the telltale connecting cord. Most of these gadgets have either a self activation mechanism or a mechanism which has to be activated manually. The briefcase camera gets activated when the briefcase is kept in a particular position.

The visuals of Shri Bangaru Laxman recorded by Tehelka.com indicate that the camera was probably at a level higher than the waist of the journalist. The use of a briefcase, which would normally have been kept on the floor, seems unlikely. It was probably concealed in some other object of day-to-day use which he kept on the table without the connecting cord attracting the suspicion of Shri Laxman or, most probably, in the sunglasses/spectacles worn by the journalist in which case the cord would not have attracted suspicion.[3]

FREEDOM OF THE PRESS AND ITS COMMON LAWS–ORIGIN AND GROWTH

The Constitution of India, in Article 19(a), guaranteed the freedom of speech and expression as a fundamental right of a citizen and the apex judiciary was quick to read the freedom of the press into this guarantee. So, any law that abridges this freedom had to validate itself by satisfying the provisions of Article 19(2) under which reasonable restrictions can be put. Consequently, these laws will need to bear a reasonable nexus to the grounds mentioned in 19(2); these grounds being the security and integrity of the nation, friendly relations with foreign states, public order, decency or morality or in relation to contempt of court, defamation or incitement to an offence. Furthermore, the restriction in question should be 'reasonable'.

The basic principle of democracy is that 'deliberative forces shall prevail over the arbitrary' and its foundations are on free election based on reason. Since no electorate is free unless it is informed, true representative democracy cannot exist without freedom of speech. Justice Holmes reflects that a 'marketplace of ideas' where free trade and competition in ideas ensure the discovery of truth, required that individuals be ever vigilant against attempts to check the expression of ideas that they loathe. The freedom of the press developed as a parallel concept, in the context of developments in mass communication. The growth and development of representative democracy was so intertwined with the development and proliferation of the press that it has long been considered an institutional limb of modern democracy. It was considered vital for the sustenance of a democracy that rival political parties be able to express alternatives to government opinion, unfettered and in public.

As soon as printing was invented in the 15th century, obstacles were set-up in order to prevent the new invention from influencing public opinion through the free circulation of news and ideas. In the English-speaking world, Henry VIII introduced press licensing in 1536. Printers and writers were the first to fight for the simple right to print and the press in Internal Vigilance and Sting.

England was the first country in Europe to fight for press freedom. Newspapers and gazettes became part of the English political spectrum with the setting up of modem political institutions in the 17th century. Parliament gradually gave up enforcing the Licensing Act as from 1679, and it was finally abolished in 1694. Newspapers no longer needed state approval and no longer needed authorization to be published, a major landmark—in this respect, England can be seen as the cradle of press freedom.[4]

The Right to Privacy: Theoretical foundations and the Interaction with the Freedom of Expression

In India, the right of privacy has a two-fold source.

Apart from the common law, the Supreme Court has recognized a constitutional origin as well. So, firstly, a private action for damages may lie for an unlawful invasion of privacy. The 'right to be left alone' is also implicit in the right to life and liberty guaranteed by Article 21. However, this right is to be balanced with the freedom of expression guaranteed in Article 19(l)(a). Hence, the state cannot impose any prior restraint on the freedom of the press on the grounds that the concerned would offend the privacy of any individual. No remedy will lie before publication.[5]

Thus under Indian law, the extent to which a person can claim a right to privacy is dependant on his public status. A person who welcomes media interest in his life will not be able to claim a right to privacy as easily as a 'private individual'. Further, in the absence of any 'public issue', the publication of material that invades the privacy of any individual can invite an action for damages.

Needless to say, the interface between freedom of the press and privacy, in the context of a 'sting operation' is quite vague. For instance, does a Bollywood actor qualify as a 'public personality'? Is the expose of the 'casting couch' phenomenon a 'public issue'?

The Supreme Court of India has concluded that the fundamental rights to privacy and a fair trial flow out of the broader right to life contained in Article 21 of the Constitution. In Kharak Singh v. State of Uttar Pradesh, the Supreme Court held that the right to privacy was an "essential ingredient of personal liberty" which is "a right to be free from restrictions or encroachments."[6]

FREEDOM OF THE PRESS IN INDIA

Freedom of the press (or press freedom) is the guarantee by a government of free public press for its citizens and their associations, extended to members of news gathering organizations, and their published reporting. It also extends to news gathering, and processes involved in obtaining information for public distribution.

With respect to governmental information, a government distinguishes which materials are public or protected from disclosure to the public based on categorisation of information as sensitive, classified or secret and being otherwise exempted from disclosure due to relevance of the information to protecting the national interest. Many governments are also subject to sunshine laws or freedom of information legislation that are used to define the ambit of national interest.

In the Indian Constitution, the word "press" is not mentioned. The press in India derives its freedom as an interpretation of the Article 19(l)(a) of the Constitution which states:

> "All citizens have the right to freedom of speech and expression."

Many restrictive and repressive laws have been used to curb the freedom of the press in India. Some of the more severe laws are the Official Secrets Act and Prevention of Terrorism Act (PoTA). Under PoTA, any person could be arrested and put into indefinite undisclosed detention by the police or the Army, if they felt that the person had been in contact with a terrorist or terrorist group and could be a danger to the state's security. This prevented journalists from using their full range of sources, and compelled them to use safer sources such as government officials, which reduced the efficiency of the press dramatically. PoTA has since been abolished by the United Progressive Alliance government.

The notion of the press as the fourth branch of government is sometimes used to compare the press (or media) with Montesquieu's three branches of government, namely legislature and in addition to it the executive and the judiciary. Sir Edmund Burke is quoted to have said: "Three Estates in Parliament; but in the Reportpooopers' Gallery yonder, there more important far than they all, sits the fourth estate, The Press."[7]

INVESTIGATIVE JOURNALISM AND STING OPERATION

Setting a trap to nab wrong doers is no doubt an accepted method of a criminal investigative process. In corruption cases, apprehending the bribe-taker in the act is accepted as a clinching evidence of his culpability. But catching someone on camera engaged in the sex act does not necessarily establish any. If a sting operation of the kind set-up by the private channel suggests anything at all it is the tendency of some officials and politicians to misuse their positions. That is neither proof of past misconduct or the certainty of such behaviour in future. In the novelty of catching some action on camera, one should not make the mistake of viewing a towards criminality as proof of actual wrongdoing.

However the following norms should be looked into going for any kind of sting operation:

Sting operations are to be mounted only on persons against whom some evidence of criminality exists and sting operation is considered necessary for getting conclusive evidence.

Permission for sting operations must be obtained from appropriate courts or the attorney general. This safeguard has been laid down since those who mount a sting operation themselves commit the offence of impersonation, criminal trespass and making a person commit an offence. (Remember that 'Cheating by Impersonation' is a crime under Section 416 of the Indian Penal Code.)

Where there is evidence of editing of tapes and films, there is an automatic presumption that the recording is probably not authentic.

There must be a concurrent record in writing of the various stages of the sting operation.

Sting journalism is not new to India. Years ago, an operation by an online news site called Tehelka caught top politicians and army officers taking bribes from journalists posing as businessmen. It was widely praised as investigative journalism carried out in the public interest. Today, almost all television news channels in India routinely use spy cameras to expose corruption.

But in a society that remains more buttoned up than those in the United States or Europe, the Indian news media have been reluctant to report on the private lives of public figures. In the land that gave the world the Kama Sutra, the ancient guide to carnal relations, public displays of affection by couples are discouraged. Bollywood movies showed their first on-screen kiss only a decade ago, and television remains strictly controlled.

INVESTIGATIVE JOURNALISM

Investigative journalism is a branch of journalism that usually concentrates on a very specific topic and typically requires a lot of work to yield results. It is an in-depth article or series of articles based on research and investigation, usually over a long period of time. The subject often involves legal or controversial issues, such as mafia, the tobacoo industry; now-a-days political controversies are forming a major part of investigation.

During the 1972 campaign for the White House, when Richard Nixon was seeking a second term in office, five persons, acting on orders, broke into the Democratic national offices in the Watergate complex in Washington and planted electronic eavesdropping devices. Their purpose remains unclear till date. Bob Woodward and Carl Bernstein, reporters with the Washington Post, became curious when a short news item appeared regarding a burglary at the Watergate office of democratic Party and began to make inquiries. Through their investigations, it was discovered that it was not a simple act of burglary but a case of political corruption and manipulation involving the highest office in the land.[8]

Investigative Journalism is a distinctive aspect of the work undertaken by the media. Essentially an information-gathering exercise, it looks for facts that are not easy to obtain by simple requests and searches, or those that are actively being concealed, suppressed or distorted. Where such investigative work involves the use of covert methods, it raises issues that tend to further blur the line between law and ethics. An informed citizenry—the bedrock of a democracy—holding the government accountable through voting and participation, requires investigative journalism. In many cases, the subjects of the reporting wish the matters under scrutiny to remain undisclosed rather buried. A healthy democracy cannot sustain itself on asymmetric dissemination of information. The political elite are sensitive to news; and news about economic or political wrongdoing can trigger judicial or quasi-judicial scrutiny. Various methods are employed for their fact-finding—the study of often neglected sources like archives, phone records, address books, tax records and license records; anonymous sources; and going undercover. It is often suggested that anonymous sources are double-edged—on the one hand they may provide especially newsworthy information such as classified or confidential information about current events, information about a previously unreported scandal, or the perspective of a particular group that may fear retribution for expressing certain opinions in the press; but the downside is that the condition of anonymity may make it difficult or impossible for the reporter to verify the source's statements. By going undercover, the reporter tries to infiltrate a community by posing as somebody friendly to that community.

The Bhagalpur Blindings provide a lesson in the crucial contribution that journalistic research can make in creating public awareness of human rights, more so in a society in which entrenched abuse is likely to be overlooked. Over three years, from 1979 to 1982, policemen blinded 33 criminals in Bhagalpur Jail using acid. Codenamed Operation Gangajal, a report carried by The Indian Express, the incident became a national scandal and 14 policemen were suspended. Of the 14 policemen, 13 were acquitted and reinstated in service. When The Indian Express brought the issue into national focus, the Supreme Court accepted it as a writ petition. In Bhagalpur, many people campaigned for the suspension of the policemen, arguing that such punishment deterred crime more effectively than protracted legal cases. It took a sustained campaign on the rights of prisoners along with the impact of the pictures of the blinded men to touch the public conscience.

A journalist once said, "News is something someone somewhere doesn't want to be published—all the rest is advertisement."[9] That may be considered a far-fetched definition in today's media world which considers advertisements the lifeblood of journalism and a starlet delivering a baby more attractive news than a wave of suicides among exploited farmers.

However, any newsperson worth his/her salt knows that uncovering a hidden story is far more challenging and satisfying than covering a prime minister's foreign tour or hunting for Page 3 gossip in a celebrity party. Regrettably, this breed of committed reporters is fast vanishing, thanks to the bulldozing forces of the market that are converting the media profession in India into an enterprise like any other industry producing consumer goods.

Modern investigative journalism is a discipline, rigorous and demanding. Modern journalism, despite its many aberrations, is considered the most effective monitor and upholder of democratic values. And the powerful instrument to fulfill this obligation is investigative reporting. Democracy involves accountability of elected representatives and civil servants. There are many mechanisms for checks and balances, but these can be abused, circumvented, ignored or made ineffective. Investigative reporting steps into this vacuum to scrutinize and expose the wrong-doings of those in authority which hurt public interest, and make them accountable to the people.

The importance of the "organic" relationship, as described by Walter Lippman, between a healthy democracy and the free press need not be elaborated here. Enough it to say that one cannot sustain without the other. Indian media is so intoxicated with its so-called freedom (freest press in the world, one might say) that it fails to understand that it is also equally underdeveloped and fragile, that freedom carries certain grave responsibilities and that as upholder of democratic values and freedom (not just another profit making industry), it has some specific obligations and duties towards the society. It is so obsessed with itself that it does not realise that it is throwing to winds its credibility, respectability and power by not attending to its basic obligations.

For investigative reporting to flourish, what is required is: an independent and pluralistic media which is fearless, committed to democracy, universal human values; journalists with commitment who can identify problems and have the grit, perseverance, patience and skills to do research; owners and editors professionally non-partisan and without vested interests (above selfish ends).

What goes under the name of investigative journalism (with some honourable exceptions) in India, can hardly be taught in a journalism school as classic investigative journalism. The so-called investigative reporting in India in the Bofors case, Fodder scam, Jain Dairy Case, Petrol Pumps largesse scandal and even Satyendra Dubey's murder case, have been either rankly partisan political exercises or halfhearted attempts to show off the fearlessness of those media units. Has anyone followed Satyendra Dubey's case to the end? Who are the murderers? Are they arrested? Who leaked Satyendra's confidential letter from the PMO? Is that person booked? And the mafia contractors of the Golden Quadrilateral? Has any paper or channel pursued them?

One remembers the sensation caused by Arun Shourie's series of 'investigative' stories on the then Chief Minister, A.R. Antulay of Maharashtra, in early 1980's. Shourie, then, was acknowledged as the pioneer of modern investigative journalism in India. One also remembers the first sentence of his first story. Paraphrased in memory, it ran something like this ."..look at these political rats; how they run when cornered..."[10] Now, any news editor worth his/her salt would spike that story. It broke all the tenets of not only investigative journalism, but also of ordinary reporting. Shourie's stories were written in a style that was blatantly partisan and spiteful. Moreover, he had not uncovered anything that had not been published earlier, that too, with much more detail, in local newspapers. Antulay's sins of omission and commission, his acceptance of cheques for his public trust in front of TV cameras, was public knowledge in the entire state of Maharashtra. But Shourie, instead of writing scathing comment pieces on the edit page, wrote 'investigative' news stories on the front pages of his newspaper!

POLITICAL EXPEDIENCE

Bofors, St. Kitts, none of the stories wes followed thoroughly and with the rigour that investigative journalism demands. The pursuit was half-hearted; the stories tapered off occasionally, but were revived vigorously whenever a political occasion demanded.

No doubt, there have been laudable attempts at exposing some major scandals at local or state levels. But, often, the exposure is made in one sensational burst and then the press loses interest. The story tapers off or is not followed at all. Clearly, the Indian media has not nourished the discipline of classic investigative reporting. The political, economic and social scenario of India is so complex and rotten and the media's credibility, despite its enormous power, is so low that even conscientious bureaucrats do not dare to blow the whistle. One whistle-blower who dared was murdered. And the press has nearly forgotten him.

BASIC REQUIREMENTS OF INVESTIGATE JOURNALISM

It is to be emphasized here even at the cost of repeating that for investigative reporting to flourish, what is required is: an independent and pluralistic media which is fearless, committed to democracy, universal human values, journalists with commitment who can identify problems and have the grit, perseverance, patience and skills to do research and owners and editors professionally non-partisan and without vested interests.

We have a fantastically free press, so free that it does not have a professional self-regulatory mechanism to monitor fundamental ethics of the press. Not even the journalists' associations; these are more interested in begging for more perks from the government and corporate bodies than in the health of their own profession. Many journalists may have the aptitude and skills for investigative journalism. But their owners and editors do not have the will, even if they have the resources, to encourage them. The owners and the editors, too, have multiple vested interests—in political parties, individual leaders, corporate bodies and so on.

THE ETHICS OF THE 'STING' IN INVESTIGATING JOURNALISM

Most discussions about ethics in investigative journalism have focused on the methodology. What methods are valid to reveal wrongdoing? Is deception legitimate when the aim is to tell the truth? Is any method justifiable no matter if there are discouraging working conditions and presence of the difficulties in getting information? Can television reporters use hidden cameras to get a story? Can journalists use false identities to gain access to information?

Operation Westend brought some particularly acute questions to the fore. Many argued that a vast gulf existed between 'snaring' or 'tempting' people into accepting 'gifts' or 'bribes'; and the exposure of corruption regarding specific deals. Is it ethical to hold someone responsible for a crime that would not have been committed if the undercover journalist had not encouraged the act? Also, how ethical was it to use prostitutes in order to expose corruption in defense deals? Tarun Tejpal, Tehelka editor, had justified the methods by saying that 'extraordinary circumstances justified the use of extraordinary methods'.

Clearly, there can be no consensus on the ethics of sting operations when the methods and objectives of each operation vary so vastly. In fact, the legal implications of reporters' actions are, by far, more clear-cut than the ethical issues involved. Ethics, dealing with distinguishing right and wrong, uses philosophical principles to justify a particular course of action. Any action can be justified ethical, depending on what framework is used to justify it, and what values are prioritized. Fortunately for this particular dilemma, the media's cherished values are not a matter of much debate. What journalists and editors need to determine is—who will benefit as a result of the reporting? If journalism is committed to democratic accountability, then the question that needs to be asked is whether the public benefits as a result of specific investigative reports. Does the press fulfill its social responsibility in revealing wrongdoing? Whose interests are being affected? Whose rights are being invaded? Is the issue at stake a matter of legitimate public interest?

One can debate endlessly about the ethics of these issues, and not be any closer to resolution, except where motive is clear. Most people would consider the sting operation on Dilip Singh Judeo as unethical because it was motivated—not by concerns of informing the citizens, but for political one-upmanship. The 'reverse sting' on Ajit Jogi and his son falls in the same category.[11]

At best, a case by case analysis may be undertaken to distinguish ethically right journalistic method from wrong. However, if one were to move beyond ethics and enter the realm of law, the determination of what is legally right method is easier. Such an enquiry is also apt in the context of the much anticipated Broadcasting Bill. Undoubtedly, the starting point for any such discussion has to be the freedom of the press.

In such circumstances, what does a restless committed journalist do? He takes a hidden camera with him and broadcasts countrywide bulletins of responsible people accepting bribes. If documents, receipts, accounts, papers or files are not forthcoming as proof, here's how the journalist furnishes the proof. Live on screen TarunTejpal and Tehelka's sting operation and subsequent imitations by others have raised a hornet's nest questioning the ethical propriety of this kind of journalism. A positive outcome indeed!

MEDIA CREDIBILITY

The press is losing credibility because of its blatant partisanship and rank commercialism. So, take the camera and expose. Never mind, it is one-time exposure of a part. But the proof is there, clearly visible on the screen to make an impact on the minds of the people. This will at least shake the people and those who are concerned, out of their slumber.

No, this is not investigative journalism. But it is the sting. An occasional sting operation made with professional commitment may serve the cause for the time being. But that is no alternative to investigative journalism. To build its credibility and ensure its freedom under democracy, the media in India will have to turn to serious investigative reporting.

The Tehelka style of investigative journalism has brought about a change in the way one looks at news, amidst new notions of editorial freedom. Stirring stuff like the kind shown in stings has a fair amount of shock value.

There is no denying the fact that a sting operation is by far the most effective way of exposing the truth. With a society and a system of governance that defies transparency, the doubting public demands credible proof. Being 'caught in an act' on camera leaves little scope for evasive answers by those who shamelessly manipulate the system for vested interests.[12]

Public figures are often reminded that they have nothing to hide from the public, which has a right to know everything. The stinging truth, however, is the easy conscience with which corruption is tolerated and allowed to plague the political system.

OPERATION WEST END

Newsgathering acquired a new meaning with Tehelka's, 'Operation West End', which left the common man with deep revulsion for the political system and contempt for those in the defence establishment who are willing to trade national interest for vested interests.[13] It is not just governance but also other systems of everyday life, which if left unchecked, spell disaster for the common man. Also, the argument that it is virtually impossible to discover the real state of affairs through normal ways of investigation, deserves a fair hearing.

The most explosive sting by Tehelka in recent times is the one, exposing the twists behind the Best Bakery case. Zaheera Sheikh, who has become a symbol of the Gujarat carnage, has been continuously changing her testimony in the case. The Tehelka tapes allege that Zaheera was paid Rs 18 lakh by a BJP MLA.

EFFECTIVENESS OF STING OPERATION

They are familiar sights on our TV screens these days: The grainy, curiously distorted images, the awkward camera angles, the unclear audio and the anchors promising startling revelations just ahead. They're sting operations; the exposes conducted by journalists in much the same manner as investigative agencies conduct undercover operations. And what's more, they're flourishing: Indeed, the current age could be called the year of the sting operation.

MAJOR STING OPERATIONS IN INDIA

Aaj Tak

Tihar jail Bani Ghoos Mahal: Officials at Tihar Jail taking bribes.

Ghoos Mahal- 82 employees of the Delhi sales tax office taking bribes.

Operation Duryodhan: 11 MPs caught taking bribes to raise questions in Parliament.

Star News

Ayaash IG: Jharkhand IG suspended for sexually exploiting a tribal woman.

Doctor selling infants from a hospital.

Operation Chakravyuh: MP's caught misusing MPLAD funds.

Wife caught on camera beating her husband.

NDTV India

Delhi policeman taking a bribe to hand over the body of a man to his family.

Railway Policemen extorting money from passengers

India TV

Bihar MLAs having sex with call girls.

Holy men sexually exploiting women devotees.

Operation Casting Couch: Actor Shakti Kapoor propositions journalist posing as actress.

Operation Casting Couch: Actor Aman Verma takes journalist posing as an actress to his bedroom.

Sahara Samay

Corruption in Delhi PWD.

Kokh Mein Qatl

Titled Kokh Mein Katl (murder in the womb) has highlighted the severity of the discrimination against the girl child and the risk involved in conducting such operations. The operation was launched by a team of journalists in Rajasthan. It was a campaign based on the personal commitment of the team. With this operation, the genre of sting operation has entered a new era.

Suppression and discrimination of women was the starting point of this operation run jointly by Sripal Shaktawat, the Bureau Chief, Rajasthan, Sahara News and Dr. Meena Sharma, a freelance journalist. Sripal Shaktawat has been crusading against the social malpractices and atrocities especially crime against women for over a decade while Meena has been a young freelance reporter committed to the social upliftment of the society. Both of them have given new meaning to the sting operations led by media. Meena left her assignments with the local media and her college lecturership to devote herself to the operation. They planned to launch a sting operation in February-March, 2005 to expose the breed of doctors conducting illegal abortions after sex determination in the state. They travelled a distance of 13,000 km across the districts of Rajasthan, MP, Gujarat, and Haryana.

This sting "Kokh Mein Katl" was telecast on Sahara channel from 4th April, 2006. The team had footage of about 100 doctors. Out of them, 80 were telecast. Some of the footages were held back because of the poor quality. Together, the team travelled a distance of 1300 km across the districts of Rajasthan, MP, Gujarat, and Haryana. There were pressures from the political and social circles but the team continued to resist all pressures to expose the killer Doctors. The local media and journalist associations and social groups came in open support of the sting team.[14]

Shakti Kapoor Stung by Sting Operation

Shakti Kapoor is one of the topmost villains of Bollywood. But one sting operation claims to have revealed that he is a 'bad guy' in real life too. He has been filmed purportedly making verbal and physical advances against a young woman and casting aspersions on several film personalities in a sting operation conducted by a private TV channel.

Kapoor did not deny making the advances but maintained he was set-up (trapped). He claimed he had not made any specific statements about his fellow stars but only spoke in generalities. The sting was conducted by producer,

Suhaib Ilyasi, for his "India's Most Wanted" programme that has now shifted to the India TV channel. The channel aired the 40-minute clip. In it, Kapoor is seen to be making sexually explicit verbal and physical suggestions to an India TV reporter posing as an aspiring film star. The reporter is told of various "services" that would have to be provided if she were to make it big. Kapoor then turns his wrath on Ilyasi and the cameraman when he discovers he is being filmed. "Kapoor had the choicest of verbal abuses reserved for us when he realised what happened. He threatened us with dire consequences and even said he would stab the girl,"[15] Ilyasi said. "It was a trap," Kapoor later told a press conference. "This girl had been in touch with me for close to five months, calling me up in the middle of the night and asking for roles. She even sweet-talked me into meeting her. Any man would fall for this," he claimed.

Arushi Talwar Case

The Arushi Talwar case has raised several troubling questions for the media and the police, questions that strike at the heart of the process of investigation and news reporting. When the CBI finally conceded it could not find any evidence against Talwar, many thought it was all over. But a day later —when Rajesh Talwar walked out of Dasna jail, there was more of the same. Fifty days on, and there's no sign of fatigue, no end in sight to the media frenzy. "Please let me spend some time with my family. In the past 50 days, I have not been able to share my grief with anyone," Talwar said. The murder was a classic whodunit for the media. But it was the UP police that provided fodder for speculation. A press conference addressed by IG, Meerut Zone, Gurdarshan Singh, days after the murder added fuel to fire. "Arushi and Hemraj were aware of the extra-marital relationship of Doctor Talwar. And slowly they both developed intimate relationships," he said. Friends of the Talwar Family, ordinary citizens as well as the Women and Child Development Minister expressed outrage. Renuka Chowdhary demanded that Singh should be suspended and charged for character assassination of the victim. Faced with a bungling police force, the media, in a way, decided to play cop. The two families—Talwars and Durranis—continued to be taunted and harassed the moment they stepped out of their house, by an army of reporters. After the CBI took over the case on June 1, it added two other suspects. But it was still Rajesh Talwar who was hounded by the media. When his bail application was rejected, most of the media and their viewers felt vindicated. Warnings from CBI Director, Vijay Shankar—"We will keep reminding the media what its limits are," he said—did not help. New versions kept doing the rounds. Media critics say techniques such as reconstructions run the risk of distorting facts. "Any case that is still under investigation, I am not sure if you have the ethical right to do reconstructions and make a crime show out of it," says media critic, Shohini Ghosh. India records over 30,000 cases of homicide every year. There have been floods, terror attacks and political developments of national significance. But none of these has been able to distract media's attention from the Noida double murders. In fact, according to a study conducted by the CMS, special programmes on the case hogged almost 40 hours out of a total 92 hours of prime time between May 16 and June 7. Just how much is too much? Going by the media's continued obsession with the case, it seems even too much is too little.[16]

CNBC Awaz regularly conducts sting operations on issues concerning consumer rights and private sector malpractices. Stings have also become commonplace on crime shows, though these have no wider impact.

Nevertheless, the most publicized topic for stings remains government corruption. The Tehelka expose was on corruption in arms deals, Operation Duryodhan on MPs taking bribes to raise questions in Parliament, Operation Chakravyuh exposed misuse of the MPLAD fund, while Aaj Tak's "Ghoos Mahal" was on corruption in Tihar jail and a sales tax office. The CNN-IBN expose showed us a UP minister willing to transport narcotics. Kairali TV also recently carried out a sting exposing a state minister. All these sting operations dealt with misuse of power by the authorities—crooked politicians, government officials and policemen.

These are all remarkable examples of the power of the

media. Sting operations have unflinchingly exposed the rot in the system and brought corruption into focus. Though a lot of what they reveal is depressing, none of it is especially surprising. Stings have only confirmed what were once mere suspicions or allegations. They have also put pressure on politicians and bureaucrats to take action against their colleagues caught with their hands in the till. News channels usually insist that their sting operations are done in public interest. They point out that stings are expensive, unpredictable affairs. Large sums of money go into paying bribes; budgets cannot be fixed in advance and can increase dramatically. And after all that, there is no guarantee of success.

Violation of Law and Sting Operation

Sting operations have raised many questions relating to citizen's privacy or violation of existing laws. Thanks to technology explosion, in the coming years, India besides making progress in several fields, will also be entering the age of sting operations and phone tapping. At the rate at which politicians are vying with each other in claiming that their phones are being tapped, a time may come when anyone whose phone is not being tapped will probably feel deprived or convinced that he needs to do something drastic to get his phone tapped or become a victim of sting operations.

The feeling of being deprived and not being considered important enough to be target of a sting operation or telephone tapping may put you into a category of a second class citizen and force many to seek different ways to become a VIP who is a target of telephone tapping and sting operation. If one were to believe all the stories floating around, one will have to reach a conclusion that every second person in our cities is working for a detective agency or some state organization in the profession of telephone tapping for a fee.

The Government which was quick to act in case of cyber law by enacting legislation on the subject to prevent its misuse has not acted promptly enough in case of sting operations or telephone tapping. This requires action as these sensitive areas are no more the monopoly of public sector; many private players have entered the field. As indicated in a recent case, the network run by a private company was involved in phone tapping case. As such, the need for having proper legislation to make the process foolproof and to discourage its misuse.

As for the sting operations, every channel is competing to undertake such operations to improve their ratings or viewership despite recent disclosures that such operations have not added many in numbers. But as sting operations have become a fashion, no channel would like to be left behind. This has raised many important questions relating to citizen's privacy or violation of existing laws. There is no doubt that new technology which can be obtained for a measly sum of a few lakhs of rupees has made these operations easy and simple.

On the issue of phone tapping, Parliament must draft a law to lay down rules under which such operations can be undertaken. The authority which can authorize such operations must be specified and the reasons for ordering such a probe specified. The private agencies should be debarred from indulging in the same and stiff punishments including closure of their professional operations should be made mandatory in case they are found guilty of undertaking such activities. It is strange that the mushroom growth of detective agencies, security agencies, indulging in illegal methods to recover bank loans are being allowed without any legislation to govern their working.[17]

Even the highest court in the country has commented on the misuse of data released by telephone companies which is used by many institutions including banks to harass the subscribers by making calls soliciting business at all odd hours and thus harassing them. This activity has neither been curtailed nor regulated despite observations by the Supreme Court on the subject. Telephone companies which allow the release of data for small gains probably could also be guilty of allowing tapping for considerations. The effective way to check this menace will be to ask agencies investigating such cases to also suggest legal amendments to safeguard the users of telephones.

As for sting operations, a time has come when media organizations like the Press Council of India should step forward and regulate this activity. In case they fail to do so, the job of censorship or regulating TV channels will fall on the Government which will be worse than the original crime as it would give them power to introduce censorship through the backdoor. In this entire debate, one must keep in mind the fact that as new technologies develop, they will provide many new benefits but will also open doors for their misuse by unscrupulous agencies in public as well as private sector.

The Government and media organizations must remain vigilant and deal with all such activities before they get out of control. The possibilities of invading the privacy of individuals have become very easy with new aids available. So, the temptations to use them for short-term gains will remain strong unless the regulators are equally alert. Recently, the controversy on these issues instead of trying to resolve the problems, has become a part of political upmanship with ridiculous demands being made to suggest that an inquiry be conducted by Chief Ministers.

The leaders occupying such offices may have many qualities but are, by no stretch of imagination, capable of conducting inquiry or doing so professionally. This work must be done by professionals. The politicians who, by misusing official agencies, create doubts about their bonafides. They are also the first to cry foul when they are at the receiving end. Solution lies in more active role by agencies like Election Commission and courts to preserve the independence of agencies who are expected to do such work as per our Constitution and laws of the country.

With India becoming a major economic power, several multinationals are in the fray and prospects of using the media to serve selfish interests have become real. Ethics in print or electronic media has become a live issue because of recent developments like increasing use of sting operations using hidden or miniature cameras, inducements like presenting live models and other forms of inducement by them. At the same time, in print media, the influence of industrial houses has become a major factor either through heavy investments or indirect help in the form of equity building. These dangers are expected to grow in days to come with laws governing foreign investments being relaxed everyday. Under the circumstances, a time has come when the Government and professional bodies of journalists should become aware of these dangers and take steps to check the menace before it starts undermining the credibility of Indian media.

The issues were very simple in olden times when the media was owned or controlled by a few big industrial houses called: "Jute Press": The situation has totally changed today as the media has become a huge empire requiring investments in several crores of rupees. In many cases, the reverse engineering has taken place where the newspaper barons have entered other industries to join the category of large industrial houses. The result is that the shape of media is undergoing a change. This change will pick up fresh momentum when foreign investment caps are relaxed or removed altogether.[18]

As of now, the international magazines have started their local editions and giants like Wall Street journal, New York Herald and Tribune have either started selling their services to local newspapers or started publishing their own editions. The old style protection provided to journalists has also disappeared as nearly all newspapers of standing are employing journalists on contract thus doing away with job security or professional protection. The entire edifice built under the guidance of Press Commissions and several Wage boards appointed by the Government has become a matter of history as it does not really exist anymore.

Under the circumstances, the dangers of media being misused by local industrialists or any foreign agencies has become real. After all, with India well poised to become a major economic power, several multinationals are likely to enter. The prospects of using the media to serve selfish (business) interests have become real. Such political manipulations were hinted at when, on the eve of last elections to the Lok Sabha, the ruling National Democratic Alliance (NDA) was accused of unduly influencing the media by launching a campaign "India shining" on the eve of elections which gave a bonanza in terms of several crores of rupees for the print as well as electronic media.

Yet another danger posed by such manipulations was hinted at during the Enron controversy when the American giant was reported to have spent several million dollars for so called "education of media and other decision-makers."[19] As the media become more and more of an industry with very little regulations, the dangers of such misuse will increase to the point where they can pose a serious threat to our economy and country. In recent times, many instances of misuse of media have been brought to public notice, but not much has been done to check these abuses. For instance, the publication of pictures and items by newspapers for cash consideration in local pages is being practiced by some established newspapers. These newspapers have also reduced the office of Editor to being a product manager only. These developments have created a situation where more serious forms of media exploitation can take place to the advantage of a particular group.

The latest instance of such misuse has been brought out by several members of Parliament in their representation to Prime Minister, Dr Manmohan Singh, Finance Minister P. Chidambaram and other officials. They have pointed out in their letters that in the recent controversy between siblings of largest industrial house in India, Reliance, the large-scale misuse of media has taken place. It is no secret that selected channels like CNBC, Aaj Tak and newspapers like Asian Age were regularly publishing stories damaging to elder brother in control of RIL. Without going into the merits of the stand taken by newspaper or TV channel, one fact stands out that these were also beneficiaries of large investment from Reliance Capital, a company controlling mutual funds under the management of Mr Anil Ambani, the younger brother.[20]

The MPs have rightly demanded that such nexus between media and industrial houses needs to be investigated by official agencies like SEBI and others. At stake is not only the reputation of these channels and publications but of the entire media. The facts brought out by MPs clearly bring out that around the time when this campaign started, the organisations also benefited in terms of more investment by company under the control of one brother. The investments in these companies can hardly be justified on the basis of the sordid state of their finances or future prospects. It is certainly a case for the Press Council of India to look into and Government to investigate. As this is not the first or the last battle being fought for control of an industrial empire, the role of media must remain neutral and transparent at all times.

Eminent Supreme Court advocate and member of Rajya Sabha from Jharkhand, R.K. Anand, is firmly of the opinion that to expose corruption in the high places, both the media and legal community are justified to use the sting operations as an instrument of exposure where gathering normal evidence under the normal provisions of the Indian Evidence Act is made impossible by the men and women in exalted positions.

Answering a question, Anand posed an equally strident question, "If a Prime Minister, a Home Minister or a Chief Minister is corrupt, how does one gather dependable information against them which can be cited in courts of law as reliable evidence? His own answer was that in such cases, the media, often with the support and collaboration of the legal profession, had resorted to sting operations. He cited the ruling of a British court in a sensational sting operation against a top British leader involved in bribery and sex scandal to expose corruption in high places, the media was justified in using sting operations. Since the Indian law is mostly based on the English law, the implementation is obvious (on British court ruling line).

UNDERCOVER OPERATIONS

An undercover operation is an investigative technique in which an operative either an undercover agent who assumes a covert identity or purpose, or a confidential informant who takes action to gain evidence or information which would be unavailable but for the target's reliance on the operative's covert role.

The undercover technique may be used in relation to criminal violations enforceable under the investigative jurisdiction of the IRS. The use of undercover operations is an essential technique in the detection and investigation of criminal activity involving tax and money laundering offenses. Undercover does not include the temporary assumption of a pretext identity for the purpose of protecting the integrity of surveillance.

They may use undercover activities and conduct undercover operations, pursuant to these Guidelines, that are appropriate to carry out its law enforcement responsibilities. These guidelines do not apply to investigations utilizing confidential informants, cooperating witnesses or cooperating subjects, unless the investigation team also utilizes an undercover employee. The FBI, through the development of internal policy, may choose to apply these Guidelines to certain confidential informant, cooperating witness, and cooperating subject operations by referring such matters to the Undercover Review Committee pursuant to Section IV, Paragraph (D)(6).[21]

Under this authority, the FBI may participate in joint undercover activities with other law enforcement-agencies and may operate a proprietary to the extent necessary to maintain an operations cover or effectiveness. All joint undercover operations are to be conducted pursuant to these Guidelines.

Undercover activities are classified as either Group I or Group II. All Group I undercover operations must be approved by the Chief, Criminal Investigation (CI). Group II undercover operations are approved by the Director, Field Operations

AUTHORIZATION OF UNDERCOVER OPERATIONS

Any official considering approval or authorization of a proposed undercover application shall weigh the risks and benefits of the operation, giving careful consideration to the following factors:

The risk of personal injury to individuals, property damage, financial loss to persons or businesses, damage to reputation, or other harm to persons;

The risk of civil liability or other loss to the Government;

The risk of invasion of privacy or interference with privileged or confidential relationships;

The risk that individuals engaged in undercover operations may become involved in illegal conduct restricted in paragraph IV.

The suitability of Government participation in the type of activity that is expected to occur during the operation.

Undercover Operations Which May be Authorized by the Special Agent

The establishment, extension, or renewal of all undercover operations to be supervised by a given field office must be approved by the SAC if the undercover operation does not involve any of the factors listed in paragraph IV.C.

(a) Initiation of investigative activity regarding the alleged criminal conduct or criminal enterprise is warranted under any applicable departmental guidelines;

(b) The proposed undercover operation appears to be an effective means of obtaining evidence or necessary information. This finding should include a statement of what prior investigation has been conducted and what chance the operation has of obtaining evidence or necessary information concerning the alleged criminal conduct or criminal enterprise;

(c) The undercover operation will be conducted with minimal intrusion consistent with the need to collect the evidence or information in a timely and effective manner;

(d) Approval for the use of any informant or confidential source has been obtained as required by the Attorney General's Guidelines on Use of Informants and Confidential Sources;

(e) Any foreseeable participation by an undercover employee in illegal activity that can be approved by the SAC on his or her own authority is justified by the factors noted in paragraph H;

(f) If there is no present expectation of the occurrence of any of the sensitive or fiscal circumstances listed in paragraph C, a statement to that effect.

2. Undercover operations may be authorized pursuant to this sub-section for upto six months and continued upon the renewal for an additional six-month period, for a total of no more than one year. Undercover operations initiated pursuant to this subsection may not involve the expenditure of more than $40,000 ($100,000 in drug cases of which a maximum of $40,000 is for operational expenses).

3. The SAC may delegate the responsibility to authorize the establishment, extension, or renewal of undercover operations to designated Assistant Special Agents in Charge. The delegation of this responsibility by the SAC should be in writing and maintained in the appropriate field office.

SENSITIVE CIRCUMSTANCES

In all undercover operations involving any sensitive circumstances, the SAC shall submit an application. The application shall be reviewed by appropriate supervisory body or by personnel. If favourably recommended it would be sent to the Undercover Review Committee for consideration. The application shall then be forwarded to the Director or a designated Assistant Director, who may approve or disapprove the application.

For purposes of these Guidelines, sensitive circumstances are involved if there is a reasonable expectation that the undercover operation will involve:

(a) An investigation of possible criminal conduct by any elected or appointed official, or political candidate, for a judicial, legislative, management, or executive—level position of trust in a Federal, state, or local governmental entity or political subdivision thereof;

(b) An investigation of any public official at the Federal, state, or local level in any matter involving systemic corruption of any governmental function;

(c) An investigation of possible criminal conduct by any foreign official or government, religious organization, political organization, or the news media;

(d) Engaging in activity having a significant effect on or constituting a significant intrusion into the legitimate operation of a Federal, state, or local governmental entity;
(e) Establishing, acquiring, or using a proprietary;
(f) Providing goods or services which are essential to the commission of a crime, which goods and services are reasonably unavailable to a subject of the investigation except from the Government;
(g) Activity that is proscribed by local law as a felony or that is otherwise a serious crime—but not including the purchase of stolen or contraband goods; the delivery or sale by the Government of stolen property whose ownership cannot be determined; the controlled delivery of drugs which will not enter commerce; the payments of bribes which are not included in the other sensitive circumstances; or the making of false representations to third parties in concealment of personal identity or the true ownership of a proprietary (this exemption does not include any statement under oath or the penalties of perjury).
(h) A significant risk that a person participating in an undercover operation will be arrested or will supply falsely sworn testimony or false documentation in any legal or administrative proceeding;
(i) Attendance at a meeting or participation in communications between any individual and his or her lawyer;
(j) A significant risk that a third party will enter into a professional or confidential relationship with a person participating in an undercover operation who is acting as an attorney, physician, clergyman, or member of the news media;
(k) request to an attorney, physician, member of the clergy, or other person for information that would ordinarily be privileged or to a member of the news media concerning an individual with whom the news person is known to have a professional or confidential relationship;

(l) Participation in the activities of a group under investigation as part of a Domestic Security Investigation or recruiting a person from within such a group as an informant;

(m) A significant risk of violence or physical injury to individuals or a significant risk of financial loss;

(n) Activities which could result in significant claims against the United States arising in tort, contract or for compensation for the "taking" of property;

(o) Untrue representations by a person participating in the undercover operation concerning the activities or involvement of any third person without that individual's knowledge or consent.

ENTRAPMENT DEFENCE

The entrapment defence is the principle means by which the government's use of "sting" operations are regulated. Where it applies, the entrapment defence exempts from criminal liability individuals who were encouraged by an agent of the government to commit what would otherwise be an offence. The critical issue is how to define the circumstances distinguishing "entrapment" from ordinary and acceptable undercover operations. Entrapment doctrine must draw some line, between permissible and impermissible undercover police tactics or between defendants whose conduct in such circumstances does or does not justify conviction, or something else.

Most jurisdictions recognize a subjective test for entrapment, which exculpates a defendant whose crime was (a) encouraged or "induced" by the government, if (b) the defendant was not predisposed to commit such crimes. Inducement and redisposition are murky ideas. Inducement requires something more than creating a mere opportunity for the defendant to commit the crime. Courts often merge the inducement inquiry into the predisposition inquiry, by asking whether the police did enough to induce a non-redisposed individual to commit the crime. Where the courts treat inducement as a genuinely independent element, it seems mostly to eliminate the entrapment defense in cases where the government agent did not even encourage the crime. Thus, inducement means persuasion; if police are merely observing events, even when they created criminal opportunities, they have not induced the crime.

In practice, undercover agents often do encourage crime. The cases, therefore, routinely turn on predisposition. Courts often use predisposition to mean the defendant was willing, in the sense of not reluctant, to commit the crime. A typical jury instruction provides:

Where a person has no previous intent or purpose to violate the law, but is induced or persuaded by law enforcement officers or their agents to commit a crime, that person is a victim of entrapment, and the law forbids his conviction. On the other hand, where a person is predisposed to commit an offense that is, ready and willing to violate the law at the first opportunity, the fact that these government officials or their agents afford him the opportunities to do so does not constitute entrapment.[22]

The government bears the burden of proving predisposition. Prosecutors tend to prove this element with evidence that the defendant exhibited no reluctance when she accepted the government's inducement, possesses knowledge or abilities useful only for committing the offense, or has committed similar offenses or acts in the past. Thus, when the issue is raised, the prosecution can introduce otherwise inadmissible evidence concerning the defendant' s reputation past crimes, and past bad acts.

LAW ENFORCEMENT CONTROLLED OPERATIONS BILL

Criminals will use any method to commit crimes and protect themselves and their ill-gotten gains. The purpose of this bill is to allow law enforcement agencies to use similar methods to fight crime while at the same time providing a strict system of accountability for the use of otherwise unlawful activities.

The bill provides for the authorisation, conduct and monitoring of operations involving what might otherwise be unlawful activities. These are to be known as controlled operations. This bill will achieve four things. Firstly, it will provide undercover officers with protection against criminal prosecution for offences committed in the course of a controlled operation. Secondly, it will put in place a tight accountability mechanism for the approval and oversight of controlled operations.

Thirdly, it will remove any doubt as to the legal status of evidence obtained in the course of a controlled operation. Controlled operations will be used by the Police Service, the independent Commission Against Corruption, Crime Commission and the Police Integrity Commission in the fight Against crime and corruption. Undercover operations are an important investigative tool. They allow law enforcement agencies to infiltrate criminal groups and to obtain evidence to prosecute for the crimes these groups commit. In some cases, undercover officers have to commit offences themselves in the course of investigation.

For example, in a drug operation, an undercover operative posing as a buyer cannot actually take possession of drugs without technically committing an offence. Furthermore, evidence obtained in a controlled operation may be subject to challenge in court. The admissibility of evidence collected during undercover operations has been under a cloud since 1995.

POLICY ON USE OF REVENUES FOR UNDERCOVER OPERATIONS

The following three sources of revenue be designated as restricted: Drug Enforcement Administration Forfeitures, Controlled Substance Tax Funds, and Local Courts Undercover Restitution. These restricted revenues shall be spent only for law enforcement purposes and shall be used to enhance law enforcement, not to replace local dollars. These revenues shall be spent in the following order: (1) Drug Enforcement Administration, (2) Controlled Substance Tax Funds, and (3) Local Courts Undercover Restitution. The policy was adopted on May 6, 1991.

The justification for undercover operations generally has been expressed as follows:

Covert investigative techniques are often the most

efficient, effective and, in the case of the most virulent strains of criminality, such as organised and major drug related crime, the only practical way of obtaining evidence for the purposes of prosecuting and convicting those responsible.

TRIAL BY MEDIA

The right to a fair trial is at the heart of the Indian criminal justice system. It encompasses several other rights including the right to be presumed innocent until proven guilty, the right not to be compelled to be a witness against oneself, the right to a public trial, the right to legal representation, the right to speedy trial, the right to be present during trial and examine witnesses, etc. In Zahira Habibullah Sheikh v. State of Gujarat, the Supreme Court explained that a "fair trial obviously would mean a trial before an impartial Judge, a fair prosecutor and atmosphere of judicial calm. Fair trial means a trial in which bias or prejudice for or against the accused, the witnesses, or the cause which is being tried is eliminated."[23] However, sensationalised news stories circulated by the media have steadily gnawed at the guarantees of a right to a fair trial and posed a grave threat to the presumption of innocence. What is more, the pervasive influence of the press is increasingly proving to be detrimental to the impartial decision-making process of the judiciary. Such news stories cannot easily be defended under the auspices of freedom of expression.

IMPACT OF PRE-TRIAL PUBLICITY

Sensationalised journalism has also had an impact on the judiciary. For example, in upholding the imposition of the death penalty on Mohammed Afzal for the December 2001 attack on the Indian Parliament, Justice P. Venkatarama Reddi stated, "the incident, which resulted in heavy casualties, had shaken the entire nation and the collective conscience of the society will only be satisfied if the capital punishment is awarded to the offender." A 'media trial' began almost immediately after Afzal's arrest. Only one week after the attack, on 20 December 2001, the police called a press conference during the course of which Afzal 'incriminated himself' in front of the national media. The media played an excessive and negative role in shaping the public conscience before Afzal was even tried. Similarly, S.A.R. Geelani, one of Afzal's co-defendants in the Parliament attack case, was initially sentenced to death for his alleged involvement despite an overwhelming lack of evidence. Large sections of the Indian media portrayed him as a dangerous and trained terrorist. On appeal, the Delhi High Court overturned Geelani's conviction and described the prosecution's case as "at best, absurd and tragic." Jayendra Saraswati, head abbot of Kanchi Kamakoti Peetham, was accused of killing two mill-workers as sacrifice, based solely on newspaper reports. The Andhra Pradesh High Court in Labour Liberation Front v. State of Andhra Pradesh held that the writ petition filed to force the authorities to investigate relied upon incorrect facts that should have been verified. The court observed that "once an incident involving prominent person or institution takes place, the media is swinging into action and virtually leaving very little for the prosecution or the Courts..."[24]

IMPACT ON THE RIGHT TO LEGAL REPRESENTATION

There has been extensive media coverage of police investigations of 'serial-killings' in Noida in the outskirts of New Delhi. The owner of the house where the corpses were found, Mohinder Singh Pandher, and his domestic help Surendra Kohli, are suspected of having committed these crimes. Influenced by media coverage, much of it proclaiming that the two men had already confessed to the killings, the local Bar Association announced that it had decided that no advocate from Noida would defend Pandher and Kohli in court. Likewise, when eminent lawyer Ram Jethmalani decided to defend Manu Sharma, a prime accused in a murder case, he was subject to public derision. A senior editor of the television news channel CNN-IBN called the decision to represent Sharma an attempt to "defend the indefensible."[25] This was only one example of the media-instigated campaign against the accused. The media assumption of guilt clearly encroaches upon the right to legal representation—a critical component of the right to fair trial —and may also intimidate lawyers into refusing to represent accused persons.

REGULATORY MEASURES

The Press Council of India (PCI) was established to preserve the freedom of the press and to improve the standards of news reporting in India. Under the Press Council Act 1978, if someone believes that a news agency has committed any professional misconduct, the PCI can, if they agree with the complainant, "warn, admonish or censure the newspaper", or direct the newspaper to, "publish the contradiction of the complainant in its forthcoming issue." Given that these measures can only be enforced after the publication of news materials, and do not involve particularly harsh punishments, their effectiveness in preventing the publication of prejudicial reports appears to be limited. Along with these powers, the PCI has established a set of suggested norms for journalistic conduct. These norms emphasise the importance of accuracy and fairness and encourage the press to "eschew publication of inaccurate, baseless, graceless, misleading or distorted material." The norms urge that any criticism of the judiciary should be published with great caution. These norms further recommend that reporters should avoid one-sided inferences, but attempt to maintain an impartial and sober tone at all times. But significantly, these norms cannot be legally enforced, and are largely observed in breach. Lastly, the PCI also has criminal contempt powers to restrict the publication of prejudicial media reports. However, the PCI can only exercise its contempt powers with respect to pending civil or criminal cases. This limitation overlooks the extent to which pre-trial reporting can hamper the administration of justice and brand innocent people guilty.[26]

Heinous crimes must be condemned and the media would be justified in calling for the perpetrators to be punished in accordance with the law. However, the media cannot usurp the function of the judiciary and deviate from objective and unbiased reporting. While a media shackled by government regulation is unhealthy for democracy, the implications of continued unaccountability are even more damaging. Steps need to be taken in order to prevent media trials from eroding the civil rights of citizens, whereby the media have a clearer definition of their rights and duties, and the courts are given the power to punish those who flagrantly disregard them. The judiciary has been critical of the overactive and prejudicial reporting by the media. In the Labour Liberation Front case, Justice L. Narasimha Reddy lamented the "abysmal levels to which the norms of journalism have drifted." In M.P. Lohia v. State of West Bengal, the Supreme Court cautioned the publisher, editor and journalist of a magazine that had reported the facts of a case that was sub-judice, thus "interfering with the administration of justice." The Indian Law Commission's recent report entitled Trial by Media: Free Speech vs. Fair Trial Under Criminal Procedure (Amendments to the Contempt of Court Act, 1971) has made recommendations to address the damaging effect of sensationalised news reports on the administration of justice. While the report has yet to be made public, news reports indicate that the Commission has recommended prohibiting publication of anything that is prejudicial towards the accused — a restriction that shall operate from the time of arrest. It also reportedly recommends that the High Court be empowered to direct postponement of publication or telecast in criminal cases. The credibility of news media rests on unbiased and objective reporting. It is in the media's interest to ensure that the administration of justice is not undermined.[27]

COURT CONCERN OVER 'TRIAL BY MEDIA'

Expressing concern over "trial by media," the Delhi High Court said that the functions of the court could not be usurped by any other authority in a civilised society. "Fairness of trial is of paramount importance as without such a protection, there would be trial by media which no civilised society can and should tolerate,"[28] Justice J.D Kapoor observed while pronouncing the verdict in the Bofors pay-off case. Stressing that the streams of justice have to be kept clear and pure, the court said "there is nothing more incumbent upon courts of justice than to preserve their proceedings from being misrepresented, than to prejudice the minds of the public against persons concerned before the case is finally heard." Terming the Bofors case "a nefarious example which manifestly demonstrates how the trial and justice by media can cause irreparable, irreversible and incalculable harm to the reputation of a person and shunning of his family, relatives and friends by the society," the court said such a person is ostracised, humiliated and convicted without trial. ``All this puts at grave risk due administration of justice," Justice Kapoor observed. The court cited the recent case of Punjabi Pop singer Daler Mehndi, whose discharge was sought in a human trafficking case ``after his humiliation and pseudo trial through media as they (police) have not been able to find the evidence sufficient even for filing the chargesheet."[29]

JESSICA LAL CASE

The Jessica Lal murder trial had peculiar feature of being reported in the Press and especially in Delhi newspapers. Instead of targeting the alleged killer, or worrying about the possibility of him going, now that all the main eyewitnesses claim to have seen nothing, most of our crime reporters are pointing the needle of suspicion at Bina Ramani and her daughter, Malini. Some newspapers have gone so far as to demand that the Ramanis be arrested. The demand is both bizarre and interesting because, just as when the murder took place on April 29, 1999, the Press seems to be playing an active role in trying to get Jessica's alleged killer off the hook. At the time of the murder, please remember, most Delhi newspapers seemed to give their gossip columnists the task of investigating the case. This was apparently because Bina and Malini were celebrated socialites familiar on the gossip columnist circuit. Alas, once a gossip columnist always a gossip columnist, so instead of crime stories we got details of Bina's glamorous parties and famous friends and Malini's seductive clothing. We learned almost nothing about the ugly, little world of Manu Sharma nor did we hear anything about why the police work in the case was so shoddy as to amount to criminal negligence. So illogical was the manner in which Jessica's tragic, needless murder was reported that if you were a casual reader, you may have ended up concluding from the stories that serving liquor without a licence — which Bina did in the Tamarind Cafe — was a bigger crime than murder. Something similar is beginning to happen again and this time round, it will almost certainly work towards getting Manu Sharma out of jail and off the hook. Let us examine what has happened since the trial began. The most important aspect of it is that four key eyewitnesses have stood up in court and said that they did not see Manu Sharma actually pull the trigger. That at least some of them are lying should be obvious to even the most of crime reporters and we should have had at least one story that attempted to investigate why they were suddenly afraid to stand by their earlier statements. But, nobody seems interested in this at all. Manu's father is a powerful Punjab politician who, for many years, was one of the pillars of the Congress. It does not need much investigation to know that in our fair and wondrous land, politicians have many ways of influencing the police to go easy when it comes to getting their delinquent sons off the hook. Ever since Jessica was murdered, Delhi has buzzed with rumours of influence being used to change of the case but for mysterious reasons crime reporters seem either oblivious of these rumours or too scared to investigate them. So, instead of the Sharmas being targeted, it is the Ramanis they are going after. Most stories have hinted that the police have been protecting them by not charging them with "destruction of evidence." No story so far has even attempted vaguely to point out that the "evidence" would be irrelevant any way if the police cannot find anyone who admits to seeing Manu pull the trigger. In Tamarind Café, Manu tried to escape. Bina's husband, George, chased after him while she took Jessica to hospital. The police, for their part, took so long to arrive at the scene of the crime that Manu or one of his pals was able to return and drive his car away. The murder weapon also disappeared. Meanwhile, the small amount of blood that stained the spot where Jessica was shot was cleaned up—possibly in the routine course—by the restaurant's staff. Now, the interesting thing about the Press demanding that the Ramanis be arrested and charged is that this would ensure that Manu goes free because if they are treated as co-accused, they cannot also be credible witnesses. So, there would be nobody left to give any evidence at all. If nobody admits to have at least seen the alleged killer in the Tamarind Cafe that night then the case is closed before it starts and Manu goes free. As it is, he will probably find it quite easy now to get bail. This has been the game the Sharmas have wanted, played all along and it has truly disturbed the Press, that it should become a vital part of it. Even more disturbing if you consider that this is far from being the only case in which the media has allowed itself to be used in this fashion. Trial by the media has become so prominent these days that the police use it regularly to cover up for shoddy police work. [30]

PRIYA RAJVANSH MURDER CASE

In 2008, in Mumbai, newspapers played a willing and eager role in helping the police make its case against Chetan Anand's sons in the Priya Rajvansh murder case. Neither of the two accused was physically present when she was killed but the police made a case against them on the alleged statement by a maid servant whom they had taken into custody. The Press made no effort to investigate what had really happened and the result was that the two Anand boys were tried and condemned so completely in the media that it is hard to see how they can hope now for an unprejudiced trial.

In every other country, there is respect for the idea of a case being subjudice which means that when a matter is under judicial deliberation it cannot be commented on. The Indian Press appears to have forgotten that the idea exists. The Indian justice system has become one of our most serious problems. It takes so long for justice to be done that even murder cases take between ten and twenty years to be decided. The result is a backlog in our courts that, according to conservative estimates, would take 324 years to clear. Justice so delayed can hardly be considered justice. The problem is so grave that it will need a monumental effort on the part of the government and the judiciary to deal with it. But, meanwhile, it has to be the responsibility of the Press to ensure that we do not add to the problem by allowing crime reporters to become willing handmaidens of the police in organising trials by the media.

The entire media has jumped to the instant conclusion, on the persuasion of the police and the political establishment, that Shah is guilty of playing footsie with the mob. In the process, they have ignored the actual evidence before the courts. Answering a mobster's telephone call is not exactly a crime. It was just another way of staying alive. Yet the media has deliberately chosen to present the facts of the case in an unfair and prejudicial manner. Shah is guilty, but, till the courts decide, we must, in the best traditions of justice and fair play, presume him innocent. We cannot, in fact, we must not prejudge him. Unfortunately, that is exactly what the media has done and made it virtually impossible for him to get a fair trial.[31]

CHAND MOHAMMAD AND FIZA

The questions after probing questions fired at Chand Mohammad and Fiza today were unsparing, but the couple survived the trial by media. The woman for whom Chand lost his chair showed flashes of her training as a lawyer when she counter-questioned a reporter who told her to recite a verse from the Quran if he could read one off from his scripture. "You look like a Hindu. Can you recite the Hanuman Chalisa?" Fiza shot back when the reporter told the couple, who had turned Muslim to marry, to prove their faith. "Do not bring religion into everything," she continued angrily, her husband looking on uneasily at the raging war of words. The "missing" couple had surfaced some 10 days and announced on TV that they had converted to Islam and married. Chand, 43, has two children by first wife Seema and Fiza, 35, is a divorcee. Chand was sacked as Haryana deputy chief minister soon after the news broke. Fiza was fired as the assistant advocate-general. Today, at an event at Delhi Press Club, neither showed signs of any regret. "For love, I can sacrifice everything," Chand said, appearing the milder of the two. Nettled by a journalist on whether he had converted only because Islam allows a man to take four wives, he merely said: "From childhood, I was inclined towards Islam." If he was so keen, why did he delay his conversion so long? "My timing is my personal choice," he replied, opting not to answer whether he intended to take a third and a fourth wife. Fiza gave her reply a more philosophical spin. "Parmeswar (God) or Allah comes into one's life first and then people," she said. Another reporter then fired the obvious question: What came into their lives first --- Allah or love? The couple replied that they did namaaz every day. Fiza claimed she had "not done any injustice" to Seema as she "still respects" her. Chand said he was trying to meet Sonia Gandhi to explain why he had re-married. Fiza, who answered most of the questions on her husband's behalf, suddenly went meek when asked if she would enter politics. "It is up to my husband. If he allows me, I will surely do so."[32]

ERAL FAMILY MASSACRE CASE

A court in Godhra convicted 11 people for murdering a family in Eral village of Panchmahal district during the 2002 riots in Gujarat. Eight persons were awarded life imprisonment for burning alive the seven-member family and raping two of their girls in the village on March 2. The verdict gives a ray of hope to people fighting to get justice in courts hearing hundreds of riot cases. The verdict comes at a time when the media has again alleged Chief Minister Narendra Modi and his government's complicity in the riots. A sting operation by Tehelka, the newsmagazine, on Friday showed people accused of murdering and attacking Muslims in the 2002 boasting that Modi shielded and encouraged them.[33]

Does the conviction of the 11 people in the Eral family massacre case days after the Tehelka case indicate the media is building a moral pressure on the justice system? Salve, amicus curiae to the Supreme Court in the riots cases, said the media cannot influence the judiciary but it can certainly build pressure on the Gujarat police. "The manner in which the police has been investigating the riots is known to all. Our criminal justice is in such despair; thank God and the media for keeping issues alive." Dholakia, director of Parzania, a movie on the riots which was banned in Gujarat, said many families who suffered in 2002 believe the law doesn't care for them. "Like the family in my film, many people have not got help from the law. They named people who were involved in the riots but there was no support from the law. So, yes, the media has played major role in keeping the issue alive,"[34] said Dholakia.

SOME OTHER CASES

In the case of Nadeem Saifi. The British courts have actually admonished our investigators for the inept job they have done and yet the media, slavishly parroting the establishment, persists in painting him guilty. Shankar Sharma, accused of trashing Yashwant Sinha's dream budget. Ketan Parekh, charged with rigging the stock market. Fardeen Khan, caught with a gram of cocaine for his own use. Salman Khan, accused of diverting his local earnings into foreign exchange. All the people put through hell to make headlines that can sell their newspapers or lure viewers for the news shows. This is what the media has finally come to. Selling instant justice so that more people buy newspapers lured by hot headlines. So that more people watch the news and TRPs go up, more advertising revenue comes in. Media is only about making money.

There was a time when the media was more sedate but more responsible because it was not trying to hawk its wares in a competitive market where the shrillest shriek draws the most attention. It was trying to bring us the truth. The truth as it honestly saw it. Journalists were not under pressure to push up ratings or sales. So they did their work with serious intent, with conviction, with courage and integrity. They did not pronounce people guilty without making a serious attempt to study the charges, investigate them, come to their own independent conclusions, without fear or favour. They did not blindly print what law enforcers claimed, what the bureaucracy said or what politicians planted on to them. That is why people trusted them.

Everyone manipulates the media to serve his own interests or hurt his rivals. If they cannot do this on their own, they hire spin doctors. In the process, justice is compromised, fair play is lost, truth is injured. What we get are doctored facts and convenient conclusions. We get planted stories that influence the course of justice and compromise our rights as citizens of free India. In fact, if the media is not careful, it could destroy the very foundations of this civil society.

With globalisation exposing the Indian media to the callousness in the functioning of the market at an international level, which provides greater as well as wider access to information, there is a need to understand the tendencies and practices that blur reality. In the changing world order media, needs to put in place systems that restore the confidence of the people. The media has yet to come to terms in resisting the temptation of building brand images, which blur the other aspects of reality on vital issues like combating communalism and problems of the common people. Media organisations must realise the need to draw out a system of control to prevent the necessary process of investigation degenerating into a "trial by the media."

The Director of the IDC, Pramod Kumar said that while in the era of globalisation, media has been able to question the creation of stereotypes, it also has a responsibility of reporting issues related to communalism, keeping in view the impact it can have on the sensibilities and reactions of the Indian diaspora. It is in this context where the "frog in a well, equipped with a telescope" syndrome needs to be understood, as he drew out the extreme localisation of news even by the established newspapers, which till recently claimed national credentials.[35]

Facing Rape Charge, Goa Minister's Son

Panaji, December 10, 2008 (IANS) Counsel for Goa Education Minister, Atanasio Monserrate's son, Rohit, told the court that his client has been harassed and convicted by the media for the rape of a 14-year-old German girl "even before the trial." "The media has been investigating the case more than the police are. Rohit has been subjected to a lot of unfair media scrutiny even before the trial started," Rohit Monserrate's lawyer, Atmaram Nadkarni, told IANS. The case came up for hearing at the Panaji bench of the Bombay High Court after Chief Justice, Swatanter Kumar, took suo moto cognizance of the rape. At the last hearing on November 21, 2008, Justice Kumar, in his show-cause notice to the state, asked why the case should not be handed over to the Central Bureau of Investigation (CBI) for probe and why should not the bail granted to Rohit by a lower court be cancelled. The court also grilled the police as to why the other influential accused in the case, Warren Alemao, was not arrested by the police. Warren is nephew of two cabinet ministers, Churchill Alemao and Joaquim Alemao. Meanwhile, in an embarrassing disclosure, the Goa police, in an affidavit, told the court that Rohit was not absconding as was construed in the chief justice's order of November 21, 2008. "Rohit was never absconding. The police did not want to arrest him as the victim was not willing either to give her statement or allow a medical examination," Superintendent of Police (North) Bosco George told the court. In his submission to the court, state Advocate General, Subodh Kantak, said, Rohit was arrested before the girl's statement was recorded by a local magistrate. The sensational rape case caught the attention of the national media as sons and kin of three ministers and one BJP legislator were probed, which was riddled with inadequacies. Justice Kumar and Justice S.A. Bobade of the Bombay High Court, while taking up the case, said: "If reports of the newspapers are correct even to some extent, then they demonstrate the apathy of the police machinery towards the rule of law. It is not only obligatory, but mandatory for the investigating agency to effectively and expeditiously progress with the investigation of a case once the FIR is registered."[36]

Uma Khurana Case

Among the numerous sting operations carried out since

the revelation of the casting couch, the latest involving Uma Khurana stands out as one of the most disturbing. The sting alleged that Uma Khurana, a mathematics teacher at Sarvodaya Kanya Vidyalaya in Delhi, was pushing her students into prostitution. The sting, aired on the TV channel Live India, led to a large-scale riot on Asaf Ali Road. Uma Khurana was almost lynched by a violent mob. In the latest development, the police said that they have no evidence against Uma Khurana. The sting was a frame-up and was allegedly motivated by a petty dispute between Virendra Arora, a businessman, and Uma Khurana. Arora's friend, Prakash Singh, the journalist with LiveIndia channel who masterminded the sting, asked a friend, Rashmi Singh, a reporter with a small Noida newspaper, Nirbhik Prehri to pose as a student who was pushed into prostitution by Khurana. A study of the unedited tapes showed that Uma Khurana refused to admit to any prostitution ring or provide any students for prostitution. The police has now arrested Rashmi Singh for cheating. The whole sting was motivated by petty revenge on the part of the businessman who gave the journalist a tip-off and a desire for cheap publicity on the part of the channel. The operation focused chiefly on the sexual angle in the whole story, which is a whole deal more glamorous than say corruption in the education system. Corruption has been the country's bane and it starts early--right in our schools. If the schools are a breeding ground for illicit liaisons and undue favors, is it surprising then that we have not been able to do away with corruption? But, somehow, the channels do not seem to highlight such instances. Growing up in small towns in the country, I know for a fact that teachers coerce students to join their private tuitions, lest the student should fail in exams. Some teachers resort to bribes to leak examination papers, while others look for favours in kind. Students oblige, parents give in. Who wants to take on a hassle for a few rupees more? There are sting operations that bring out corruption in the bureaucracy, but as the bureaucracy functions in India, these operations lead nowhere. Taking action on those found guilty is a long-winded process, and no one seems to have the patience, nor the inclination to wait for the outcomes. It's just convenient to bring out stories that do not deserve more than a day's worth of attention. Close on the heels of the Uma Khurana sting operation in Delhi, comes another one from down south. Professor Suryanarayan of Osmania University met almost the same fate as the maths teacher from Delhi—minus the public thrashing. The charge here is the professor sought sexual favours from students in lieu of a doctorate degree. Again, the focus of the story seemed sex, and not the moral responsibility education entails.[37]

Media is regarded as one of the pillars of democracy. Media has wide ranging roles in society. It plays a vital role in moulding or at least influencing the opinion of the society and it is capable of changing the whole view-point through which people perceive various events. The media can be commended for starting a trend where the media plays an active role in bringing the accused to book. Freedom of media is defacto the freedom of the people as they should be informed of public matter.[38] It is thus needless to emphasise that a free and a healthy press is indispensable to the functioning of democracy. In a democratic set-up, there has to be active participation of people in all affairs of their community and the state. It is their right to be kept informed about the current political, social, economic and cultural life as well as the burning topics and important issues of the day in order to enable them to consider to form broad opinion in which they are being managed, their issues tackled and society and business administered by the government and their functionaries. To achieve this objective, people need a clear and truthful account of events, so that they may form their own opinion and offer their own comments and viewpoints on such matters and issues, and select their future course of action. The right to freedom of speech and expression is contained in Article 19 of the"constitution. However, the freedom is not absolute as it is bound by the sub clause (2) of the same article. However, the right of freedom of speech and expression does not embrace the freedom to commit contempt of court.[39] The media has again come in focus in its role in the trial of Jessica Lal murder case. The concept of media trial is not a new concept. The role of media was debated in the Priyadarshini Mattoo case and, likewise, many other high profile cases. There have been numerous instances in which media has been accused of conducting the trial of the accused and passing the 'verdict' even before the court passes its judgment. Trial is essentially a process to be carried out by the courts. The trial by media is definitely an undue interference in the process of justice delivery. Before delving into the issue of justifiability of media trial, it would be pertinent to first try to define what actually the 'trial by media' means. Trial is a word which is associated with the process of justice. It is the essential component in any judicial system that the accused should receive a fair trial.

In Sushil Sharma v. The State (Delhi Administration) and Ors[40] it was held by the Delhi High Court that: "Conviction, if any, would be based not on media's report but what facts are placed on record. Judge dealing with the case is supposed to be neutral. Now if what petitioner contends, regarding denial of fair trial because of these news items, is accepted it would cause aspersion on the Judge being not neutral. Press reports or no reports, the charge to be framed has to be based on the basis of the material available on record. The charge cannot be framed on extraneous circumstances or facts but on the material available on record. While framing the charge, the Court will form prima facie view on the basis of the material available on record. The apprehension of the petitioner that he would not get fair trial is perfunctory and without foundation. None of the news items, if read in the proper prospective as a whole, leads to the conclusion that there is any interference in the administration of justice or in any way has lowered the authority of the Court. The Trial Court has rightly observed that after the charge sheet has been filed, if the Press revealed the contents of the chargesheet, it by itself and by no stretch of imagination, amounts to interference in the administration of justice." Even in highly sensitive cases, the session trial has been conducted by the courts of Sessions without fear or favour. For example, to count a few cases which are commonly known as 'Billa Ranga Case', 'Baba Nirankari", "Sudha Gupta" and of "Shalini Malhotra" see the other aspect. One cannot gag the press. The Indian courts have emerged as the most powerful courts in the world with virtually no accountability. But every institution, even the courts, can go wrong. Every institution including the judiciary has its share of black sheep and corrupt judges are also there. The judiciary is peopled by judges who are human; and being human, they are occasionally motivated by considerations other than an objective view of law and justice. It would be foolhardy to contend that none of them, at least some of them, and at least some times, are motivated by considerations of their own personal ideology, affiliations, predilections, biases and indeed even by nepolistic and corrupt considerations. In stifling all criticism by the threatened exercise of the power of contempt against media, the issue in a democratic society is not to insulate judiciary even when things go wrong. Ultimately, one of the issues of vital concern is the accountability of the judiciary itself. In order to stifle free speech and comments on the court judgements, even an occasional exercise of this power is enough to deter most persons from saying anything that might annoy their Lordships. Perhaps the most important reason for the lack of reforms in the judiciary is the reluctance of the Press to write about and discuss the state of affairs within it for fear of contempt.

In Saibal Kumar Gupta and Ors. v. B.K. Sen and Anr,[41] it was held by the Supreme Court that: "No doubt it would be mischievous for a newspaper to systematically conduct an independent investigation into a crime for which a man has been arrested and to publish the results of that investigation. This is because trial by newspapers, when a trial by one of the regular tribunals of the country is going on, must be prevented. The basis for this view is that such action on the part of a newspaper tends to interfere with the course of justice whether the investigation tends to prejudice the accused or the prosecution. There is no comparison between a trial by a newspaper and what has happened in this case." The Ins and Outs of Media Trial—English View—is that High-profile civil litigation is not just decided in the courts; it also is decided in the court of public opinion. Courts and legal commentators are increasingly recognizing that the media, through the way it covers litigation, has a very real impact on the resolution of individual lawsuits. Common sense dictates that it is within a lawyer's role, therefore, to work with reporters on their stories to ensure accurate reporting. Many defence attorneys in high-profile cases, though, flinch at the idea of saying anything to reporters out of concern that such conversations could be misconstrued as an attempt to affect the jury pool or persuade a judge or jury. For this reason, rules and beliefs have developed as to how lawyers may appropriately engage the media to mitigate its impact on their clients.[42]

Pro-Plaintiff Media Bias Litigation involving well-known companies or individuals always has grabbed the attention of the news media, especially when it involves sensational charges. The magnitude of the coverage and the filter through which the media reports on litigation can create a "clear plaintiff bias in civil cases." While small companies can find themselves under the media spotlight in a particularly novel or "bet the company" suit, the media tends to focus on allegations against established and respected corporate defendants. These larger companies tend to have household names, and allegations against them can make good "copy"—even if the allegations are seemingly spurious, commonplace or unproven. The same is true for litigation involving celebrity defendants.[43]

In covering litigation, particularly corporate litigation, the media has an inherent bias that favours plaintiffs. When charges are made public, the media automatically reverts to the basic elements of story telling and casts the lawsuit in traditional protagonist-antagonist terms. The defendant, simply by being on the wrong side of the "v," becomes the "villain" to the plaintiff's "victim," whether or not the actual charges have any factual basis or legal merit. Reports frequently lead with the plaintiff's injury or allegations and only include the corporate position as a response. These stories rarely are counterbalanced by positive stories about the defending company. Because companies would rather not draw attention to any litigation, they usually do not seek publicity for their victories. Even if they did, reporters often would not see corporate litigation victories as particularly newsworthy. Goliath is supposed to beat David; that is not"news.[44]

THE NATURE OF BIAS IN HIGH-PUBLICITY CASES

A larger issue is the complex nature of juror bias and how that bias predisposes a juror towards one side in a case. It is no secret that we all have biases. The difficulty comes from understanding how those biases may ultimately affect the viewing of evidence and the deliberations in a case. Because the ramifications and remedies of this issue are far-reaching, the courts have elected to take the "I instruct you not to be biased" approach. As a result, the court can attempt to reform any juror who expresses bias by appealing to his or her fear or by appealing to the juror's inherent sense of fairness ("Don't you think you could set aside those initial impressions and only consider evidence from the witness stand?"). Rare is the juror who would not be intimidated by an admonishment from the court or who does not think of himself or herself as a fair and unbiased person. In fact, most jurors struggle mightily against their initial impressions. Several issues make it more difficult for jurors in high-publicity cases. Jurors want to appear fair and unbiased in front of the court and the press. Jurors want to sit on sensational trials. Jurors have a hard time distinguishing between impressions formed by pre-trial publicity and impressions formed in court. Jurors mostly do not understand or acknowledge their own biases. They themselves sometimes do not know the strength of their impressions and opinions. When in a high-conflict situation, such as juror deliberations, jurors revert to their initial impressions, experiences, and opinions. The courts make it relatively easy to conceal or not reveal a conscious or unconscious bias. These issues were highlighted in Mr. Simpson's civil trial. Despite having stated numerous times in their questionnaires that they believed him to have been guilty at various times during the presentation of the criminal trial, more than 30% of these jurors were not excused because they stated that they were not willing to put their opinions and impressions aside in the civil case.

The Additional Pressure on Judges in High-Publicity Trials

The media create a series of unconscious pressures on a juror in a high-profile trial. Jurors know that they are being watched by the world. They are not only making a decision for themselves, but they are making a statement for their family, co-workers, community and society as a whole. This elevates their verdict to a level beyond the evidence. In interviewing jurors after the trial of Hollywood, many jurors expressed how they hoped that the police would use their resources more wisely than to prosecute victimless crimes. When talking about the testimony of Dr. Irwin Golden, who was the coroner in the Simpson case, juror Marsha Rubin-Jackson said: "But it comes to the point in this particular case where Dr. Golden has made thirty errors. Now, you can't tell me this man has not made errors on previous autopsies. But this just happened to be a case that came to the court as a 'high-profile' case and the problems were brought to everyone's attention."[45]

It becomes clear that the media had a more negative influence rather than a positive effect (except for a few exceptions here and there). The media has to be properly regulated by the courts. The media cannot be granted a free hand in the court proceedings as they are not some sporting event. The Law Commission also has come up with a report on 'Trial by Media: Free Speech vs. Fair Trial under Criminal Procedure (Amendments to the Contempt of Court Act, 1971)' Report number 200 prepared in 2006. The report is still pending in the Parliament as such the researcher could not get a copy of the report. It will be available to the public once it is discussed in the Parliament.

The most suitable way to regulate the media will be to exercise the contempt jurisdiction of the court to punish those who violate the basic code of conduct. The use of contempt powers against the media channels and newspapers by courts have been approved by the Supreme Court in a number of cases as has been pointed out earlier. The media cannot be allowed freedom of speech and expression to an extent as to prejudice the trial itself."What lessons does the Jessica Lal fiasco teach us? There is definitely a case for intensifying efforts to upgrade the quality of policing. There is at the same time a need to improve judicial performance. For instance, the Jessica trial took nearly seven years to get completed. Hardly anyone has commented on this. Will it be unreasonable to demand that this should be taken up by the Delhi High Court as a kind of case study to find out why there was such delay? The public would like to satisfy themselves that the failure was not because of judicial lethargy, but rather because of several extraneous factors such as police indifference and wanton delaying tactics on the part of the defence. The current popular perception is that judicial accountability is an unrealisable dream. It is for the judiciary to prove this perception wrong. The above analysis reveals the gravity of the situation as it persists in India. An ideal proposal will be that the Indian press and the Indian people are not at present democratic enough to allow the press to intrude in the judicial process. What will an ideal proposition be is not to allow the media trial at this moment. It's definitely an ideal proposition to allow controlled media reporting of the cases, once the media is supposed to come out of the profit and sensational considerations. The media has to play the role of a facilitator rather than tilting the scales in favour of one or the other party.

Notes and References

1. http://www.pbs.org/newshour/bb/media/july-dec98/lawyers_10-19a.html
2. http://www.jastor.com
3. McNAir, B., The Sociology of Journalism (London: Arnold Press), 1998, pp. 21-37.
4. http://www.jour.sc.edu/news/convergence
5. Natarajan, S., A History of the Press in India (Bombay: Asia Publishng House), 1967, pp. 21-29.
6. *Ibid.*
7. Krishnamurthi, Nadig, Indian Journalism (Mysore: University of Mysore), 1966, pp. 41-49.
8. Jones, Steve, Encyclopaedia of New Media (C.A.: Sage Publications), 2003, p. 30.
9. Rao, Bhaskara, N., G.N.S. Raghavan, Social Effects on Mass Media in India (New Delhi: Gyan Publishing House), 1996, pp. 28-29.
10. www.indianexpress.com
11. Das, Ajay, Sting Operation by Media (New Delhi: Discovery Publishing House), 2007, pp. 198-99.
12. Singh, Manorma, Sting Operation (New Delhi: Discovery Publishing House), 2007, pp. 48-50.

13. www.indiatoday.com
14. Singh, Manorma, Sting Operation, *op. cit.*, pp. 48-50.
15. *Ibid.*
16. www.merinews.com
17. Pavlik, J.V., Journalism and News Media (New York: University Press), 2001, pp. 41-59.
18. *Ibid.*
19. Weaver, D. (ed.), The Global Journalist (New Jersey: Hampton Press), 1998, pp. 4-53.
20. Wilson, J., Understanding Journalism: A Guide to Issues (London: Routledge), 2006, pp. 114-128.
21. Singh, Manorma, Sting Operation, *op. cit.*, p. 51.
22. Tunstal, J., Journalist at Work (London: Constable Press), 2001, pp. 11-32.
23. www.merinews.com
24. India Today, "Media Trial", January, 2002.
25. www. CNNIBN.com
26. Krishnamurthi, Nadig, Indian Journalism, *op. cit.*, pp. 78-84.
27. www.jstor.com
28. www.merinews.com
29. *Ibid.*
30. Singh, Tavleen, "Jessica Lal: Trial by Media", The Tribune, June 2, 2001,
31. www.timesofindia.com
32. www.the tribune.com
33. www.hindustantines.com
34. *Ibid.*
35. Journalism: Principle and Practice (London: Sage Publication), 2004, pp. 41-52.
36. *Ibid.*
37. www.merinews.com
38. Kapil Sibal, The Hindustan Times, New Delhi, May 4 2001.
39. The State of Bombay v.: P., AIR1959Bom182.
40. 1996 CriLJ 3944.
41. AIR 1961 SC 633.
42. Steven B. Hantler, et al., Extending The Privilege To Litigation Communications Specialists In The Age of Trial By Media, 13 CommLaw Conspectus 7 CommLaw Conspectus 2004.
43. Paul Pringle, Hush-Hush High-Profile Cases: Dome of Silence Caps Celebrity Cases; Authorities: It's in Defendants' Best Interests, L.A. TIMES, Mar. 22, 2004, at A1 (citing a lawyer as saying, "There seems to be an insatiable appetite for these trials.").
44. As just one example, a Westlaw search shows that when a jury returned a verdict for $58.5 million dollars against Chrysler in Debbs v. Chrysler Corp. in 1999, many of the nation's daily newspapers

covered the verdict and the allegations. When a Pennsylvania appellate court overturned that verdict in October 2002, the decision received scant coverage, which was mostly contained to legal trade publications. 810 A.2d 137 (Pa. Super. Ct. 2002).

45. Armanda Cooley et al., Madam Foreman: A Rush to Judgment? 162 (Dove Books 1995).

Impact and Analysis

India has entered a space age in communication technology. This has increased manifold the social impact for good or ill of the media of mass communication. It is the need to promote critical awareness among policy makers and managers as well as the audience of the media.

The broadcasting system was owned and run by the government prior to India's independence. It provided entertainment to the middle and upper classes who could afford to buy a radio receiver in the pre-transistor age, and purveyed such information as was not adverse to the interests of the British authorities. Soon after the transfer of power, Jawaharlal Nehru said on 15th March 1948, while replying to a debate on external publicity in the Constituent Assembly which functioned as the provisional parliament of India : 'My own view of the set-up for broadcasting is that we should approximate, as far as possible, to the British model, the British Broadcasting Corporation : that Is to say, it would be better if we had a semi-autonomous corporation under the government, of course, with the policy controlled by the government, otherwise being not conducted as a government department but as a semi-autonomous corporation'. Nehru's impulses were liberal but he did not always act on them. The continuance of All India Radio as a government department during all the 17 years of Nehru's prime ministership was one of many instances in which a shadow fell between his perception and his practice.

A great difference would have been made to radio's role in free India had he remembered and acted on the recommendations of a sub-committee on communication of the National Planning Committee formed by the Congress in 1937 with Nehru as chairman. The sub-committee's report laid great emphasis on the potentiality of radio as the only literacy-free medium of mass communication then available. Sharing the socialist inclination of Nehru, and convinced that development had to be powered and guided by the state, the sub-committee used the expression 'State propaganda' for what is now connoted by the term 'development communication'. "The principal functions of broadcasting," the report said, (a) dissemination of news an useful information; (b) adult education and fighting rural ignorance; rural ignorance; propaganda by the State; (d) entertainment.

The sub-committee's report called for an innovative approach to broadcasting hardware, stating that, "many problems of communication engineering are peculiar to the country and their solution can only be obtained by carrying out investigations in the country itself." Broadcasting was envisaged as the most effective link between "the vast majority of the population who are still illiterate and a large section of the women who do not go out into the public, on the one hand, and the progressive part of India on the other." Radio, the report said, should provide "an easy channel for bringing to the masses useful information on agriculture, animal husbandry, current political thought, etc." The planning for broadcasting had to serve the objective of providing populous regions of the country with first-grade service, and installing community receivers on a wide scale in the rural areas."

The approach was thus oriented to rural development, and there was lively awareness of the need not only to put out broadcasts of relevance to the village population but to provide access to radio to the rural poor through the facility of community listening.

The role of communication in development as

envisaged in the document on the First Five Year Plan was in line with the approach of the National Planning Committee's subcommittee. The Plan document, published in December 1952, had in Chapter VIII, a section on 'Reaching the people' which said: "A widespread understanding of the Plan is an essential stage in its fulfillment. An understanding of the priorities which govern the Plan will enable each person to relate his or her role to the larger purposes of the nation as a whole. The Plan has, therefore, to be carried into every home in the language and symbols of the people, and expressed in terms of their common needs and problems ... with the assistance of creative writers and artists, which has to be specially enlisted. All available methods of communication have to be developed and the people approached through the written and the spoken word no less than through radio, film, song and drama. Above all, steps have to be taken to provide literature and information for the people in simple language on a scale equal to the needs of the country."

Post-independence reality turned out to be very different from this vision of decentralized communication which would be bottom-upward as well as top-down, and supportive of progress towards an egalitarian social and economic order. Radio continued to serve with entertainment and information the middle and upper classes. The transistor revolution did not alter the role of radio. Instead of serving the new mass audience with information relevant to improvement of their living conditions, All India Radio regaled them with tinsel film music and brought them commercial messages such as this one from Modern Bread, a unit which was meant to control of the Central public sector the 'commanding heights' of the economy: mummy, mummy, modem bread'. Children in the majority of Indian families neither eat packaged and branded bread, nor do they mummy their mothers. The failure to utilise the advent of the transistor to turn radio into an Instrument for democratising communication and conveying to the rural and urban poor locally relevant and useful information reflected the elitist orientation of free India's economic growth.

The course of planned development began to take an

elitist turn even in Jawaharlal Nehru's days. This was perhaps because of the time and energy that, as Prime Minister, he devoted to International affairs as his own Foreign Minister (and it is tragic that he failed in this field of his own choosing in the handling of Kashmir and of India's relations with China). He tried to replicate in India both the Soviet model of heavy Industrial development and the Chinese Communist model of cooperative joint farming, without the instrumentality of a totalitarian system in which a single party stifles the expression of dissent and liquidates dissenters. The regime of government controls, permits and licences introduced by the bureaucracy in the name of socialism was taken advantage of by unscrupulous politicians, businessmen and civil servants for self-aggrandisement.

Nehru's own vision, even if dimmed over the years, remained basically egalitarian. In the course of a letter to Chief Ministers on 7th June 1961, Nehru said: "We should think in terms of concentrating on production of goods that a person or family with an income of Rs. 500 per month or so might require. From this point of view, a bicycle is far more important in India today than a motor car, even if a small one." Considering the then value of the rupee, Nehru obviously had in mind the middle class rather than the poor. Subsequently, towards the close of his life, he noted with anguish that the Five Year Plans had made little difference to the living conditions of the masses. While replying to a debate on planning in the Lok Sabha in December 1963, Nehru said : "One thing that distresses, me very greatly is that there are a good number of people in India who have not profited by planning, and whose poverty is abysmal and most painful. I begin to think more and more of Mahatma Gandhi's approach."

It too that long for Nehru, though he had been a close lieutenant of the Mahatma, to realise that only the Gandhian approach of decentralised, labour-intensive production, and of compassion and sharing, would enable India with her vast under-employed manpower to achieve self-reliant economic growth. Not surprisingly, Nehru's successors were unable to act in accordance with Gandhi's talisman: "Recall the face of the poorest and the weakest man whom you may have seen, and ask yourself if the step you contemplate is going to be of any use to him."

There has been a sea-Change in the attitude of the commercial advertising. Mahatma Gandhi excluded advertisements altogether from his journals. He was against the multiplication of wants (as distinct from needs), and expressed the wish in the course of an article in 'Young *India' in October* 1919 that there were, for each province, only one advertising, medium-not a newspaper-containing innocent, unvarnished notices of things useful for the public. Annie Besant, after she acquired the 'Madras Standard' and ran it as the daily *'New India'*, from 1914, wrote to a friend that the first thing she did was to "clear off all the coarse advertisements."

In *The Discovery of India*, written in 1944, Jawaharlal Nehru said: "The advertiser is one of the symbols of our age with his continuous and raucous attempts to delude us and dull our powers of perception and induce us to buy unnecessary and even harmful products." In an address to the All India Newspaper Editors' Conference at Allahabad on 16th February 1946, he said: "The quality of advertisements appearing in some newspapers sometimes pains me. I appeal to the editors that they should exercise a strict censorship over advertisements so that undesirable advertisements are not accepted." Referring to commercial advertisements carried by Radio Ceylon and other foreign broadcasting systems, Nehru said in 1963: "Personally I react strongly if an advertisement comes through radio. My reaction is never to encourage that advertiser. What does he mean by interfering with my peace of mind? It angers me when it suddenly comes in; it upsets me."

In order to counter the pull of Radio Ceylon which was broadcasting Indian film songs, the Vividh Bharati channel was introduced in Nehru's time, on 3rd October 1957-. But it did not adversely affect popular taste because film music at that time was not the organized noise that much of it is today but had a lyrical quality and aesthetic appeal. Though radio listenership went up with the introduction of the Vividh Bharati service by more and more stations, creating an audience of tempting size for the commercial advertiser, it was out of the question for A. 1. R. to go commercial as long as Nehru was Prime Minister.

After commercials were introduced on Ist November 1967, during Indira Gandhi's prime ministership, the standard of Vividh Bharati began to decline, along with the quality of film music which began to be dominated by love songs ranging from the inane to the lewd. Vivid Bharati also began to carry commercial advertisements promoting the sale of consumption goods of interest to the growing urban middle class and to the affluent, but of no relevance to the urban poor and the majority of India's rural population. To the extent that these latter have exposure at all to television, advertisements on TV have a disorienting effect and serve to provoke envy, frustration and crime.

On the destabilising effects of the consumerist culture associated with industrialism, Jawaharlal Nehru said in the course of the Maulana Azad Memorial Lecture delivered by him in November 1959: "We see the effects of rapid technological changes more especially in young men and women today. There is a tendency to criminality, alcoholism, destructiveness, eroticism, in addition to a cynical and negative attitude towards life and work. In a world of constant change, and without any assurance of certainty, the hedonistic principles of life have a strong appeal. These tendencies are present more in the developed societies than in India or other under-developed countries. But it is important to note them because similar forces are likely to affect our life too." The words have proved prophetic.

Indira Gandhi, who succeeded her father as Prime minister after Lal Bahadur Shastri's brief tenure, was also aware of the pursuit of more and more wants to the detriment of moral integrity. Unmindful of the contradiction between precept and action, she went on to say in an address to the United Nations General Assembly in New York on 28th September 1983 : "In this age of instant globe-encircling information technology, the media dazzle eyes and fill ears with Images and reports of affluence. Even the modest expectations of our people are far beyond our present means."

Why did the government-owned electronic media go in

for commercial advertising, despite the warnings of Mahatma Gandhi and Jawaharlal Nehru? The reason lies in the need felt by those who have led the country after Nehru for the building of their image at the personal level as well as for propaganda in favour of the policies and performance of the governments headed by them at the Centre. This could be done day after day through the news and current affairs programmes of All India Radio and Doordarshan, since both are run as government departments.

The four metropolitan cities—Calcutta, Bombay, Madras and Delhi—are the centres of publication of many of India's oldest and largest circulated daily newspapers. Several of them were critical of some of the Central Government's policies even in Jawaharlal Nehru's time, and more so of the populist policies of Indira Gandhi during and after the Congress split of 1969. The electronic media operated by the Central Government came to be regarded by the ruling party as weapons with which to counter the Press which was privately owned. Soon there grew a division of labour under which the citizen received from radio and television only good news, favourable to the Government and it was left to the Press to report what was going wrong.

There was an additional reason for the Central Government concentrating its energies on addressing the urban audience. The middle classes and the affluent who form the bulk of the population in cities and towns could afford to buy their own receiving sets. There was no need to organise community access to the electronic media. All that the Government had to do was to make the audio and visual fare popular enough to attract a large clientele. This it proceeded to do with total disregard for the aesthetic standards and moral health of society. Cheap film music became the main pulling power of radio. Feature films, far too many of them laden with sex and violence, and song and dance sequences compiled therefrom became the chief attraction of Doordarshan. The new mass audience, mainly urban and with Increasing purchasing power in its hands, attracted the commercial advertiser in a big way. This brought in, specially in the case of Doordarshan, commercial revenue to supplement budgetary provisions for expanding the reach of the electronic media through additional stations and relay transmitters.

Oldest of the modern media of mass communication, the Press has by and large served India better than the others, both before and after independence. Press played a socially purposeful role in the pre-independence period and the early years of freedom. In contrast to the scope afforded to the socially conscious communicator by newspapers, both of which are in the private sector, monopoly control of radio by the Government since before independence, and of television since its advent in the 1960s, has proved stultifying.

It is the middle class that contributes most of the personnel of all the mass media. But since the Press, besides being free of government control, is relatively less market driven than films with their large budgets and generally short life, (many newspapers have from time to time exemplified the idealism that marks the more attractive of the two faces of the middle class) Jawaharlal Nehru said of the Janus-like middle class in the course of his presidential address at the Lucknow session of the Congress on 12th April, 1936: "Being too much tied up with property and the goods of the world, it is fearful of losing them, and it is easy to bring pressure on it and to exhaust its stamina. And yet, paradoxically, it is only from the middle class intellectuals that revolutionary leadership comes, and we in India know that our bravest leaders and our stoutest comrades have come from the ranks of the middle class."

The beginnings of the Press in India revealed both the faces: newspapers as commerce and as social mission. The first printed periodical, the *Bengal Gazette,* which appeared in Calcutta on 29th January, 1780 was a commercial venture and it illustrated the nexus that often exists between newspapers and politicians. Though published on Indian soil, the weekly was meant for English-speaking foreigners residing in India, not for Indians. James Augustus Hicky, the publisher and editor, openly sided with the Governor-General, Warren Hastings, in the in-fighting between two factions in the Governor-General's Council. The opposition to Warren Hastings was led by Philip Francis, whose ambition was to become Governor-General himself. The journal would lampoon Elijah Impey, Chief Justice of the Supreme Court and a friend of Warren Hastings, as 'Foolbundy' (pul in Hindustani means bridge) in an obvious reference to a contract for maintaining bridges which the Chief Justice had secured for a relative. Warren Hastings and his wife were also boldly satirised. The types of Hicky's press were seized and his journal was suppressed in 1782 after Philip Francis decided to leave India. Warren Hastings for his part patronised a rival weekly, the *India Gazette,* which was given postal facilities not available to Hicky.

We have witnessed two centuries later, to a similar struggle between some journals affiliated with rival barons of industry who, in turn, enjoy the support of rival princes of the State. A conspicuous example is the campaign carried on in recent years against each other by the Ambanis of Reliance Industries who own the *Observer* group of publications and Nuslia Wadia, of Bombay Dyeing, who is a director of the *Indian Express.*

A half-way house in the emergence of a truly Indian Press was marked by the journals brought out, early in the 19th century, by Christian missionaries in Bengal. Though published by foreigners, these journals were addressed to Indians, and some of them were in Indian languages. They promoted the dual objectives of promoting—the Christian, religion and the British Empire. It was in order to counter the attacks on Indian religions which these missionary journals carried, and to assert national self-respect, that the first Indian newspapers, property so called, were established by Raja Ram Mohan Roy (1772-1833), the initiator of India's renaissance in the modem period. Born in a well-to-do family he represented the finer of the two faces of the middle class.

Raja Ram Mohan Roy advocated, through the journals launched by him in the 1820s—the weeklies *Sambad Kaumudi* in Bengali and Mirat ul *Akhbar* in Persian and irregular in publication, the *Brahmunical Magazine,* a brief-lived magazine in English—many social reforms that were to become part of the plank of the nationalist movement. These included abolition of Sati or the custom, already on the wane in most parts of the country, of Sati or the burning of the widow on the funeral pyre of her husband, equality before the law, and modem education through the English medium. He did not press for representative government, it being too soon for that—with an entrenched imperial power and a people steeped in illiteracy and superstition and with little sense of a national identity; the affiliation of caste was, at that time, all that mattered for self-identity. But Raja Ram Mohan Roy's readiness to assert national self-respect is evident from his courageous criticism of the brash methods of the foreign missionaries who reviled the religious beliefs and practices of Indians, both Hindus and Muslims.

The role of the Press acquired a new dimension with the advent of daily newspapers in the 19th century. Several of them were moderate or conservative, both with regard to political and social issues: some were moderate in their politics but radical in their attitude to social reform or vice versa, and some others were radical both in politics and on social issues without necessarily subscribing to the tactics of law-breaking in the name of Satyagraha.

The complexity of the scenario is illustrated by the instance of Annie Besant (1847-1933) and her daily newspaper New *India.* Having fought and suffered in England for many causes—as a free—thinker, trade unionist and proponent of planned parenthood—she became a theosophist, found in India her spiritual home, and settled at Adyar, in Madras, in 1907. Through New *India* which she ran from 1914, Annie Besant advocated a political line that was bold in comparison with the petitionary politics of the then Congress leadership. In 1916 the British authorities demanded a security from Annie Besant for "the better conduct of her publications." It was to protest against this action that young Jawaharlal Nehru, then practising law at Allahabad, made his first public speech in June 1916.

Annie Besant was chosen, while under internment as punishment for her advocacy of self-government for India, as president of the 1917 Congress session at Calcutta, becoming the first woman to be so honoured. But her popularity declined when she refused to endorse Gandhi's movement in 1919 against the Rowlatt Bills, his advocacy of Non-Cooperation, and support to Khilafat. She held that there was nothing in the two Bills to which an honest citizen could take exception, and that, instead of non-cooperation, the best men and women should enter the legislative councils and press for the transfer of greater power to the people's representatives. Civil disobedience, she warned, was "rearing huge obstacles in the way of the first Home Rule government."

The over-simplification and consequent misrepresentation in branding a person as a 'moderate' or a 'radical' is illustrated also by the case of Bal Gangadhar Tilak. He was a conservative in his attitude to social reform, while being a radical in politics; he coined the pledge 'Swaraj is my birthright, and I shall have it.' Though Tilak suffered imprisonment and deportation, he was for a constructive response to any move that the British were prepared to make in the direction of self-government, such as the Montagu Reforms Act of 1919.

Gandhiji was an exemplar of educative journalism. His first journalistic venture was 'Indian Opinion', a weekly brought out in 1904 in South Africa. It was published in four languages—English, Gujarati, Hindi and Tamil in order to reach all the major elements of the Indian population in Natal and the Transvaal. It is characteristic of Gandhiji that while, on the one hand, he utilised the journal to ventilate the grievances of Indians who were grossly discriminated against by the regime of the white colonists, he also exhorted his countrymen to give up unsanitary habits, to overcome feelings of difference based on caste or religion, and to observe truthfulness in their business dealings.

After returning finally to India in 1915, Gandhiji conducted three weekly journals: 'Navajivan' (1919-31) in Gujarati; 'Young India' in English (1919-32); and 'Harijan' in English from 1933 till his martyrdom in 1948. So widespread was the interest in Mahatma Gandhi's views that what he wrote in these journals was news.

"I have taken up journalism", he wrote in 1919, "not for its sake but merely as an aid to what I have conceived to be my mission in life. My mission is to teach by example the matchless weapon of Satyagraha which is a direct corollary of non-violence. To be true to my faith, I may not write merely to excite passion. The reader can have no idea of the restraint I have to exercise from week to week in the choice of topics and my vocabulary. It is training for me." And in his autobiography: "One of the objects of a newspaper is to understand the popular feeling and give expression to it; another is to arouse among the people certain desirable sentiments; and the third is fearlessly to expose popular defects."

A major consequence of Gandhiji for Indian journalism was the emergence of new dailies as radical alternatives to the nationalist but somewhat staid Indian-owned newspapers of long standing. These emerged as a third alternative to the loyalist newspapers, many of them British-owned, and to the newspapers which were once described by Nehru as 'immoderately moderate'.

In the 1920s, as modern journalism was just taking form, writer *Walter Lippmann* and American philosopher *John Dewey* debated over the role of journalism in a *democracy*. Their differing philosophies still characterize a debate about the role of journalism in society and the nation-state. Lippmann understood that journalism's role at the time was to act as a mediator or *translator* between the *public* and policymaking elites. The journalist became the middleman. When elites spoke, journalists listened and recorded the information, distilled it, and passed it on to the public for their consumption. His reasoning behind this was that the public was not in a position to deconstruct the growing and complex flurry of information present in modern society, and so an intermediary was needed to filter news for the masses. Lippmann put it this way: The public is not smart enough to understand complicated, political issues. Furthermore, the public was too consumed with their daily lives to care about complex public policy. Therefore the public needed someone to interpret the decisions or concerns of the elite to make the information plain and simple. That was the role of journalists. Lippmann believed that the public would affect the decision-making of the elite with their vote. In the meantime, the elite (i.e. politicians, policy makers, bureaucrats, scientists, etc.) would keep the business of power running. In Lippman's world, the journalist's role was to inform the public of what the elites were doing. It was also to act as a watchdog over the elites, as the public had the final say with their votes.

Effectively that kept the public at the bottom of the power chain, catching the flow of information that is handed down from experts/elites.

Dewey, on the other hand, believed the public was not only capable of understanding the issues created or responded to by the elite, it was in the public forum that decisions should be made after discussion and debate. When issues were thoroughly vetted, then the best ideas would bubble to the surface. Dewey believed journalists should do more than simply pass on information. He believed they should weigh the *consequences* of the policies being enacted. Over time, his idea has been implemented in various degrees, and is more commonly known as *"community journalism."*

This concept of *community journalism* is at the centre of new developments in journalism. In this new paradigm, journalists are able to engage citizens and the experts/elites in the proposition and generation of content. It's important to note that while there is an assumption of equality, Dewey still celebrates expertise. Dewey believes the shared knowledge of many is far superior to a single individual's knowledge. Experts and scholars are welcome in Dewey's framework, but there is not the hierarchical structure present in Lippman's understanding of journalism and society. According to Dewey, conversation, debate, and dialogue lie at the heart of a democracy. While Lippman's journalistic philosophy might be more acceptable to government leaders, Dewey's approach is a better description of how many journalists see their role in society, and, in turn, how much of society expects journalists to function. Americans, for example, may criticize some of the excesses committed by journalists, but they tend to expect journalists to serve as watchdogs on government, businesses and other actors, enabling people to make informed decisions on the issues of the time.

Journalists around the world often write about the *governments* in their nations, and those governments have widely varying policies and practices towards journalists, which control what they can research and write, and what press organizations can publish. Many Western governments guarantee the *freedom of the press*, and do relatively little to restrict press *rights* and *freedoms,* while other nations severely restrict what journalists can research and/or publish. Journalists in many nations have enjoyed some privileges not enjoyed by members of the general public, including better access to public events, crime scenes and press conferences, and to extended interviews with public officials, celebrities and others in the *public eye.* These privileges are available because of the perceived power of the press to turn public opinion for or against governments, their officials and policies, as well as the perception that the press often represents their consumers. These privileges extend from the legal rights of journalists but are not guaranteed by those rights. Sometimes government officials may attempt to punish individual journalists who irk them by denying them some of these privileges extended to other journalists. Nations or jurisdictions that formally *license* journalists may confer special *privileges* and *responsibilities* along with those licenses, but in the *United States* the tradition of an independent press has avoided any imposition of government-controlled examinations or licensing. Some of the states have explicit *shield laws* that protect journalists from some forms of government inquiry, but those statutes' definitions of "journalist" were often based on access to printing presses and broadcast towers. A national shield law has been proposed. In some nations, journalists are directly employed, controlled or *censored* by their governments. In other nations, governments who may claim to guarantee press rights actually *intimidate* journalists with threats of arrest, destruction or seizure of property (especially the means of production and dissemination of news content), torture or murder. Journalists who elect to cover *conflicts,* whether *wars* between nations or *insurgencies* within nations, often give up any expectation of protection by government, if not giving up their rights to protection by government. Journalists who are captured or detained during a conflict are expected to be treated as civilians and to be released to their national government.

Journalists' interaction with sources sometimes involves *confidentiality,* an extension of freedom of the press giving journalists a legal protection to keep the identity of a *source* private even when demanded by police or prosecutors; withholding sources can land journalists in contempt of court, or in jail. The scope of rights granted to journalists varies from nation to nation; in the *United Kingdom*, for example, the government has had more legal rights to protect what it considers sensitive information, and to force journalists to reveal the sources of leaked information, than the United States. Other nations, particularly *Zimbabwe* and the *People's Republic of China*, have a reputation of persecuting journalists, both domestic and foreign. In the *United States*, there has never been a right to protect sources in a *federal* court. Some states provide varying degrees of such protection. However, federal courts will refuse to force journalists to reveal sources, unless the information the court seeks is highly relevant to the case, and there's no other way to get it. Journalists, like all citizens, who refuse to testify even when ordered to can be found in *contempt of court* and fined or jailed.

Social media has changed journalism. The Web is now the sole distribution channel for newspapers that can no longer afford to publish hardcopy, and those that don't follow the best practices of social media may see their brands marginalized in cyberspace as well. Social journalism, an extension of those practices, is now an essential component of any news organization's strategy. Citizen journalists post photos of fast-breaking events, and cover stories from a different angle than legacy news organizations, but it's the premeditated watchdog or advocacy role that defines a social journalist. Another factor is the network effect: people using social media to communicate and collaboratively produce content. Editors are still important, but the pieces are shaped by crowd dynamics and the velocity of information. Here's a look at the past, present, and future of social journalism.

The Past—As Mark Glaser of the PBS site media shift *points out* in his summary of Dan Gillmor's "We the Media," a book about grassroots media, the people who recorded the Los Angeles police beating of Rodney King nearly thirty years later did so out of a sense of social duty: they could have turned off their cameras, but kept them rolling, and contacted mainstream media with the results. This was a crowd of social journalists who broke the story before any editor could slow it down. The *Independent Media Center,* formed in 1999 to cover the World Trade Organization protests in Seattle, was an early aggregator of social journalism. Run by a collective of alternative journalists and activists who provided minimal editing, the IMC allowed individuals to upload their own coverage of political events. Today, Indymedia hosts a network of IMCs serving cities around the world. In 2005, social journalists responded to Hurricane Katrina by filing coverage from the field that was more detailed, and often more accurate, than that seen on mainstream media. Sites like the *Interdictor,* self-described as "A small pocket of New Orleans web guys blogging, running off a generator, with a web cam," provided a firsthand account of the disaster. One person even declared a *Katrina Blog Relief Day* in an attempt to start a groundswell movement.

The Present—The *Huffington Post* might not be the first organization that comes to mind when talking about today's social journalism, but it's actually a leader in this area. Last year, it co-sponsored Off the Bus, *described by director Amanda Michel* as a "citizen-powered campaign news site." The idea was to offer alternative coverage of the presidential election by ordinary people, but the process uncovered a market that Michel describes: "Our market was defined by our access to on-the-ground information that other news outlets lacked, and collaborative, crowd-powered methods of newsgathering that made some traditional journalists uncomfortable. Private fundraisers, official campaign conference calls, volunteer meetings, and rallies—where mainstream reporters found themselves stuck in pens—were our specialty. We wanted to tell stories inaccessible to the national press. This required replacing objectivity with an ethic of transparency..."

The Future—Rosen's *Flying Seminar in the Future of News* cites Dan Conover's piece *"2020 vision: What's next for news"* as a definitive source for predictions. Conover, a reporter turned blogger, offers a number of observations about the next decade of journalism. He talks about the continued demise of newspapers: the metro dailies in major cities, not the "web/print nationals" (New York Times, Washington Post, Wall Street Journal), or local papers serving communities of up to 30,000 readers. His assertion that the *Semantic Web* and open-source technologies will drive revenue from sources other than advertising and paid subscriptions anticipates data-mining and machine-readable news feeds, and he even mentions the trend of *newspapers opening up their APIs,* correctly pointing out this won't mean much unless developers and end-users are given more freedom. Conover offers a cautionary statement about crowd funding, citing *Spot.us,* a Bay area site where writers and individual donors can collaborate to fund stories. He says that "volunteers" who are paid neither directly nor substantially will produce much of the next decade's writing, editing and producing. The future of social journalism will be driven by *disintermediation,* the replacement or removal of middlemen in the supply chain. This has already happened on the revenue side, with Craig list *(http://www.blipper.com)* and other online resources taking classified ads from newspapers. As the newspaper industry consolidates, and social media matures, journalists will increasingly work as independents, forming transient relationships with multiple publishers. A handful of national brands will survive, and hundreds, perhaps thousands of new microbrands will flourish. The public good will be preserved, and society will be more transparent.

The Indian media, especially, the electronic news channel, exceeds its limits in reporting an issue. Rather than playing the role of a responsible Press, certain news channels go berserk reporting cynically just to increase their channel's (Television Rating Point) TRP.

Breaking News: Three children born to a woman; the statues of Gods are drinking milk; a boy reborn, recalls his past life and the list accrues with such breaking news.... A time will come when these kinds of news will be flashed on various channels to increase the television rating point (TRP) of the news channels. Out of 1.12 billion populations, our country suffers with the low literacy rate (though the literacy rate rose to 65.38 per cent, people are still unable to read and write efficiently). The people who belong to the group of illiterates are unable to understand their right to information. The electronic media targets them and show programmes, according to their needs. Moreover, news channels play a major role in misleading these people. A large section of our countrymen, are still superstitious in practice and are easily misled by elites. Thus, news channels overcome the expectations of these people. Many among us watch such news out of anxiety and gradually this anxiety merges with our faith.Breaking news (as the essential part of the news channels) should throw light on the subject that is important for the masses and the nation and owes to its interest. A few years back, it was flashed that a boy fell in a deep ditch. This could be a news because it is well known to us that a single boy or a girl takes his or her stand in making a prosperous nation, but the way it was telecast ie a full 24-hours live telecast was somewhat an exaggerated form of the issue. The misuse of breaking news could be avoided by showing, the news, relevant to the nation's interest. The channels should cover those issues, which matters rank and file, but do not mislead them. It is true that some people want to see the 'masala' news. Therefore, the sole responsibility lies on the shoulders of electronic media to act as an eye-opener and take initiatives to guide people to the right path.

Media plays a vital role in the upliftment of the rural masses. It widens mental horizons for better perception of information that help the people to be update on the information super-highway, transporting people to a modern society. Media plays a very vital role in the development of social life. It enhances or widens the horizons of people. Mass media add to the knowledge levels of the masses. It helps elevate intellectual level to new heights.

It is synonymous with a liberating force because they can break the bonds of distance and isolation. It transports people from a traditional society to the advanced or modern society, i.e. also known as great society because it has the availability of all those means and instruments, which are required for receiving information first hand.

This feature help the masses of a nation develop the quality of empathy. High empathetic capacity is the personal style of West. In India most people are apathetic towards the need of others. A non-traditional society is urban, highly literate, industrial and participant.

A traditional society is predominantly rural, partially

illiterate, agriculture based and non-participant. It develops people by kinship into communities that are isolated from one other and from a centre. It also means that there is no urban-rural division of labor in this society and that is lacks the bonds of interdependence. The horizons of people are limited because their decisions involve other known people in known situations. On the contrary, in a modern society, the operations are done through consensus individuals, who make personal decisions on public issue. These must occur quite frequently with others to arrive at rational society-friendly decision.

Mass media creates curiosity by disseminating information among the masses. In an era of information and communication networking, everyone wants to travel on the information highway because information is synonymous to power. In a modern society, the mass media presents images of distant places and events most of the times. When a traditional society moves towards modernity, it also starts depending upon mass media. Hence, the ideas generated in the minds of masses have their cues or origins in the media. Mass media promotes people, products, concepts and even nations. Ad campaigns can create history in the field of business and trade.

If the media of a developing nation is responsible, they can shift focus not only on commercial aspects of life but also on the broader socio-political canvas that can help the nation become a modern advanced society. The media can bring new customs, procedures and activities to the notice of the masses. They can also focus on the ill-effects of dowry, ostentatious marriages, drinking etc by censuring these issues and events. As such, it can change the mindset of the society from the traditional to become an advanced one. The mass media can also raise aspirations. They can motivate people to buy new or improved products, services, concepts and ideologies. They raise the aspiration levels of the masses of both advanced and developing nations. During the late seventies, the media added fuel to the fire and motivated people to say even those things that they did not want. Commercialism and materialism overcomes the 'fear to change' if the media raises aspirations of the masses through carefully planned media campaigns. The campaigns are planned so that change has to look 'natural, positive and in tune with the existing value sets of the audience'. There are many limitations for the masses though. Socially unacceptable products, imported goods, free sex, pornography, high-tech gadgets, sport cars, fashion apparel etc are some of the many things that our rural masses do not need. Hence, we can conclude that the media raises the aspirations of the urban masses largely and to some extent it raises the aspirations of the rural masses too.

In the 'excitement' of covering Mumbai terror live, the media, especially TV channels, forgot their role, namely, to be sensitive and non-melodramatic. In its anxiety they asked silly and irrelevant questions, but forgot to raise more serious issues. Television Channels drew much flak for going overboard covering the Mumbai terror live for more than 60 hours. The likes of Barkha Dutt, Rajdeep Sardesai, and Arnab Goswami, etc. etc. overworked to bring 'exclusive' reportage to the anxious audience. Doesn't matter, if they asked some silly questions to the relatives of those who were taken hostages inside Taj (like, 'Are you worried?'). They made sure that their TRP ratings shot up by over 30 points in those 60 hours.

In the bargain, as critiqued widely, two important events were almost forgotten: elections in three states and the death of V. P. Singh (Unfortunately, he died at the wrong time). But one thing was clear: the attacks did not dither the voter from coming out to vote. In fact, the average across the states was 66 per cent, much higher than what it used to be earlier. And as the results show us, the voter came out defying all odds just to make sure that only the performer got elected. The BJP's cashing in strategy on terror boomeranged, as the voter did not perceive terror as something that concerned only the ruling party. All this shows that that the voter has become more intelligent and choosy. No party, thus, is a frontrunner in the coming Lok Sabha elections.

Coming back to the live media coverage of Mumbai terror, it was sheer loss of professionalism on the part of Indian TV channels. They threw all caution to the wind and reported as if they were the only heralds of hope for those trapped inside and waiting anxiously outside, not to mention millions of hungry viewers all over. All norms of broadcast journalism were forgotten, at least for sometime. Their main concern seemed to be only TRP ratings and nothing else.

Compare this with the reportage of BBC network. They too went live to a certain extent; but they never gave a feeling of a loss of balance anywhere. Granted, that they were a foreign channel and that they did not have as much at stake in the Mumbai terror as Indian channels did. But such stakes need not overburden you to be melodramatic and, in some cases, even to the extent of loss of voice. It is true that reporters too are human and, perhaps, most of them were covering such terror live for the first time. But, whatever happened to those long years spent in training, learning news values, social responsibility, sense of proportion and so on? It is indeed unfortunate how journalists conveniently forget fundamental theories of journalism when it comes to competition. Media sets agenda and manufactures consent. This was proved decades ago by Walt Lippman, Noam Chomsky and others. The coverage of the Mumbai attacks was a fascinating example corroborating these theories. The audience was made to believe that Taj and Trident were more important (national icons!) and CST was just another railway station. We were also told that it was an attack on Indian economy. But does our economy depend only on a miniscule filthy rich people who frequent such avoidable hotels?

A quick final comment: over the last five years or so, more than 10,000 farmers have committed suicide, owing to debt and other reasons, in Maharashtra alone. But that tragedy does not seem to be a worthwhile issue for the TV channels. However, lives lost in Taj and Trident are deeply mourned. Does it mean that some lives are more valuable than others? It is true that all terror attacks should be condemned and that we cannot condone the violence that takes its toll on hundreds of innocent civilians. But all lives are equally precious and hence must be given equal weightage, if not intensity. A farmer's life is as important as the life of a wealthy man dying in the Taj or a police official dying while fighting terrorists at CST. We can only hope media will learn from their mistakes.

It's not often that Indian sports persons except cricketers get featured on the front page of newspapers. It is time for the media to create an equal space for all sports to encourage the masses towards other games beyond cricket. Sushil Kumar, Vijender Kumar and Abhinav Bindra are names, which have done India proud at Beijing Olympics. Hardly anyone knew them a few days back, may be the sports journalists had known them but now these three have become a part of history forever. Media is all over them for a small interview, a picture, for a minute of their life. Their families are being interviewed on television channels, media has reached their homes. And all the credit goes to the three stars who proved their mettle at Beijing. Else, when do the media in India get time to cover any other sports except cricket, which is their first love? Even if Dhoni buys a new car, or gets a new dog it is 'breaking news'! Or Yuvraj attends a party with a girl, it's news! Before the world cup, anything you do, make a cake in shape of bat, sing a song to wish the Indian team, it was news and the media covered it. But the same passion is never there for any other sport. These do get some coverage but that prime time attention is missing, especially in electronic media. In fact, when Abhinav was competing in the shooting event, half the Indian media at Beijing was missing, they only rushed to get his shots when he won.

Media attention also brings in money, sponsors and no doubt, Indian Cricket Board is the richest cricket board in the world. Sports other then cricket also have a story. It is not that Sushil, Abhinav and Vijender have never played for India earlier. In 2006 Doha Asian Games, Sushil got a bronze. Vijender is the Asian Games bronze medallist and the King's Cup silver medalist. Similarly, Abhinav had got a gold in 2002 Manchester Commonwealth Games and is the first Indian shooter to win a world championship gold. It was covered by media, may be as one news item or limited to sports page. Unlike this time when Bindra made to Page One as India's golden boy. Possibly, these victories in wrestling, boxing and shooting may do some good to these sports and divert attention to them. And a country like India with over a billion people should be aiming high in the next Olympics. We celebrated India's 1984 World Cup victory in cricket, but we never celebrated or even remembered Khashaba Dadasaheb Jadhav's victory, he was India's first individual (Olympic Games) wrestler to win us a bronze medal at the 1952 Helsinki Olympics. Today when Sushil Kumar repeated history they talked about him.

In today's fast life, people tend to rely on electronic media more. They get the glimpses of the news in a minute rather than going through pages of the newspapers or magazines. But, new channels today are more devoted order to increase their TRPS.

From time immemorial, journalists are considered to be 'the watch dog of the society', ever since the concept of journalism came into existence. Journalism basically started with print media, but got into our nerves through the electronic media only. The impact of the latter is considered to be much more because its the electronic media that brings the news first to our homes. In that respect print media lags behind. But the vivid analytical interpretation is only and solely provided by the newspapers. But no matter what, in today's fast life, people tend to rely on electronic media more. They get the glimpses of the news in a minute rather than going through pages of the newspapers or magazines. So, with passing of each day, the impact and effect and power of the electronic media is increasing. With power, comes responsibility. So inevitably the responsibility gets doubled. The electronic media industry should be more and more cautious on the accuracy of the information. Rather than devoting their effort to increase their channel's television rating points (TRP) and moulding the news value for entertaining the audiences, they should actually be conscious on providing the accurate information to the society. Not all news can be given an entertainment value...that's what they should learn. Political, social and human interests stories, business stories all are given as much entertainment element to it, to gather audience. This violates the norms of journalism. Who will remind the big stars of the media industry...the so-called 'well known news organisations of the country'? Unnecessary lengthening of the stories, dramatisation of crucial issues– all these are responsible for the degradation of the credibility. The common mass who depends on this medium for their information source, are being basically fooled. Being ignorant of 'behind the scene' scenario, they are unable to raise their voices. But we, who are socially responsible citizens and somewhat related to the media industry and are aware of such confusion, we can lead the revolt against such a volation of journalism.

These days, news channels telecast entertainment bytes besides news, just to improve ratings. They believe news relating to peoples problems does not sell. But if the channels really want people to like those, they have to focus on peoples problems. Now-a-days one can often get confused while watching news channels on television. One must have had those experiences, in which while watching a comedy show or a reality show or some dance programme, the show suddenly stops and a news anchor starts sharing her views about the programme as news. Then you focus at the channel name and find it is a news channel. This has become the present scenario. Almost all news channels are telecasting very long clips of several programmes of different entertainment channels. The worse thing is that the news readers present it like very important news concerning the nation. They try to create a thrill about the programme to add viewer ship. Do the news channels really exist for this kind of presentation? Probably such comedy shows or reality shows and other programmes have such a great impact on the general public that it can improve the ratings of that particular channel. But will the news channels do anything to enhance the ratings of their channel?

Don't they have any moral duties? Why do they forget that it is a news channel that they have some duties towards the nation and that they have some responsibilities for the general public? Probably they have so much spare time that they don't have anything important to present within that time. Probably they don't want to prepare anything logical. Probably they don't want to listen to the problems of the general public or they don't try to anything like this. Probably they are sure that all those efforts of them will go in vain.

If they really want to be liked by the general public, they have to feel the pulse of them. The people of India may like to watch recreational programmes on their news channels but more than that they would like to watch programmes about their problems and their solutions. If you can't provide solutions to any problem, at least you can highlight the problem and make the government aware of that particular problem. News channels can reveal thousands of problems (corruption, populations, transportation, medical facilities and many more) which people are facing in their daily life. Every problem has a solution and the media are the strongest fighters in the fight against problems, whether they are related to the government or the public.

If the electronic media accept their duties and responsibilities, the general people will definitely support them. News channels will no more be avenues for refreshment for viewers but a path they can take to reach the solutions to their problems. Moreover, people can be more active and more supportive of that particular news channel

The question is not that of TRP only; electronic media is politically affected, biased and motivated by different influences. The public will have to strengthen their independent source of information and will need to counter the misleading media.

The Value of freedom rests in valuing the freedom and security of others as one value it for oneself. After securing ones own stake at home, if one ventures and dare to safeguard the security and freedom of others, he is also extending the cover of his own security. Television channels adopt most insipid and frivolous methods to promote their channels and business and often compromise the quality of their programmes. For promoting Sri Lankan tourism, these channels built up hype in a completely derogatory manner, unacceptable to a prudent and rational mind. Instead of making the programme informative and scientifically acceptable, these channels made a mockery of the entire Ramayana by shouting in high-pitched voices: "Mil gaye Ram, Mil gayi Sita, ab aap dekhenge Ravan ka sharir jo is admi ne dekha hai, yeh Pushpak viman jo admi ki charbi se chalta tha." Why such nonsense should be allowed to hurt the religious feelings of thousands of people and make a mockery of great epic, Ramayana.

Why should ordinary incidents of crime be dramatised in such illustrious manner, which does not add anything in substance to any information of the viewer except perverting the brains and most of the times influencing people in a negative way and inspiring more crimes in the society. Why can't they make crime reports interesting with information that can help the viewer in some way identifying some grey areas and take precaution? Why should you present teenage sex in schools in such bad light that parent get scared of sending their children to schools?

Perhaps, people at the helm of affairs do not trust the common sense of general viewers; they do not believe that their visuals and words are effective enough and they resort to crude forms of expressions with very vulgar and primitive taste. They indulge in buffoonery and mudslinging rhetoric in serious matters of discussions supposedly being aired in public interest.

During elections and even some time before that, these channels take sides with one or the other political party. In a brazen manner the channels show their twisted slant and when charged with accusation, they claim that if 'netas' (leaders) can mislead people in the name of vote why cannot TV channels do it for TRP.

In the election analysis, one expected that there will be some meaningful debate on the serious issues of the people and the politicians will find it tough time to answer probing queries. But what one got to witness was dramatised version with background music and special thrust on the presentation of Varun Gandhi as a communal demon, a big threat emerging from a place called Pilibhit to swallow all secular forces, therefore warning the entire nation. In the entire debate, the anchors tried in utter desperation to revolve the debate for almost an hour around Varun Gandhi with a view to hype communal sentiments as was done at the time of Amarnath land row in J&K by the same channel. The channel had taken a lead in highlighting the venom spilled by PDP leader Mehbooba Mufti and had polarised the Jammu and Kashmir voter. It shows a clear nexuses of public and private owned media to divert public attention from the real issues. The media is completely hand-in-glove with the politicians who believe that progress in the balance sheet of just a few people is the progress of the entire country. The entire media is subservient to such forces for its existence. The public will have to strengthen their independent source of information and will need to counter the misleading media of doctored debates, opinions and politically motivated promos.

We live in a society that depends on information and communication to keep moving in the right direction and do our everyday activities. But today, is the information given really genuine? Can we rely on that information? Is it not sensationalised? The media plays an important role in a democratic country. It acts as a fourth institute outside the government. In the last 50 years media influence has grown exponentially with the advancement in technology. We live in a society that depends on information and communication to keep moving in the right direction and do our daily activities. But, today, is the information given really genuine? Can we rely on that information? Is it not sensationalised? Media today is no less then a Bollywood masala movie. News channels are no less than dance drama and action. They serve us everything except the news which we require. They take no time in stretching a small issue, like a bubble gum, into an hour long show. Shows like SANSANI with a tag line "Chain Se Sona Hai To Jaag Jao" are one of its kind. It takes no time in converting a five minute issue such as a rape case or a dowry case into a one hour long horror cum suspense show. Just another way of sensationalizing news. The news channels are more interested in showing what people think about SRK's six—pack—abs than the plight of the flood victims in Bihar. All the news channels are working in order to gain TRP's today and not to educate and inform the people. Every minute there is a "Breaking News." Whether a boy falling into a 20 feet deep hole or a Kareena Shahid breaking up, it's all Breaking News. Channels even sometimes cross the boundaries of ethics. The Arushi murder case for instance is a great example for crossing ethical boundaries. They actually tainted the character of a teenager who was dead. May it be blue line buses case or an UFO seen or may be some mishap in some reality show, there is not less than an hour's show program's script ready at hand.

The mass media has lost its essence today in the race for TRP's. The news channels should be run under some code of conduct, so that, they don't forget their ethics and limitations. They should provide the public with genuine and reliable news and information and not some masala Bollywood flick.

The term alleged, according to Oxford Concise Dictionary means asserted but not proved. Princeton Dictionary defined it as "supposed but doubtful." It also has synonym like claimed, asserted or charged. Is it fair to use this word in news stories?

The term allegedly is thrown around very often these days. It is used profusely in the print and electronic media. Why would a news article or story report that someone was allegedly murdered, maimed or kidnapped? Why would a report state that someone allegedly made the following statement? Why would any news report be based as well as build around the alleged action or statements or links or implication or even alleged events? The term alleged, according to the Oxford concise dictionary means asserted but not proved. Princeton dictionary defined it as "supposed but doubtful." Alleged also has synonym like claimed, asserted or charged. It also means a declaration made, but not yet substantiated. So is all the news where any statement, allegation or event is 'alleged' is unsubstantiated? The word has recently become an integral part of many stories for "legal reasons" as often "allegations are made when the story is made and later another angle appears." So is it a bid to cover the legal aspects when a story makes unsubstantiated allegations or implications? Or is a bid to simply make stories appear more that what they are? But doesn't the use of such works make the story appear less unsubstantiated and rather fishy/flimsy? Or, to a less jaded and cynical mind, is it a genuine attempt to report truthfully and objectively? Sulbha Rai, a freelance news analyst in Bangalore, feels that every news report has more than just viewpoint. She feels in a recent case of the rave raid in Bangalore there is the police's side of the story, the party goers have another story to see, so do the society's watchdogs and so the various segments of the society. "So whose story or whose versions of the truth do news agencies take as the absolute and complete truth" is the question. She subscribes to the "safety net of words that help states one party's version, yet remaining objective as well as open to another side of the story." Yet, by itself, the word in question 'allegedly' is rather harmless. It's used in legal jargon as not really an allegation but "declaring or asserting of something (believed) to be true.

In the literal sense, it means simply stated yet not proved, but in terms of news it comes across as simply attributing a statement (negative—like an accusation, or positive—like a political party claiming to have made progress or development or government as well as the opposition's statistics and 99 per cent of their statements). Amusingly what makes the media's usage of the word seem flimsy is that subjectively it uses the word. So do we assume stories where 'allegedly' is not used is substantiated and the absolute truth? So shouldn't all political, social as well as most news be littered with the word alleged, unless the editors and newshounds can cent percent prove its validity? On a final note, till the word allegedly, that is an attempt to show impartial objectivity, is not used objectively is all news for accountability? What does the reader believe, in news that is alleged or is sans the allegation of being alleged? Is the former the truth or the latter a lie? Allegedly, both are news!

More than 18 journalists have been killed by militants and unidentified miscreants in the last few years in Assam. And the shocking part is, none of the killers of these journalists have been arrested by police, so far. Media is mirror of the society but the freedom of the Press guaranteed by the Constitution is by no means absolute. More than 18 journalists have been killed by militants and unidentified miscreants in the last few years in Assam. And the shocking part is, none of the killers of these journalists have been arrested by police so far. On August 9, 1991, unidentified miscreants gunned down Ajir Asom's local correspondent in Sivasagar, Kamal Saikia. Police has so far failed to nab his killers and the family members are making the rounds of courts seeking justice. In the same year, Assam Tribune's local correspondent, Kunarmal Agarwala was killed by suspected ULFA cadres in Kampur, Nagaon. On Aug 19, 1995, suspected timber smugglers killed Northeast Times correspondent, Pabitra Narayan in Sonari, Sivasagar. In the same year, on Sept 24, unidentified miscreants killed Goreshwar journalist, Dipak Swargiary. On April 26, 1996, suspected BLT members gunned down journalist, Manik Deuri in Diphu. In the same year in May 16, Asomiya Pratidin's editor, Parag Kr Das was gunned down in broad daylight in the heart of Guwahati city. In 1997 local journalist, Panja Ali was shot dead by unidentified miscreants in Kasugaon, Kokrajhar.

In 1998, suspected mafia killed local journalist, Nurul Haq in Hojai. In 1999, photographer Alfarid Shazad and journalist Jiten Chutiya were killed in a grenade explosion inside Sivasagar SP's office. On Dec 31, 1999, suspected ULFA gunned down senior journalist, Ratneswar Sarma Shastri in Barpeta district. On March 24, 2003, journalist Dinesh Brahma fell to assassin's bullets in Dhubri district. In 2003, Amar Asom's local correspondent, Indramohan Hakasama was killed in Aagiya in Goalpara district. On Jan 6, 2005 Asomiya Khobor correspondent, Prahlad Gowala was killed in a preplanned conspiracy in Golaghat. On Oct 29, 2006, Suwalkuchi journalist, Kanak Raj Medhi died under mysterious circumstances. Last year, Hojai journalist, Mohd Musalmuddin, Kokrajhar cable TV director Bodosa Narzary and very recently Kokrajhar journalist, Jagajit Saikia were killed in cold blood. What is shocking is that the police has so far not been able to nab the assailants of these journalists. Will these journalists and their family members ever get justice? "Freedom of Press" is gaining momentum from the people, engineered by politicians, students' organisations and anti-social elements in the state. If the authorities do not take any steps, this may well send a wrong message across the world on how democracy is being threatened and how freedom of the Press is sabotaged in an egalitarian society like ours. Let media be work freely.

These challenges and opportunities are on the same line in the Darwin's theory of the 'survival of the fittest'. The closure of the 'National Herald' is a clear example of what can go wrong if a newspaper cannot keep pace with the times. How much information is needed in this over-informed society? Today, the information market is flooded with newspapers, magazines, broadcasting corporations, etc. The answer lies in only that much, which is important enough for the audience, with which they can relate themselves and fall back to pay attention. But media portrays itself as a medium, which not only provides information to masses but also supports individual interests and rights. The drift from being a representative of the mass, to catering to specialised audience aimed at small, special-interest, regional or even local markets results in segmentation of the audience. From mass to niche audiences: In the demassified media, audiences have wider choices from which to choose from whether its cable TV, Internet FM broadcasts or the numerous FM stations. They have a situation whereby different media organisations are no longer targeting a mass audience but dealing with niche audiences. For instance, audiences are now being categorised by age group or social class by different media houses. The challenge is to get hold of the viewer. For example, in case of broadcast news, the prospective viewer has a remote control in his/her hand and may switch to other channels. So one has to be a whole entity and present it in each frame to tell viewers who they are, why they are important.

Citizen Journalism

If we need to know what is happening, and the Media won't tell us; if we need to know why it matters, and Media won't tell us; if we need to know what to do about it and Media won't tell us but we have to tell the story ourselves. This trend has gained momentum nowadays with easy availability of camera phones, camcoders and user-friendly editing software, everyone who wished to make a difference can be a journalist. On the line medium: On-line medium is considered a major factor behind the demassification of the mass media. This medium brings both the media and the masses closer than any other medium. The challenge lies in providing information, which is credible and unassailable and much faster than before.

Opportunities for Journalists

Today, almost every publication and broadcast media has their own website (online editions) providing what they are already providing through their existing medium. The media has realised the potential of new technology, especially the Internet, which they see as a platform to go global and tap global market. The money factor: Setting up a newspaper and a news channel is a costly affair whereas having your own website is a much cheaper option for journalists. Media freedom: Due to demassification, the information age has witnessed huge diverts in presenting news though blogging, private websites. These trends give more freedom to journalists to express and the concept of Press Freedom remains intact.

Support to Regional Languages

Demassification revitalises the regional media in India, which somewhat enhances reporting, giving it wings to explore new ventures.

Print media also gets into new avenues with the publishing of supplements and the concept of free newspaper has come into existence. In Kolkata, a free newspaper circulates its edition to its employees travelling in company's bus service. Recently in Nepal, an 8-page weekly was launched on gay community to disseminate information about the risk of contracting HIV and AIDS through unprotected same gender sex and provides a voice to a community that alleges persecution by family members, employers and even police. These challenges and opportunities are also on the same line of the Darwin theory of the 'survival of the fittest'. The closure of the National Herald, which was instituted by Pt Jawaharlal Nehru is a clear example of what can go wrong if you are not part of the demassified reality.

Mere knowledge of a crime is not enough to be awarded death penalty under IPC Section 120B. In a democratic country like India, no innocent person should be sentenced to death. The media could play a constructive role in this regard. Some sections of the media often give their judgment without waiting for the decision of the court. We have seen it before, especially in the Aarushi murder case. The Nithari killings case is not an exception either.

Without thinking through the pros and cons of the repercussions of their behaviour, sections of the media declared Mohinder Singh Pandher as the main culprit in Nithari killings even though there are many loopholes in the case. After the failure of the state police in investigating the case, the Central Bureau of Investigation (CBI) took up the probe. The CBI has filed chargesheets in 16 cases, out of a total of 19 cases of abduction, rape and murder of four women and 15 children, mostly girls. The cases are being heard separately and while Koli has been charged with rape, abduction and murder in all the cases, Pandher is the co-accused in six.

But according to RS Sodhi, the retired judge of the Delhi High Court who agreed to defend Moninder Singh Pandher in the Allahabad High Court, there is no evidence which directly links Pandher to the conspiracy and this lack of evidence may come to his aid in the high court. In his opinion, Pandher's mere knowledge of the horrific crimes is not enough to invite a conviction like a death penalty. Interestingly, Sodhi has presided over many sensational cases, including the Jessica Lall murder case, the gruesome Tandoor murder case and the Shashinath Jha murder case. He has sent many criminals, including Priyadarshini Mattoo's killer Santosh Kumar Singh, to the gallows. Sodhi practised in constitutional, civil, criminal, land revenue and excise matters in the Supreme Court of India for 25 years. Appointed a high court judge in 1999, he retired in 2007. According to Sodhi, the judge got emotionally involved and the judgement, therefore, is not a judgment in law and may be called a judicial murder. He also said that there are no factual things on record that nail Pandher in the present case, that the trial court judge totally bypassed the facts on record and that mere knowledge of the happening was not enough to convict anyone of murder. No doubt, the house in Noida where the murders occurred belongs to Moninder Singh Pandher. It means that he must have known about the crime being committed. But you can't hold a person guilty for murder under 120 B (criminal conspiracy) for 'must have known' because it does not mean he was, in fact, in the know.

Then, what made the judge deliver such a judgement?

The immense media hype that surrounded the case may have played a role. Media should understand its limitations and do its job accordingly. Media's role should be constructive in this regard.

In a democratic country like India, no innocent person should be sentenced to death. So, everybody must think about the case at least once from a different angle.

Now it is time for the media to show some maturity. It should concentrate much more on the actual political atmosphere. Rather than commenting on assumptions it must analyse the current political scenario. The Election Commission has banned exit polls. Apparently it seems to curb the freedom of the media but a close look will reveal another story.

It seems that this time the Election Commission has begun moral policing over the media by banning dissemination of results of opinion polls and exit polls during the 48 hours before the end of the poll in case of single phase election. This has raised a question whether it is trying to curb media freedom? After the 26/11 Mumbai attack the government similarly wanted to restrict media freedom. The repeated attempt means that the media is under the scanner. But in this case it should be taken as a positive move. In the past few years we had seen that experts gave their views and analysis on the opinion polls and exit polls which later proved either misleading or wrong. The question is how a whole election process can be estimated on opinion polls and exit polls which abdicate in its purpose. Now it is almost a trend, before an election, to analyse an election by experts depending on opinion polls. Many news channels and news papers spend lots of money not only to carry out the surveys but also on experts. But as it was proved in the past elections that these are often wrong. The comments and analysis that are based on them are also misleading. Whether opinion polls and exit polls affect voters is a matter of controversy but the experts' opinion and these polls surely mislead common people.

Another aspect is that these opinion polls create a frenzy that makes the situation more complex in times of an election. On the eve of election different media gave various opinion polls. As if these are penultimate results. Different political parties react with such belligerence on these results that it takes on a war like hysteria. Moreover, our susceptible sensex reacts accordingly with these opinion polls and become more volatile.

Now it is time for the media to show some maturity. It should concentrate much more on the actual political atmosphere. Rather than commenting on assumptions it must analyse the current political scenario. People can only have a clear idea about the political spectrum when news, views and analysis are based on actual facts and figures. Proper guidance of masses is the soul of true journalism.

No less than the Advertisement Guru, indeed a demi-god of the Ad-circuit, Alyque Padamsee, has called for a ban on rape scenes in films and TV shows. Notorious for his ultra liberal views, even Padamsee is outraged. "Like Doctors and lawyers journalists should have statutory registration. There is no shame in it. If doctors and lawyers have a licence why not journalists?" This stunning suggestion came 62 years ago from an eminent editor-journalist, the late Mr. K. Rama Rao, in an address to an Andhra journalist conclave. It is instructive to note a couple of paragraphs from his address that is of considerable relevance today, as reproduced here (1944). He said: "An eminent journalist recently pointed out that journalism in India has ceased to be a calling and become trade. So far as proprietors are concerned, it is a well-organised industry, but it is not a well-organised profession, even so far as the men who produce newspapers are concerned. If the ideal that the best newspaper should be owned by its own readers cannot be realised? We must at least attempt, those who own and those who work, to adjust our angles and approaches, in common interest? The profit motive (has become) rather deep rooted in the mind of the proprietors..?..Skilled labour is the basis of trade unionism. You can regulate (entry) only on the test of skill." These observations were made a couple of years before Independence when almost the entire nationalist press was part of the national struggle for freedom. It shows that the situation, none-too-happy then, has worsened since, particularly with advent of the electronic media. Left to itself, the electronic media will reduce Kalidas to Khushwant Singh and Meerabai to Shobhaa De. This profound observation, made by a well known journalist-editor, Mr. Prabhash Joshi, at a media university meeting sometime back, underlines the seamy side of the media. It may sound a trifle exaggerated but it is the quintessential truth of the state of the media today. Both of the electronic and its forerunner, the print media, which has become an apology for tabloids — with few honourable exceptions. The term 'media' itself is the plural of 'medium' but, rightly or otherwise, has come to mean a collective noun for the entire press, the printed word as well as its electronic variety, the ubiquitous idiot box.

The proliferation of 24-hour news and entertainment channels, started by all and sundry from Rupert Murdoch to babulal panwala, is a pain in the neck. With their tireless reiteration of the trite, these channels revel in highly dramatised presentation of sex and crime stories, sensationalising senseless minor incidents, often strewn with unrelated, salacious visuals culled from old clips. Of late the use of "hidden cameras" is a new craze in stage managed shows and making tall claims of investigative journalism. Most of the news channels relegate major national events of importance to secondary or even tertiary position. Doordarshan seems to be the only exception, but it is also gradually falling in line. It is strange that terms like dress code, regulation, control, (much less 'remote control', 'censorship', etc.) have become dirty words in the lexicon of even eminent editors like Vinod Mehta as much as of the show business stalwarts like Mahesh Bhatt. Both profess to be unrelenting champions of freedom of expression, freedom of art, freedom of the press — indeed in defense of absolute unbridled freedom in everything.

Cry in wilderness A code for self-regulation of print and electronic media has long been a cry in the wilderness. In the fiercely competitive world of liberalisation and globalisation it is foolish to expect voluntary restraint from the media. The media barons, addicted to making pots of money through crass commercial ventures at the expense of social harmony and welfare, and public decency and morality, will never respond positively to the calls of self-regulation. The only remedy lies in a powerful popular movement to re-instill a modicum of sanity and obviate obscene displays. Not through violent methods adopted by Bajrang Dal, Shiv Sena, VHP or Yaqoob Khan, but by millions writing a constant barrage of protests to the bigwigs in the various channels and show business, as also by non-political public organisations. Most urgently needed is for an all powerful Media Council to replace the toothless Press Council and an empowered autonomous regulatory mechanism. It is deplorable how the incipient Broadcast Bill, still in the womb, has provoked sharp criticism mostly from professionals backed by entrenched commercial interests. "Bare bosom culture" The state of the self-styled entertainment channels, blighted by films dominating the television, is even worse. Vulgarity seems to be the new passport to wealth and fame. It is a cruel joke that the likes of scarcely clad Rekha Sawant or Mallika Sherawat protest — and protest too much. No less than the Advertisement Guru, indeed a demi-god of the Ad-circuit, Alyque Padamsee, has called for a ban on rape scenes in films and TV shows. Notorious for his ultra liberal views, even Padamsee is outraged obviously because of their inevitable baneful impact on young formative minds as much as on adults and adolescents who constitute a large chunk of viewers. The danger of teen-age pregnancy looms large and stares some of them in the face. Most of the TV shows revel in spreading the semi-nude "bare bosom" culture. Add to it the fashion parades and ramp shows exhibiting models wearing little or no clothes? Paradoxically to advertise designers who seem to be averse to all kinds of clothing. It is only Doordarshan which presents its female anchors in decent dress.

Unlike most other private channels which seem to promote what may be called the "banyan coat" dress code to their anchors and newsreaders of the fair sex which in any case proliferates all over the television these days. Conclusion with recent examples: The media is playing havoc with the cultural and moral fabric of the Indian society, as we have witnessed in recent times in the case of the Mangalore Pub incident, the Arushi case, Mumbai terror attacks, the acid attack on girls where the media sensationalised and delivered its own justice, thereby, circumventing the judicial process. In the Mangalore case, the media blew up an issuel and distorted the facts by showing women alone as being assaulted. The Arushi case was the worst of all! Given this situation, it is myth that self-regulation will work in the media. It has not worked in the west. Its better that India learns its lessons before it is too late.

Information dissemination through media helps in raising the aspirations of the masses and highlighting the need for education. Media has contributed in changing nations and societies. Thus, revolutionary changes have taken place at all levels.

Communication is power and so is information. Communication is needed for development; communication elicited is long-lasting, more meaningful and readily acceptable. Media, in the modern world, is a force to reckon with. The active role played by the media in the development of human beings in regional, national or international spheres has to be fully acknowledged. The most important endeavour in development has to be accorded to human development. In fact human development is the key to development in all other areas. Without adequately-planned, skilfully-executed and spontaneous media support, human development will prove to be a difficult proposition and remain an unachievable goal. It is therefore imperative that before we plan any development activity, we ensure that the human effort involved in the task is adequately communication-oriented. Media encompasses upbringing, human nature and personality in a number of ways. It has contributed tremendously in changing nations and societies. In spite of inequalities in our society, revolutionary changes have taken place at all levels. The role of media in highlighting women's issues and helping ameliorate their plight has been amply recognised. A large number of television serials on women such as 'Stree; kab kyo aur kaise; shakti' and several others have focused on issues like child marriages, pregnancy tests, dowry deaths, broken marriages, widow remarriage, discrimination against women at the workplace and numerous other issues. It must however be recognised that media is a tremendous force in today's world.

National and global issues are affected, influenced and shaped by media outputs. Any nation or organisation, which ignores media power does so at its own peril.

Involvement of media in development is in two ways: to help remove illiteracy and improve prosperity. All the other allied tasks are by-products of media inputs and media consumption by masses and they contribute to the welfare of the nation and the happiness of its people.

The media played a crucial role in focusing the attention of the entire country on the recent pub incident in Mangalore. However, stories about local broadcast channels being party to the attack point to a depressing trend in the Indian media. "What would you choose as a press photographer if you were to decide between clicking a photograph and saving the life of a victim?" The photographer said, "I would rather click a photograph." There is a case of a South African photographer who won the 1994 Pulitzer Prize for Feature Photography. The photograph shows a starving and emaciated Sudanese girl struggling her way to a UN food distribution centre and a vulture waiting behind her at a distance, supposedly for the girl to die so that it could feast on her.

The photograph received rave reviews. However, the photographer was criticised for failing to carry out a basic humanitarian duty. Subsequently, the photographer committed suicide out of depression but that's another story. The recent pub attack in Mangalore and the media role in it, brings ashore several such issues. It was alleged that the miscreants who attacked the hapless women in the pub took TV journalists along to cover the 'moral policing'. The whole thing, it is alleged, was orchestrated with precision with cameramen waiting for the 'action' to begin.

Subsequently, the police accused the media of not informing them about this planned attack. According to the police, the media should have alerted them so that the whole incident could have been avoided. Yes, the media could have informed the police and the police could have averted the incident. But the question is would such action by the media serve any purpose? Next time the Sri Rama Sene goes out to bring about 'order' in another pub, they may go about it quietly and inflict a greater blow. With no any media coverage, it is likely that the world will not see their hooliganism. It is widely argued, at least in media circles that but for the wide and constant reportage by media channels, the Mangalore pub attack would have gone unnoticed. In a way, it is true as it was only after the national news channels broadcast the story that the police and the government woke up to take some measures.

Even now, the whole incident refuses to die down with the Sri Rama Sene being vindicated by the apparent failure of the Karnataka state government to take stringent action. However, in the whole development, there emerged another disturbing trend. It is reported, quite convincingly that certain local broadcast channels were party to or at least part of the entire assault.

In fact, it is alleged that the Sene members made sure that TV cameras were there with them when they went on the rampage (perhaps, they were eager to show to the whole world their "chivalry" by attacking helpless women.) If it is true that these TV cameras went along with the hooligans, then it could point to a depressing trend in the Indian media. Yes, journalists have to tell, show to the whole world, the reality as it is (well, as far as possible). For this they may have to be candid. They may, at times, even have to cross boundaries. However, there is a danger of temptation to indulge in such endeavors purely for personal gains—to increase circulation, gain a few more TRPs, etc. When that happens, the media will cease to be messengers.

Bibliography

PRIMARY SOURCES

Collected Works of Mahatma Gandhi, Hundred Volumes (New Delhi: Publications Division, Ministry of Information and Broadcasting, Government of India), 1958-83.

Gandhi, M.K., Story of My Experiments With Truth, Vol. I (Tr. By Mahadev Desai from Gujarati) and Vo1. II Tr. (By Mahadev Desai and Pyarelal Nair (sic) from Gujarati) (Ahmedabad: Navajivan Press), 1927-1929.

Gandhi, Mohandas, K. Hind Swaraj, or Indian Home Rule (Ahmedabad: Navajivan Press), 1931.

Gandhi, M.K. Ethical Religion: Neethi Dharma, Tr. by A. Rama Iyer from Hindi (Madras: S. Ganesan), 1930.

Gandhi, M.K., Satyagraha in South Africa (Ahmedabad: Navajivan Press), 1972.

Gandhi, M.K., Constructive Programme: Its Meaning and Place (Ahmedabad: Navajivan Press), 1945.

Gandhi, M.K., The Bhagvadgita (Delhi: Orient Paperbacks), 1998.

Gandhi, M.K., Delhi Diary, (Prayer Speeches from 10-9-47 to 30-1-48), (Ahmedabad: Navajivan Press), 1948 (Written in third person and corrected by Gandhi)

Gandhi, M. K., Key to Health (Ahmedabad: Navajivan Publishing House), 1948

Gandhi, M. K., From Yervada Mandir (Ahmedabad: Navajivan Publishing House), 1932.

SECONDARY SOURCES

Books

Agarwala, B.R, Trials of Independence (1858-1946) (New Delhi: National Book Trust), 1991.

Ahluwalia, B.K., (ed.), Facets of Gandhi (New Delhi: Lakshmi Book Store), 1968.

Alexander, Horace G., Gandhi Through Western Eyes (Bombay: Asia Publishing House), 1969.

Ambedkar, B.R., What Congress and Gandhi Have Done to the Untouchables (Bombay: Thacker and Company Limited), 1945.

Andrews C.F., Mahatma Gandhi Ideas (London: George Allen and Unwin), 1929.

Ashe, Geoffrey, Gandhi: A Study in Revolution (London: Heineman), 1968.

Athalye, D.V., The Life of Mahatma Gandhi (Poona: Aryabhushan Press), 1923.

Azad, Maulana Abul Kalam, India Wins Freedom, The Complete Version (New Delhi: Orient Longman), 1988.

Bakshi, Rajni, Bapu Kuti (New Delhi: Penguin Books India (P) Ltd.), 1998.

Bandopadhya, Anu, M. K. Gandhi: Author, Journalist, Printer, Publisher, (Ahmedabad: Navajivan Publishing House), 1994.

Bandopadhyaya, Jayantanuja, Social and Political Thought of Gandhi (Bombay: Allied Publishers), 1969.

Bangal, Nicholas, Newspaper Language (London: Focal Press), 1993

Barnes, Margarita, The Indian Press: A History of the Growth of Public Opinion in India (London: George Allen and Unwin), 1940.

Basu, Bishwas, Your Guide to Journalism (Chandigarh: Abhishek Publications), 2006.

Bell, A., The Language of News Media (Oxford: Blackwell Publishers), 1991

Bernays, Robert, Naked Fakir (London: Victor Gollanez Limited), 1931.

Bertrandt, C., Media Ethics and Accountability System (New Jersey: Transaction Publishes), 2000.

Bhargava, Motilal, Role of the Press in the Freedom Movement (New Delhi: Reliance Publishing House), 1987.

Bhattacharya, Bhabani, Gandhi: the Writer (The Image As It Grew) (New Delhi: National Book Trust), 1969.

Bhattacharya, Bhabani, Mahatma Gandhi (New Delhi: Arnold Heineman Publishers), 1977.

Bhattacharya, Sabyasachi, The Mahatma And The Poet (Delhi: National Book Trust), 1999.

Bhattacharya, S.N., Mahatma Gandhi, The Journalist (Bombay: Asia Publishing House), 1998.

Birla, G.D., In the Shadow of the Mahatma (Delhi: Orient Longman), 1953

Birla, G.D., Bapu, A Unique Association, Four Volumes (Bombay: Bharatiya Vidya Bhavan), 1977.

Bolton, Glomey, The Tragedy of Gandhi (London: George Allen and Unwin Limited), 1934.

Bond, F. Fraser, An Introduction to Journalism (USA: McGrew-Hill Book Company), 1989

Bondurant, Joan V., Conquest of Violence: The Gandhian Philosophy of Conflict (New Jersey: Princeton University Press), 1988.

Bose, Ninnal Kumar, My Days With Gandhi (New Delhi: Orient Longman Limited), 1974.

Boyd, Barrett, The Globalization News (London: Sage Publications), 1998

Boyd Barrett and T. Rantanen, (ed.), News Agencies as Agent of Globalisation (London: Sage Publication), 1998, p. 89.

Brailsford, Henry N., Rebel India (London: Leonard Stein), 1931.

Brock, Peter, Gandhi as a Linguistic Nationalist (New Delhi: South Asia Publications), 1996.

Broomfield, J. H., "Gandhi: A Twentieth Century Anomaly" in Richard L. Park (ed.), Change and Persistence Tradition in India: five Lectures (Michigan: Michigan Papers on South and South East Asia, No.2), 1971.

Brown, Judith, Gandhi's Rise to Power: Indian Politics 1915-22 (Cambridge: Cambridge University Press), 1972.

Brown, Judith, Gandhi and Civil Disobedience: 1928-34 (Cambridge: Cambridge University Press), 1977.

Brown, Judith, Gandhi: Prisoner of Hope (Delhi: Oxford University Press), 1992.

Bush, Catherine, Mahatma Gandhi (London: Burke Publishing Company Limited), 1940.

Butterworth and Hememann, Journalism in the Digital Age (London: Pluto Press), 2000.

Cargill, Oscar, Henry David Thoreau: Selected Works on Nature and Liberty (New York: Liberty Arts Press), 1952.

Case, C.M., Nonviolent Coercion (London: George Allen and Unwin), 1923

Chadha, Yogesh, Rediscovering Gandhi (London: Century Books Ltd.), 1997.

Chandra, Bipan, et al, India's Struggle For Independence, 1857-1947 (New Delhi: Viking),1988.

Chatterjee, Partha, Nationalist Thought in the Colonial World (London: Zed Books),1986.

Chaudhary, Ramnarayan, Bapu As I Saw Him (Ahmedabad: Navajivan Publishing House), 1959.

Chenery, William L., Freedom of the Press (New York: Harcourt, Brace and Company), 1955

Choudhary, J. C., Introduction to Journalism and Mass Communication (New Delhi: Authorspress), 2007

Choudhari, Manmohan, Exploring Gandhi (New Delhi: Gandhi Peace Foundation), 1990.

Christopher, C., Dynamics of Journalism (New Delhi: Anmol Publications Private Limited), 1997.

Collins, Larry, and Lapierre, Dominique, Freedom at Midnight (New Delhi: Vikas Publishing House Private Limited), 1978.

Compbell, C. P., Race, Myth and News (Chicago: Sage Publications), 1995

Cousins, Nonnan, (ed.), Profiles of Gandhi (Delhi: Indian Book Company), 1969.

Curram, J. and M. Gurevitch (ed.), Mass Media and Society (London: Arnold Press), 2000

Dalton, Dennis, Gandhi's Power: Nonviolence in Action (Oxford: Oxford Publishers), 1998.

Datta, K. Vishnu (ed.), Journalism Today (New Delhi: Akansha Publishing House), 2006.

Dandavate, Madhu, Marx and Gandhi (Bombay: Popular Prakashan), 1977.

Das, Ajay, Sting Operation by Media (New Delhi: Discovery Publishing House), 2007.

Das, Durga (ed.), Sardar Patel's Correspondence, Six Volumes (Ahmedabad: Navajivan Publishing House), 1972.

De Burg, H. (ed.), Investigated Journalism: Context and Practice (London: Routledge), 2000.

Deluca, Anthony R., Gandhi, Mao, Mandela, and Gorbachev: Studies in Personality, Power, and Politics (London: Praeger), 2000.

Desai, Mahadev, Day to Day With Gandhi, Ten Volumes, Edited by Parikh, N.D., Sarva Sewa Sangh Prakashan, Varanasi, 1961-73.

Desai, Mahadev, The Epic of Travail Core (Ahmedabad: Navajivan Publishing House), 1937.

Desai, Mahadev, The Story of Bardoli: Being a History of the Bardoli Satyagraha and its Sequel (Ahmedabad: Navjivan Publishing House), 1929.

Desai, Mahadev, A Righteous Struggle, [A Chronicle of Ahmedabad Textile Labourers' Fight for Justice] Translated by Dave Somnath P. and edited by Kumarappa Bharatan (Ahmedabad: Navajivan Press), 1951.

Desai, M.V. and Ninan, Sevanti (ed.), Beyond those Headlines (New Delhi: The Media Foundation, Allied Publishers), 1996.

Devanesan, Chandran D. S., The Making of the Mahatma (New Delhi: Orient Longman), 1969.

Doke, J.M., M. K. Gandhi: A Patriot in South Africa (New Delhi: Publications Division, Ministry of Information and Broadcasting), 1994.

Dua, M.R., Themes in Indian Communication (New Delhi: Metropolitan), 1980.

Dyke, G., Inside Story (London: Harper Collins), 2004

Edwardes, Michael, The Myth of the Mahatma: Gandhi the British' and the Raj (London: Constable Press), 1986.

Elwin,Verrier, Gandhiji, Bapu of His People (Shillong: Assam Government Press),1950.

Erikson Erik H., Gandhi's Truth: The Origins of Militant Non-violence (London: Faber and Faber Limited), 1970.

Fischer, Louis, The Life of Mahatma Gandhi (London: Jonathan Cape Thirty Bedford Square), 1951.

Fischer, Louis (ed.), The Essential Gandhi (London: George Allen and Unwin), 1962.

Fisher, Fredrick B., That Strange Little Brown Man (Delhi: Orient Longmans), 1970.

Frost, C., Media Ethics and Self -Regulations (London: Longman Press), 2000

Galtung, Johan, The Way is the Goal: Gandhi Today (Gujarat: Gujarat Vidyapith), 1992.

Galtung, J. and M. Ruge, "The Structure of Foreign News", Journal of International Peace Research, Vol. I, 1965, pp. 65-71.

Gandhi, Manu, Last Glimpses of Bapu (Delhi: Shivlal Aggrawal and Co.), 1962.

Gandhi, Prabhudas, My Childhood With Gandhi (Ahmedabad: Navajivan Publishing House), 1957.

Gandhi, Rajmohan, The Good Boatman (Delhi: Viking), 1995.

Gangrade, K.D., Gndhi's Autobiography: Moral Lessons (New Delhi: Gandhi Smriti and Darshan Samiti), 1998.

Gaur, Sanjay, Media Journalism in 21st Century (Jaipur: Book Enclave), 2006

Ghose, S.L, Motilal Ghose (New Delhi: National Book Trust), 1979.

Ghosh, Hemendra Prasad, The Newspaper in India (Calcutta: The University Press), 1952.

Ghosh, Sudhir, Gandhi's Emissary (Calcutta: Rupa and Company), 1967.

Green, Martin, Gandhi: Voice of a New Age Revolution (New York: Continuum), 1993.

Hall, Jim, Online Journalism (Sterling: Pluto Press), 2001.

Hall, Stuart, The Rediscovery of Ideology: Return of the Repressed in Media Studies (London: Methven Publications), 1982.

Harcop, T. Journalism: Principle and Practice (London: Sage Publications), 2004.

Hargreaves, Ian, Journalism: Truth or Dare (London: Oxford University Press), 2003.

Harold Koontz, and Heinz Weihrich, Essentials of Management (Singapore: McGraw Hill Book Co.), 1990.

Heath, Carl, Gandhiji: Satyagraha or Non Violent Resistance (Madras: S.Ganesan), 1930.

Heath, Carl, Gandhi (London: George Allen and Unwin), 1944.

Herbert, J. Practicing Global Journalism (Oxford: Focal Press), 2001

Homer, A. Jack (ed.), The Wit and Wisdom of Gandhi (Boston: Beacon Press), 1951.

Horsburgh, Nonviolence and Aggression: A Study of Gandhi's Moral Equivalent to War—Mahatma Gandhi (London: Lutterworth Press), 1972.

Hoyland, John S., The Cross Moves East: A Study in the Significance of Gandhi's "Satyagraha" (London: George Allen and Unwin), 1931.

Hunt, James D., Gandhi in London (New Delhi: Promilla and Co.), 1978.

Hunt, James D., Gandhi and the Nonconformists (New Delhi: Promilla and Co.), 1986.

Iyengar, A. S., All Through the Gandhian Era (Bombay: Hind Kitabs Ltd.), 1950.

Iyengar, K.R. Srinivas, Indian Writing in English (Bombay: Asia Publishing House), 1962.

Iyer,Raghavan .N., The Moral and Political Writings of Mahatma Gandhi, Three Volumes, Oxford University Press,1987.

James R., (ed), Winston S. Churchill: His Complete Speeches (New York: New York Press), 1974.

Johnson, Stanley and Harriss Julian, The Complete Reporter (New York: The Macmillan Company), 1958

Jones, Steve, Encyclopaedia of New Media (C.A.: Sage Publications), 2003.

Jones, John Paul, Gathering and Writing the News (Chicago: Nelson Hall Inc.), 1976.

Jordans, J.T.F., Gandhi's Religion: A Homespun Shawl (London: Macmillan Press Ltd.), 1998.

Kamath, M.V., Professional Journalism (New Delhi: Vikas Publishing House), 1980.

Kapur, Sudarshan, Raising Up A Prophet: The African-American Encounter With Gandhi (New Delhi: Oxford University Press), 1993.

Karkhanis, Sharad, Indian Politics and the Role of Press (New Delhi: Vikas Publishing House), 198.

Keeble, Richard (ed.), Print Journalism: A Critical Introduction (New York: Rutledge Taylor), 2005.

Keer, Dhananjay, Dr. Ambedkar: Life and Mission (Bombay: Popular Prakashan), 1954.

Keer, Dhananjay, Mahatma Gandhi: Political Saint and Unarmed Prophet (Bombay: Popular Prakashan), 1973.

Khare, Prem Shankar, Press and Public Opinion in India (1857-1918) (Allahabad: Piyush Prakashan), 1964.

Kishore, Giriraj, Pehla Girmitiya (New Delhi: Jnanapith Prakashan), 2000.

Khosla, Gopal Das, Stern Reckonin (New Delhi: Bhawanani and Sohs), 1949.

Kothari, M.M., Critique of Gandhi (Jodhpur: Critique Publications), 1996.

Koontz, Harold and Weihrich, Heinz, Essentials of Management (Singapore: McGraw -Hill Book Co.), 1990.

Krishnamurthi, Nadig, Indian Journalism (Mysore: University of Mysore), 1966

Kriplani, Krishna, Gandhi: A Life (New Delhi: National Book Trust), 1993.

Kumar, Mahendra and Low Peter, (ed.), Legacy and Future of Nonviolence (New Delhi: Gandhi Peace Foundation), 1996.

Kumar, Satish, Mahatma Gandhi: The Man and Writer (Bareily: Prakash Book Depot), 1983.

Lester, Muriel, Entertaining Gandhi (London: Ivor Nicholson and Watson), 1932.

Limaye, Madhu, Mahatma Gandhi and Jawaharlal Nehru: A Historic Partnership 1916-1948, Four Volumes (New Delhi: Gandhi Media Centre), 1989.

Lindley, Mark: Gandhi and the World Today (1998) (Kerala: Centre for Gandhian Studies), 1999.

Lovett, Pat, Journalism in India, (Aharchandra Mooketjee Lectures April 1926) (Calcutta: Banne Publishing Company), n.d.

Mansfield, F. J., The Complete Journalist (London: Sir Issac Pitman and Sons Limited), 1944.

Manubehn, Bapu, My Mother (Ahmedabad: Navajivan Publishing House), 1949.

McNAir, B., The Sociology of Journalism (London: Arnold Press), 1998

McQuail, Denis, Mass Communication Theory (London: Sage Publications), 1994.

Meer, Fatima, Apprenticeship of a Mahatma: A Biography of Mahatma Gandhi 1869--1914 (New Delhi: Gandhi Hindustani Sahitya Sabha), 1997.

Mehta, D.S., Mass Communication and Journalism in India (Bombay: Allied Publishers Private Limited), 1979.

Mehta, Ved, Mahatma Gandhi and His Apostles (New Delhi: Penguin Books, 1976.

Menon, Narayana, The Communications Revolution (New Delhi: National Book Trust), 1976.

Meyer, Henry, The Press in Australia (Melbourne: Lanswdowne Press Pvt. Ltd.), 1968.

Miller, Corl G., Journalism (New York: Holt, Rinehart & Winston, Inc.), 2001.

Mira, Gleanings, Gathered at Bapu's Feet (Ahmedabad: Navajivan Publishing House), 1949.

Mott, Frank Luther, American Journalism (New York: The Macmillan Company), 1962

Mujumdar, Ammu Menon, Social Welfare in India: Mahatma Gandhi's Contribution (London: Asia Publishing House), 1965.

Mukherjee, Hiren, Gandhiji, A Study (Calcutta: National Book Agency Private Ltd.), 1958.

Mukherjee, Subrata, and Ramaswamy, Sushila,(ed.), Facets of Mahatma Gandhi, Four Volumes (New Delhi: Deep and Deep Publishers), 1994.

Munshi, K.M., Gandhi: The Master (Delhi: Rajkamal Publications), 1948.

Munshi, K.M., Gujarat and its Literature (Calcutta: Longmans, Green and Co., Ltd.), 1935.

Murti, V.V.Ramana, Gandhi: Essential Writings (New Delhi: Gandhi Peace Foundation), 1970.

Nair, Gopalakrishnan, N., Mahatma Gandhi and the Indian Writers (New Delhi, Gandhi Smriti and Darshan Samiti), 1996.

Nanda, B.R., Mahatma Gandhi: A Biography (London: George Allen and Unwin Ltd.), 1958.

Nanda, B.R., Mahatma Gandhi: A Pictorial Biography (New Delhi: Publications Division), 1972. -

Nanda, B. R., Gokhale, Gandhi and the Nehrus (London: George Allen and Unwin), 1976.

Nanda, B.R., Gandhi and his Critics (Delhi: Oxford University Press), 1985.

Nanda, B.R., Gandhi, Pan-Islamism, Imperialism and Nationalism (New Delhi: Oxford University Press), 1989.

Nanda , B.R. (ed.), Mahatma Gandhi: 125 Years, ICCR, Wiley Eastern Ltd., New Age International Publishers, 1995.

Narain, Jai, Gandhi's View of Political Power (New Delhi: Deep and Deep Publications), 1987.

Narain, Jai, Alternative Economics (New Delhi: Deep and Deep Publications), 2007.

Narasimhan, Bharati, (ed.), Making of Great Communicator, Gandhi (New Delhi: National Media Centre), 1997.

Narayan, Shriman, (ed), Selected Works of Mahatma Gandhi, Six Volumes (Ahmedabad: Navajivan Publishing House), 1968.

Narsimhaiah, C.D., The Writers Gandhi (Patiala: Punjabi University), 1967.

Natrajan, S., A History of Press in India (Bombay: Asia Publishing House), 1962.

Nayar, Sushila, In Gandhiji's Mirror (New Delhi: Oxford University Press), 1991.

Nayar, Sushila, Mahatma Gandhi's Last Imprisonment The Inside Story (New Delhi: Haranand Publishers), 1996.

Nehru, Jawaharlal, An Autobiography (London: John Lane), 1936.

Nehru, Jawaharlal, The Discovery of India (Bombay: Asia Publishing House), 1960.

Padhya, Prabhakar, Principles of Journalism (Bombay: Popular Prakashan), 2004

Pandhikattu, Kuruvilla, The Meaning of the Mahatma for the Millennium (Delhi: Maadhyam Book Services), 2000.

Pant, K. C., Modern Journalism (New Delhi: Kanishka Publications), 2004

Parekh, Bhiku, Gandhi (Oxford: Oxford University Press), 1997.

Parekh, Bhikhu, Gandhi's Political Philosophy, A Critical Examination (New Delhi: Macmillan), 1989.

Parekh, Bhikhu, Colonialism, Tradition and Reform: An Analysis of Gandhi's Political Discourse (New Delhi: Sage Publications), 1999.

Parel, Anthony .J. (ed.), Hind Swaraj and Other Writings, Cambridge Texts in Modern Politics (New Delhi: Cambridge University Press), 1997.

Parthsarthy, Rangswami, Basic Journalism (New Delhi: Macmillan India Ltd.), 1984.

Parthasarathy, Rangaswami, Journalism in India (New Delhi: Sterling Publishers Private Limited), 1989.

Patel, Jehangir P., and Sykes, Marjorie, Gandhi: His Gift of the Fight, Friends Rural Circle (New Delhi: Rasulia), 1987.

Pavlik, J.V., Journalism and News Media (New York: University Press), 2001.

Payne, Robert, The Life and Death of Mahatma Gandhi (New Delhi: The Bodley Head), 1969.

Pinto, Vivek, Gandhi's Vision and Values: The Moral Quest

for Change in Indian Agriculture (New Delhi: Sage Publications), 1998.

Prabhakar, Naval and Basu, Narendra, Journalism and Mass Communication (New Delhi: Commonwealth Publishers), 2007.

Prasad, Rajendra, Satyagraha in Champaran (Ahmedabad: Navajivan Publishing House), 1949.

Prasad, Rajendra, At The Feet of Mahatma Gandhi (Bombay: Asia Publishing House), 1961.

Polak, Henry S.L, M. K. Gandhi: A Sketch of—His Life and Work (Madras: Ganesan and Co.), 1918.

Polak, Henry S.L, Speeches and Writings of M. K. Gandhi (Madras: Ganesan and Co.), 1919.

Polak, Millie Graham, Mr. Gandhi: The Man (Bombay: Vora and Company), 1949.

Pyarelal and Nayar, Sushila, Mahatma Gandhi: A Biography, Ten Volumes (Ahmedabad: Navajivan Publishing House), 1965.

Pyarelal, The Epic Fast, Mohanlal Maganlal Bhatt (Ahmedabad: Navajivan Publishing House), 1932.

Pyarelal, A Pilgrimage for Peace: Gandhi and Frontier Gandhi among North West Frontier Pathans, (Ahmedabad: Navajivan Publishing House), 1950.

Radhakrishnan, N., The Quest for Tolerance and Survival (New Delhi: Gandhi Smriti and Darshan Samiti and Gandhi Media Centre), 1995.

Radhakrishnan, N., The Gandhian Concept of Sustainable Development and New World Order (Madurai: Gandhi Museum), 1997.

Radhakrishnan, N., The Sparks of Non-Violence (New Delhi: Gandhi Smriti and Darshan Samiti), 1998.

Radhakrishnan, S., Mahatma Gandhi: Essays and Reflections of His Life and Works (London: George Allen and Unwin), 1939.

Radhakrishnan, S. (ed.), Mahatma Gandhi: 100 Years (New Delhi: Gandhi Peace Foundation), 1968.

Raghavan, G.N.S., PTI Story: The Origin and Growth of the Indian Press and the News Agency (New Delhi: PTI), 1987.

Raghavan, G. N. S., The Press in India: A New History (New Delhi: Gyan Publishing House), 1994.

Rajagopalachari, C., and Kumarappa, J.C., The Nations Voice Being a Connection of Gandhiji's Speeches in England and Sjt. Mahadev Desai's Account of the Sojourn (Ahmedabad: Navajivan Press), 1931.

Rajsekhar, T. (ed.), Modern Media and Television Journalism (New Delhi: Sonali Publications), 2007.

Randall, D., The Universal Journalist (London: Pluto Press), 2000.

Ranjeet, Swami, A Hidden Side of Mahatma Gandhi (New Delhi: Gandhi Smriti and Darshan Samiti), 1995.

Rao, Bhaskara, N., G.N.S. Raghavan, Social Effects on Mass Media in India (New Delhi: Gyan Publishing House), 1996.

Rau, Chalapathi M., The Press (New Delhi: National Book Trust), 1974.

Rau, Chalapathi M., The Press in India (Bombay: Allied Publishers Private Limited), 1976.

Reddy, E.S., Gandhiji's Vision of a Free South Africa (New Delhi: Sanchar Publishing House), 1995.

Reynolds Reginald, The True Book About Mahatma Gandhi (Bangalore: Educational Publishers), 1966.

Rolland, Romain, Mahatma Gandhi (New Delhi: Publication Division, Ministry of Information and Broadcasting, Government of India), 1990.

Rothermund, Dietmar, Mahatma Gandhi: All Essay in Political Biography (New Delhi: Manohar Publications), 1991.

Roy Chaudhury, P.C., Gandhi and His Contemporaries (New Delhi: Sterling Publishers Private Limited), 1972.

Ruben, Brent D., Communication and Human Behavior (New York: Macmillan Publishing Company), 1984.

Rudolph, Susanne Hoeber and Rudolph Lloyd I., The Modernization of Tradition: Political Development in India (Chicago: University of Chicago Press), 1997.

Rudolph, Susanne Hoeber and Rudolph Lloyd I., Gandhi: The Traditional Roots of Charisma (New Delhi: Orient Longman), 1987.

Sarkar, R. C. S., The Press in India (New Delhi: Sultan Chand and Company Limited), New Delhi, 1984.

Sengupta B. and Chowdhary R, Mahatma Gandhi and India's Struggle for Swaraj (Calcutta: Calcutta Publishing House), 1932.

Sethi, J.D., Gandhi Today (New Delhi: Vikas Publishing House), 1978.

Shankhdhar, B. M., Pioneers of Social Change in India (New Delhi: Deep and Deep), 1986.

Shankdhar, M. M., Understanding Gandhi Today (New Delhi: Deep and Deep), 1996.

Shannon, Claude E., and Weaver, Warren (USA: The Mathematical Theory of Communication, University of Illinois Press), 1949.

Sharp, Gene, Gandhi Wields The Weapon of Moral Power (Ahmedabad: Navajivan Publishing House), 1960.

Sharp, Gene, Gandhi Faces the Storm (Ahmedabad: Navajivan Publishing House), 1961.

Sharp, Gene, Gandhi as A Political Strategist with Essays on Ethics and Politics (Boston: Porter Sargent Publisher Inc.), 1979.

Sheean, Vincent, Lead, Kindly Light (New York: Random House), 1949.

Mahatma Gandhi, A Great Life in Brief (New Delhi: Publications Division, Ministry of Information and Broadcasting), 1954.

Shrivastava, K M, Radio and TV Journalism (Bangalore: Sterling Publishers Private Limited), 1989.

Shridharani, Krishnalal, War Without Violence (Bombay: Bharatiya Vidya Bhawan), Bombay,1952.

Shourie, Arun, Worshipping False Gods: Ambedkar and The Facts Which Have Been Erased, ASA Publications, New Delhi, 1997.

Shukla, A.S., Handbook of Journalism and Mass Communication (New Delhi: Rajat Publication), 2008.

Shukla, Chandrashanker (ed.), Gandhiji as We Know Him (Bombay: Vora and Company Publishers), 1945.

Shukla, Chandrashanker (ed.), Incidents of Gandhiji's Life (Bombay: Vora and Company Publishers), 1949.

Shukla, Chandrashanker (ed.), Reminiscences of Gandhiji (Bombay: Vora and Company Publishers), 1951.

Singh, J. K., Media and Journalism (New Delhi: APH Publishing Corporation), 2007.

Singh, Manorma, History of Journalism (New Delhi: Discovery Publishing House), 2007.

Singh, Manorma, Sting Operation (New Delhi: Discovery Publishing House), 2007.

Sitaramayya, B. Pattabhi, The History of Indian National Congress (Bombay: Padma Publications), 1946.

Slade, Madeleine, The Spirit's Pilgrimage (New York: Coward-McCann), 1960.

Sonnlietner, Michael W., Gandhian Nonviolence: Levels of Satyagraha (New Delhi: Abhinav Publications), 1985.

Smith, K., The Mass Media: Reporting, Writing (New York: Harper Row Publishers), 2000.

Spratt, P., Gandhism (Madras: The Huxley Press), 1939.

Tandon, P.D., and Wolseley, Roland E., Gandhi: Warrior of Non-Violence (New Delhi: National Book Trust), 1969.

Tarlo, Emma, Clothes Matter: Dress and Identity in India (New Delhi: Viking Penguin India), 1997.

Tendulkar, D. G., Mahatma Gandhi: Life of Mohandas Karamachand Gandhi, Eight Volumes (New Delhi: Publication Division, Ministry of Information and Broadcasting, Government of India) 1953.

Thiaga Rajan, S.P., History of Indian Journalism (Thanjavur: The Columbia House), 1966.

Thoreau, Henry D., Life Without Principle (London: London Press), 1905.

Thiaga Rajan, S.P., On the Duty of Civil Disobedience (London: London Press), 1903.

Thiaga Rajan, S.P., Selected Writings on Nature and Liberty (New York: Liberty Arts Press), 1952.

Thomas, Mac Combe, The History of Colony of Victor (Melbourne: Dilldown Press), 1858.

Tolstoy, Leo, The Kingdom of God and Peace Essays (London: London Press), 1936.

Tolstoy, Leo, Tolstoy's Writings on Civil Disobedience and Non-Violence (London: Peter Owen), 1968.

Tunstal, J., Journalist at Work (London: Constable Press), 2001.

P. Van den Dungen, Essays on Gandhian Politics, R. Kumar (ed.) (Oxford: Clarendon Press), 1971.

Upadhayaya, J.M., Mahatma Gandhi as a Student (New Delhi: Publications Division, Ministry of Information and Broadcasting), 1965.

Upadhayaya, J.M., Mahatma Gandhi: A Teacher's Discovery (Ahmedabad: Vallabh Vidyanagar), 1969.

Upadhayaya, J. M., (compiled), Gandhiji's Early Contemporaries and Companions (Ahmedabad: Navajivan Publishing House), 1971.

Verma, M.M., Gandhi's Technique of Mass Mobilization (New Delhi: R.K. Gupta and Co.), 1998.

Wadhwa, Priyanka, Development of Journalism (New Delhi: Murari Lal and Sons), 2007.

Wain Wright, David, Journalism Made Simple (London: Allen & Allen Company Limited) 1972.

Walker, Roy, Sword of Gold (New Delhi: Orient Longman), 1969.

Walter, W. G., An Outline of Modern Newspaper (New Delhi: Arise Publishers), 2008

Watson, Francis, Talking of Gandhi (London: London Press), 1957.

Watson, J. Media Communication: An Introduction to Theory and Process (Basingstroke: MacMillan Publishers), 1998

Weaver, D. (ed.), The Global Journalist (New Jersey: Hampton Press), 1998.

Weber, T.A., Gandhi, Panas Publishing Company (London: London Press), n.d.

Weber, Thomas Conflict Resolution and Gandhian Ethics (New Delhi: Gandhi Peace Foundation), 1991.

Weber, Thomas, Gandhi's Peacekeeping Army: The Shanti Sena and Unarmed Peacekeeping Army (New York: Syracuse), 1996.

Wellock, Wilfred, Gandhi as Social Revolutionary (New Jersey: Hampton Press), 1950.

Whale, John, Journalism and Government (London: Fontona Books), 1977.

Wilson, J., Understanding Journalism: A Guide to Issues (London: Routledge), 2006.

Wolpert, Stanley, Nine Hours to Rama (New York: Hamish Hamilton, 1990.

Wolpert, Stanley,Gandhi's Passion, The Life and Legacy of Mahatma Gandhi (New York: Oxford University Press), 2001.

Wolseley, E.Roland, (ed.), Journalism in Modern India (Bombay: Asia Publishing House), 1953.

Woodcook, George, Gandhi (New York: Fontana), 1972.

Woodcook, George, Who Killed the British Empire (New York: Fontana), 1974

Yogananda, Paramhansa, Autobiography of a Yogi (New York: The Philosophical Library), 1946.

Zakaria, Rafiq, Gandhi and the Breakup of India (Mumbai: Bharatiya Vidya Bhavan), 1999.

Periodicals and Journals

Gandhi Marg, Gandhi Peace Foundation, 221-223 (New Delhi: Deen Dayal Upadhyaya Marg),

Journal of Gandhi Smriti and Darshan Samiti (New Delhi: Gandhi Smriti and Darshan Samiti)

Journal of Peace and Gandhian Studies, A Quarterly of Gandhi Media Centre, Delhi.

Articles

"Special Issue on Hind Swaraj", The Aryan Path, Sept., 1938

Dasgupta, Swapan, and Koppikar, Smruti, "Nathuram Godse on Trial Again", India Today, August 3, 1998

Porter, William E., "Journalism", International Encyclopedia of Social Sciences, Vol. 8,

Patel, Avaan, "Gandhi on Canvas", The Hindu, New Delhi, Sunday, March 28, 1999.

Pinto,Vivek, "Gandhi :Writing for Change", Folio: Reaching Out, The Hindu, Chennai, April 8, 2001.

Sundaram, Geeta, "The Gandhi Oberschule", The Hindu, New Delhi, Sunday, January 3, 1999.

Vanna, Ravindra, "Godse's Testament", The Hindu, New Delhi, August 30,1998.

Balachandran, P.K., "Godseism Without Gandhi", Reflections: The Hindustan Times, New Delhi, August 16,1998.

Brown, Judith, M., "Gandhi: Will He Be Relevant?", A Future Past and Present, The Hindustan Times, Special Issue, 2001, New Delhi, January, 2001.

Chowdhry, K., "Gandhi Failed, Like All Saints", The Hindustan Times, New Delhi, January 30,1998.

Cole, Kris, "Ten Steps to Good Communications for Managers", The Hindustan Times, New Delhi, December 8, 1998.

Dalmia, Yashodhara, "The Mahatma As Muse", The Hindustan Times, HT City, New Delhi, July 28, 1999.

French, Patrick, "Gandhi Was My Number One Hero", The Hindustan Times, Sunday Magazine, New Delhi, January 25, 1998.

Ganguli, Amulya, "The Mahatma in Sepia," The Hindustan Times, New Delhi, September 27, 1997.

Ganguli, Amulya, "The Spectre of Godse", The Hindustan Times, New Delhi, July 27, 1998.

Inder Jit, "Parliament Ignores Gandhi," The Hindustan Times, New Delhi, October 1, 1997.

Jagmohan, "Gandhi and the Removal of Spiritual Illiteracy", The Hindustan Times, New Delhi, October, 3, 1997.

Khan, Maulana Wahiduddin, "The Gandhi I Knew," The Hindustan Times, New Delhi, January 30, 1996.

Madan,T.N., "Victory Without Fulfilment", The Hindustan Times, New Delhi, December, 28, 1997.

Mukhetjee, Subrata, "Gandhi's Theory of the State", The Hindustan Times, New Delhi, February 2, 1999.

Nanda, B.R., "Gandhi and the West", The Hindustan Times, New Delhi, January 30, 1998.

Narayanan,V. N., "Dumbing Down Of A People", The Hindustan Times, Sunday, New Delhi, February 1, 1998.

Padgaonkar,Lalita, "A Lifetime of Tolerance", Interview of Narayan Desai, recepient of 1998 UNESCO-Madanjit Singh Prizefo the Promotion of Tolerance and Non-Violence, The Hindustan Times, New Delhi, November 1, 1998.

Salil, Kuldip, "Gandhi is Glad" (a poem) in Singh, Khuswant, "With Malice Towards One and All", The Hindustan Times, New Delhi, January, 30, 1999.

Singh, Natwar, K., "The Eternal Pilgrim", The Hindustan Times, Sunday Magazine, New Delhi, January 25, 1998.

Sharp,Gene, "The Gandhian Way Today", The Hindustan Times, New Delhi, January 30, 1999.

Narayanan, K.R., "Media: A Distorting, Magnifying Mirror," The Hindustan Times, New Delhi, April 28, 1997.

Polak, R.S.L., "Gandhiji As I Knew Rim", Nostalgia, The Hindustan Times, New Delhi, January 26, 1995.

Kumar; Ravinder, "A Prophet of Modernity?", The Hindustan Times, New Delhi, January 30, 1999.

Bakshi, Rajni, "A Tale of Two Yogis", The Times of India, New Delhi, February 24, 1999.

The SGI Newsletter/Special, Tokyo, 1996 "Gandhi: A Tireless Speaker and Writer"

Sharma, Jai Narain, "The Great Nuclear Debate: A Gandhian Perspective", The Tribune, Chandigarh, May 27, 1998.

Naipaul, V.S., "Christianity Didn't Damage India Like Islam", Outlook, Milleneum Special, November 15, 1999.

Special Issue on Gandhi as a Journalist, Vidura, Journal of the Press Institute of India, New Delhi,Vo1.35., Issue No.1, January -March, 1998.

Gandhi Memorial, Place Number, Vishwa Bharati Quarterly, Shantiniketan, 1949. News Items

"'Gandhi Comers' to come up in schools", The Hindu,New Delhi, September 24,1999.

"Mahatma Gandhi's Rare Letters to Be Auctioned", The Hindustan Times, New Delhi, July 8, 1998.

"Too Late, But SA Honours Gandhi", The Pioneer, July 24, 1997, p. l.

Brochures

The Sulabh Movement: Human Development Approach to Sanitation, Brochure issued by Sulabh International Social Service Orgnanisation, New Delhi.

Websites

http://www.pbs.org/newshour/bb/media/july-dec98/lawyers_10-19a.html

http://www.jastor.com

http://www.jour.sc.edu/news/convergence

www.indianexpress.com

www.indiatoday.com

www.merinews.com

www.CNNIBN.com

www.timesofindia.com

www.the tribune.com

www.hindustantines.com

http://www.ap.org

www.jour.sc.edu/news

www.mediacentre.org/content

www.journalism.co.uk/news

www.ojr.org/ojr/workplace

www.africanews.org

http://www prescouncils.org.

http://www.actionsites.com

Index